Cosmopolitan Vistas

COSMOPOLITAN VISTAS

AMERICAN REGIONALISM AND LITERARY VALUE

TOM LUTZ

CORNELL UNIVERSITY PRESS

ITHACA AND LONDON

First published 2004 by Cornell University Press
First printing, Cornell Paperbacks, 2004

Printed in the United States of America

Library of Congress Cataloging-in-Publication Data
Lutz, Tom.
   Cosmopolitan vistas : American regionalism and literary value / Tom Lutz.
      p. cm.
   Includes bibliographical references and index.
   ISBN 0-8014-4263-X (alk. paper) — ISBN 0-8014-8923-7 (pbk. : alk. paper)
    1. American literature—History and criticism—Theory, etc.   2. American fiction—History and criticism—Theory, etc.   3. Internationalism in literature.   4. Cosmopolitanism—United States.
5. Social values in literature.   6. Regionalism in literature.   7. Local color in literature.   I. Title.
   PS25.L88 2004
   810.9—dc22

                                    2004001486

Cornell University Press strives to use environmentally responsible suppliers and materials to the fullest extent possible in the publishing of its books. Such materials include vegetable-based, low-VOC inks and acid-free papers that are recycled, totally chlorine-free, or partly composed of nonwood fibers. For further information, visit our website at www.cornellpress.cornell.edu.

Cloth printing   10 9 8 7 6 5 4 3 2 1
Paperback printing   10 9 8 7 6 5 4 3 2 1

Where you come from is gone, where you thought you were going to never was there, and where you are is no good unless you can get away from it. Where is there a place for you to be? No place.

—Flannery O'Connor, *Wise Blood,* 93

It's a world of laughter, a world of tears,
It's a world of hopes and a world of fears.
There's so much that we share, that it's time we're aware,
It's a small world after all.

—Richard M. Sherman and Robert B. Sherman, "It's a Small World"

Even the most inclusive social scheme must stop somewhere.

—Henry James, *The American Scene,* 240

The whole field of human experience was never so nearly covered by imaginative literature in any age as in this; and American life especially is getting represented with unexampled fullness. It is true that no one writer, no one book, represents it, for this is not possible. . . . The world was once very little, and it is now very large.

—William Dean Howells, *Criticism and Fiction,* 68

Contents

Cosmopolitan Vistas

Discipline and Hubris

For pure hubris, no statement in the history of literary criticism has more impressed me than this one by the literary critic René Girard: "My theory," he said in the early 1980s, "most economically accounts for all phenomena."[1] And it is worth noting that Girard was not talking about literary phenomena but about quite literally all phenomena. By the 1980s various new forms of literary criticism—based in structuralist and poststructuralist literary theories, cultural theory and cultural studies, historicism of various kinds, women's studies, ethnic studies, and multidisciplinary approaches—had moved from the fringes to the center of the academic study of literature. Literary scholars, no longer content with our traditional jobs—the editing, explicating, and evaluating of literary texts—acquired global ambitions, and the world was our oyster. Ever since, many of us have been busy explaining just this to central administrations, students and their parents, trustees, and legislatures: that literary training is very possibly the best way to prepare students for life in the information age, since we can teach them to analyze the most complex forms of information in the world—literary texts and their contexts—and that we are therefore the discipline best equipped to prepare students for a postmodern world constructed of dense, complex signs.

The literary scholar's job, according to the current consensus, is not to make aesthetic discriminations and judgments but to research instead, according to Cary Nelson, Paula A. Treichler, and Lawrence Grossberg, "the history of cultural studies, gender and sexuality, nationhood and national identity, colonialism and postcolonialism, race and ethnicity, popular culture and its audiences, science and ecology, identity politics, pedagogy, the politics of aesthetics, cultural institutions, the politics of disciplinarity, discourse and textuality, history, and global culture in a postmodern age."[2] Nelson et al. straightfacedly apologize for this list being too partial, unable to encompass all the present and future fields that are or will be covered under the rubric of cultural studies. They worry that, in producing such a list, they might appear too narrow-minded, and so are quick to reassure their colleagues that any list of topics, even one that, like this one, includes the entire history of the world, is inadequate to express the breadth of our comprehensive ambitions.

I have been and continue to be as guilty of such disciplinary imperialism as anyone, writing about medicine, politics, neuroscience, anthropology, music, and on and on, as if my work in an English department outfitted me to analyze "all phenomena." This book, conversely, might seem to be a very different kind of project, a throwback to an earlier time in the discipline. I developed the basic argument in response to the existing scholarship in a fairly minor subfield of the very traditional (since the 1920s) field of American literary studies. The study of regionalism, especially late nineteenth-century local color literature—the work of Sarah Orne Jewett, Mary Wilkins Freeman, Hamlin Garland, and the lesser lights—is a specialist's endeavor, and further, my insistence on analyzing the "literary value" of these texts conjures up the cobwebbed attic of New Critical, New Humanist, and earlier forms of conservatism. The same tendencies that have helped expand our disciplinary purview (especially that loose alliance of critical activities that now gather under the cultural studies umbrella), have made evaluation off-limits, have left it tainted by, indeed invalidated by, what has been seen as literary evaluation's exclusionary, hierarchical, antidemocratic, traditionalist, and therefore reactionary politics.

Instead of falling for what Fredric Jameson called "the false problem of value," critics are now required either to disavow evaluative literary judgments or to cop to their own place of elite privilege, their own exclusionary biases.[3] To engage in discriminations about literary value, even to declare, for instance, that Henry James is a better novelist than Zane Grey or Thomas Dixon, is simply "leisure-class gossip," and such "debaucheries of judiciousness," as Northrop Frye called them almost fifty years ago, are theoretically considered more appropriate at cocktail parties than in professional discourse.[4] But I am going to argue that literary critics continue to make such discriminations and that the prime literary values that provided the ground for nineteenth-century regionalism are very similar to those that are implicitly agreed on today across not only much of the academy but by the larger literary public—that public against which academics now find themselves pitted. Our relation to literature is closer to that of our immediate and more distant literary ancestors than we in the academy sometimes like to assume. The nineteenth century's realists and sentimentalists, the writers of the Harlem Renaissance and of the Southern Renaissance and their critics, the firebrands who issued in the new canon and the traditionalists who struggled to save the old, the supporters and detractors of Oprah's Book Club, the antiacademic *littérateurs* who shun all scholarly discourse, and the most obscure Ivy League literary theorists all share some central beliefs.

What we share is what I will call *literary cosmopolitanism:* briefly, an ethos of representational inclusiveness, of the widest possible affiliation, and concurrently one of aesthetic discrimination and therefore exclusivity. At the same time that it embraces the entire world, in other words, literary cosmopolitanism necessitates an evaluative stance, and it is this doubleness, this combination of egalitarianism and elitism, that has animated American literature since the Civil War. Literary cosmopolitanism is a way to describe literary taste and at the same time suggest that literary distinction and discrimination over the last 150 years has always been political, not just in the trivial sense in which all discourse is political or because of literature's class parameters, but precisely because, as I will explain, it has been tied so closely to an ethos of textual density and overdetermination. This cosmopolitan ethos, very different from the literary federalism of the *Salmagundi* circle, for instance, or European aestheticism, continues to be the central informing base of American literary culture, academic and nonacademic alike.[5]

If I am therefore renouncing a certain kind of disciplinary hubris, I am enacting another kind: I aim to talk not just about regionalist fiction but about what literature, the old-fashioned Literature with a capital "L," has to offer and has been offering for the last century and a half. Already a sizable part of my audience will balk, since Literature, scholars now agree, is a historically constituted, always-changing construct; by Literature I mean those texts deemed to have aesthetic value above and beyond those considered subliterary, a distinction not everyone makes, but which is nonetheless recognized as necessary: one cannot study the history of canon formation, or argue for new canons, for instance, without reference to it; one obviously cannot have an admissions process for an MFA writing program, jury a book award, decide what should be included in the Library of America, or make arguments for the value of literary study, like those I just referred to, without it. The argument for the complexity of the literary text as a sign system, I will argue, is also a corollary to American arguments about literary value throughout this long period.

Some readers will have an allergic reaction to the elitism implied by the capital L, and will argue that working-class poetry, popular fiction, or any other group of texts we might see as the opposite of elite Literature has just as much value as the work of Henry James for his minute audience. Class politics, they might say, not "literary value," determines what ends up in the honorific, capitalized category. This argument, I will show, develops from the same literary ethos, from the same urge to inclusiveness that I am describing as literary cosmopolitanism. Over and over again, the popular texts championed by anti-elitist literary scholars are defended on cosmopolitan grounds, just as cosmopolitanism informs criticisms of classic Literature's class politics. Critics who enthuse about literary value are accused of being apolitical, of not considering the political impact of texts, but even the writing of literary regionalists such as Hamlin Garland, who most clearly and loudly espoused partisan positions in their non-literary writings, produced fictions that were politically cosmopolitan. Partisan literature, purely didactic literature, has been considered subliterary whenever such judgments have been made in America since the middle of the nineteenth century, at which time the cosmopolitan vista and the literary purview began to become inseparable. J. H. Morse, in a review of local color writing in 1883, to take just one of many examples, took it as axiomatic that "all good art resents the imposition of a too formal didacticism."[6] The classic American literary text is, at one and the same time, committed to representing the political issues of its day and committed to neutrality in relation to them. The classic text, as the New Critics were fond of pointing out, is complex, ambiguous, multifaceted, multifarious, and it achieves this complexity not, as some New Critics seemed to imply, by removing itself from the world of social and political reality, but by thoroughly immersing itself in that world.

The "bloody crossroads" was Lionel Trilling's nickname for the intersection of politics and aesthetics in literary culture: I want to suggest that instead of violence we have a kind of meld, that our politics—the politics for which we in academia have been pilloried of late even more than for our excesses of theoretical elaboration—and our aesthetics—which we have been discussing primarily as historical artifacts—together stem from the same cosmopolitan ethos. And this ethos of literary cosmopolitanism provides a common ground that unites the many disparate, warring factions of what continues to be a literary community—that group of readers whose work or leisure involves the reading of literary texts.

The politicizing of explication in the contemporary academy and the disdain for literary evaluation have, for many readers, exceeded the limits of credibility and relevance, cutting academic literary discussion adrift not just from the larger culture but from literary culture itself as it lives outside the academy and inside it, in the form of creative writing programs. Alvin Kernan announced the "Death of Literature" in 1990, John Ellis pined for "Literature Lost" in 1997, Robert Scholes described the "Rise and Fall of English" in 1998, and, in his role as president of the Modern Language Association, Edward W. Said lamented in 1999 the "disappearance of literature itself from the curriculum" and its replacement by "fragmented, jargonized subjects."[7] I also hope to show what is literary about the literary wars that have been waged since the waning of the New Criticism in the 1970s, how the scholarly tendencies and desires at the center of feminist, progressive, Marxist, postcolonialist, and postmodern movements have been bred by the very literary values held, much more explicitly, by their combatants in these culture wars. I am going to argue that we all, in very fundamental ways, ascribe to these cosmopolitan values, however much we disagree on what those values require of us. The argument that Literature is a very different kind of writing from political tracts and requires a very different kind of reading does not, in the end, carry with it a specific ideology. And at the same time, the desires to escape elitism, to increase the relevance of literary study and to expand its purview, to open the literary field to more kinds of authors, more kinds of readers, more kinds of texts, more diverse and larger populations—these desires are not perversions introduced by 1960s radicals, they are not inimical to literary evaluation, and, most important, they do not signal an epistemic or ethical break from pre-1960s literary culture. These desires, in fact, have been at the center of American literary culture since the Civil War, and they remain at the center of what constitutes the best of American literature, both within the academy and without.

This book is my apologia for both my discipline and its central object of study, then, a defense of the literary in the context of a discipline that, as everyone seems to agree, is in crisis. The disappearance of literature, the disappearance of academic jobs, the disappearance of university presses, and the scaling back of everything else have occasioned a number of proposals, including recent MLA president Stephen Greenblatt's, in which he (like his counterparts a hundred years ago), suggests that "we should not be thinking about looking inward, but about the ways literature and the teaching of language are intellectually and culturally and socially part of the larger world."[8] This may just seem to add fuel to the fire, since it is in part exactly this urge to increased contextualization that has led literature, as Said put it, to disappear from the curriculum. What I am going to offer is a new way to think of literature's relation to its society, one that is always already political, but not one that therefore has a very specific politics. Literary cosmopolitanism is an ethos that the discipline of literary studies can and should embrace, an ethos that academics should be happy to promulgate and teach. It is an ethos, as I hope to show, that though often observed in the breach and rarely set forth explicitly these days, still saturates the best of what we read and write.

The writing of this book has spanned many years and I have had an enormous amount of material and intellectual help from students, research assistants, colleagues, friends, and family. I want to mention in particular Paul Mandelbaum, Kevin Kopelson, Ken Cmiel, Kathleen Diffley, Harry Stecopoulos, Corey Creekmur, Matt Brown, and Doris Witt, who helped me think the project through, read parts or the whole of the book, and argued with me beyond the call of duty. Robert F. Sayre was my first interlocutor for this project, and he edited and published an early version of these ideas in *Recovering the Prairie* (University of Wisconsin Press, 1999). Some sections rely heavily on essays published in *Black Orpheus*, ed. Saadi Simawe (Garland, 2000) and in *Little Magazines and Modernism*, ed. Adam McKible and Suzanne Churchill (Ohio State University Press, 2004), and I thank the editors for their comments. I also want to thank the University of Iowa, especially the College of Liberal Arts and the Department of English, for their support; the Department of English at the University of South Carolina, especially Susan Courtney, Greg Forter, and Robert Newman, for important feedback; Catherine Jurca and Cindy Weinstein and members of their Huntington Library seminar in 2001; and audiences at the University of Illinois Chicago, the American Studies Association, the Midwest Modern Language Association, the American Literature Association, Carnegie-Mellon University, and the California Institute of the Arts. I would like to thank once again Jay Fliegelman, David Halliburton, Rick Maddox, and Mary Pratt for teaching me at the beginning of my career, and other colleagues at Iowa—especially Judy Aikin, Roger Aikin, Melissa Deem, Ed Folsom, Joni Kinsey, Brooks Landon, Rob Latham, Kathy Lavezzo, Susie Phillips, Laura Rigal, David Wittenberg, Barbara Welch-Breder, and Hans Breder. I would also like to thank my colleagues in Los Angeles—especially Betsy Amster, Leo Braudy, Sande Cohen, Barry Glassner, and Steve Molton—and elsewhere—especially Carrie Bramen, Nancy Glazener, Andrew Hoberek, June Howard, Paul Levine, Adam McKible, and Joel Pfister—for intellectual and literary conversations. Thanks to my students and former students Douglas Anderson, Susanna Ashton, Jason Brickey, Jeff Charis-Carlson, Pat Eamon, Lyn Eliot, Jim Hall, Susan Hwang, Josh Kotzin, Jon Miller, Elyce Myers, Angela Nepodal, Sean Scanlan, James Sprengelmeyer, Ned Stuckey-French, Jeffrey Swenson, Keith Wilhite, and others in my regionalism seminars in 1999 and 2001. Thanks go to Jesse, Yarrow, and Cody Lutz, John Stefaniak, Jonathan Penner, Stacy Title, Pam Galvin, Joel Goldberg, Margot Frankel, Elena Song, Dorothy Braudy, the Cheviot Hills poker mafia, the Winers and the Gordons, the Blue Tunas and the Blues Patrol for the life outside. Melanie Jackson helped make this possible, as did Carol Lutz, who introduced me to the wide world of the literary life. Thanks especially to Laurie Winer, my local cosmopolitan, for the past, present, and future.

TOWARD A THEORY

Art's Region

In 1996 a symposium was held at the University of Iowa on "Images and Functions of the American Prairie." The participants included ecologists, biologists, prairie restorationists, political historians, geographers, landscape architects, painters, photographers, art historians, literary historians, and eco-activists. Most were not just professionally interested in the prairies, but, like Robert F. Sayre, one of the organizers, had a personal dedication to the region, and one that was already politicized. As the self-designated heirs of a long line of prairie regionalists from the worlds of social thought, art, literary studies, folklore, and politics, the participants were the kind of people who have, among other things, helped maintain an interest in the Midwest as a distinct cultural region and a steady market for regionalist writing about the area. They also shared a cross-professional ideology that I found remarkably similar to, as well as significantly different from, the ideology of literary writers and critics who, beginning in the 1860s and 1870s, developed a particular way of talking about regional and cultural difference, and thereby a particular way of understanding culture itself from the standpoint of cultural workers.

The symposium was organized in conjunction with an exhibit curated by Joni B. Kinsey and titled *Plain Pictures,* which charted the history of visual representations of the prairies from the eighteenth century to the present. As part of the program, four artists who represent the Midwestern landscape, and whose paintings and photographs were being exhibited, spoke about their work and then took questions from the audience. In their responses to questions about politics and representation, the artists repeatedly returned to formal, artistic considerations. In her presentation and in response to questions, Genie Patrick, who paints softly geometrical scenes of the Iowa countryside, spoke of her training in abstract art, of the Clement-Greenberg-spawned directive to consider the canvas a two-dimensional space. Even when pushed toward political questions of land use and environmentalism she replied in formalist terms, "My work has always been involved with abstract shapes and linear rhythms"; "I consciously look for these painted flat shapes in the landscape"; and "I paint the formal art elements I find in nature." Someone asked if the two fence posts and tree in one painting were meant to suggest the relationship between nature and culture. "Yes, perhaps," she explained, "but I was more interested in the fact that they form a triangle."

When participants asked Fred Easker why he had chosen to paint a certain roadside view near his home in Iowa, and whether the stop sign and other touches of modern life were added to make a political point of some kind, he said, no, they were just there, so he painted them. When pressed for a reason for choosing that particular scene to paint (the question suggested that the incursion of modernity had influenced his decision at least subconsciously), Easker looked intently at his own painting and said: "I was really taken by this line," outlining with his hand the rolling horizon that formed the centerline of his painting. "I just really liked this line." Keith Jacobshagen, who paints the landscape around Lincoln, Nebraska, was asked similar questions: Why, members of the symposium asked, assuming that the answer was obvious, do you show that large, late twentieth-century grain elevator in the distance? "Because it's there," Jacobshagen answered. "I drive out into the country, and I paint what I see." But do you think you chose that scene because of the intrusion of the industrial world into the landscape? "Well, the industrial world is everywhere," Jacobshagen answered, "and I suppose I chose the prospect I did because that was one of the elements." He stopped and looked at the represented elevator and said, "It is a nice shape, isn't it?" He was the last artist to speak, and the audience had been getting more and more pointed in its attempts to elicit authorial intentions that matched their reading of the paintings. Jacobshagen continued gently to rebuke their questions, asking them to remember that, as he finally put it, "the language of art is not in the subject."

William Carlos Williams made a similar statement in an essay on Marianne Moore's poetry: "Local color is not, as the parodists, the localists believe, an object of art."[1] For Williams, whose epic *Paterson* might easily be considered urban local color, locality was one of several lines that needed to intersect in a work of art, but it was their aesthetic intersection, not the lines themselves, that was central to the work of art. Just as "white is the intersection of blue and green and yellow and red," Williams wrote, "it is this white light that is the background of all good work" (311). Other authors, identified even more easily as literary regionalists, have made similar arguments, sometimes, like Williams, denying they are primarily local writers. William Faulkner, for instance, claimed that he wrote about people like those in the communities surrounding Oxford, Mississippi, simply because it was easier than writing about other people. At the University of Virginia in 1957, Faulkner responded to a question about whether his characters were "regional" or "universal" by saying:

> I feel that the verities these people suffer are universal verities—that is, that man, whether he's black or white or red or yellow still suffers the same anguishes, he has the same aspirations, his follies are the same follies, his triumphs are the same triumphs. That is, his struggle is against his own heart, against—with the hearts of his fellows, and with his background. And in that sense there's no such thing as a regional writer, the writer simply uses the terms he is familiar with best because it saves him having to do research. That he might write a book about the Chinese but if he does that, he's got to do some research or somebody'll say "Ah! you're wrong there, that ain't the way the Chinese behave." But if he uses his own region, which he is familiar with, it saves him that trouble.[2]

Slightly—but only slightly—tongue in cheek.

Some writers, of course, embrace their regional status and are happy to be marketed (to national and international audiences) as regional writers. Larry Brown, for instance, whose writing career began in Oxford, Mississippi, some years after Faulkner's, presents himself as a local writer, someone who has stayed in the town where he was born (but not raised—he returned as an adult), someone who writes organically about people like himself and his neighbors. "Geography has something to do with the creation of the characters that live in it," he told an interviewer in response to a question about Southern writing. "My characters come out of the land that is around me that I see every day, that is rural Lafayette County, Mississippi. That's just about the only way I know how to explain it."[3] His publisher identifies him as a practitioner of "grit lit," in which the characters are so close to the earth that they wear their dirt proudly.[4] The press releases describe Brown as a longtime fireman, a working-class local guy who began writing late, almost as an afterthought, and his down-home affability and diction add to the picture of an accidental author speaking the authentic voice of the local, somewhat oppressed citizenry. "I have a high school diploma and was lucky to get that," he told the same interviewer in April 2000. "I was such a dumbass that I failed senior English and had to go to summer school. Since then, I've read books to educate myself." But at a reading in 1997, in response to the question of how he began writing, he expressed a more expansive view of his literary world (and his education): he had read Dostoyevsky, Tolstoy, Joyce, and Conrad in college courses, he said, directed by a professor who had, he felt, opened not just the world of literature for him, but the world itself. Reading the classic texts of Western literature at the University of Mississippi, he said, he decided *"That* is what I want to do. I want to write *literature.* Like *that."*[5] In contrasting Brown's self-portrait as a near-dropout natural chronicler and his self-portrait as an epiphanic collegiate apprentice to the Great Tradition, I do not mean to expose yet another case of inauthenticity in the literary marketplace. I want instead to suggest that this doubleness—in which an appeal to local commitments, unadulterated by even the cosmopolitan gloss of a liberal arts education, is coupled with a commitment to Literature as a universal, cosmopolitan, honorific category—is at the center of what makes regional writing regional literature, and that a similar doubleness is at the center of American literature itself over the last 150 years. Aesthetic concerns, in this tradition, are sometimes denied in favor of social commitments, and social commitments are sometimes denied in favor of aesthetic concerns, but, when pushed, most writers and readers, unlike the visual artists at the Iowa symposium, can honestly articulate both.

The frustrations that the academic participants felt with the artists' lack of political engagement at the symposium is mirrored by a related discomfort among literary academics with universalist remarks such as Faulkner's (at the level of human desire) or Williams's (at the level of aesthetics). One of the common multicultural pieties is that the anguishes and aspirations (and aesthetics) of white, black, yellow, and red, of upper and middle and lower classes, of homo-, hetero- and other sexualities, are in fact different, and that those differences cannot be resolved into universal categories. From this perspective Toni Morrison writes about black women not simply because that choice does away with the need for research but because it is her artistic responsibility, and Scott Momaday (whose research, while a graduate student at Stanford, centered on the nineteenth-century Massachusetts patrician poet Frederick Goddard Tuckerman) writes about Native Americans in the Southwest against a background that is not exactly Williams's "white light." Universal verities and universal aesthetics are off-limits in contemporary criticism, as is, indeed, the kind of literary evaluation suggested by Faulkner when he claimed that writers are not concerned with their reception in their own time but in their reception in "2057 or 4057," when, one assumes, the politics of literary consumption will be different, as will the "material bases" of aesthetic judgment. But the local color boom after the Civil War, where literary cosmopolitanism took on its basic form, can show us that social and aesthetic commitments are far from mutually exclusive.

Trilling coined the term "bloody crossroads" in an essay about Vernon Parrington, an obviously politicized critic whose progressive history of American literature was published between 1927 and 1930. "It is possible to say of V. L. Parrington that with his *Main Currents of American Thought* he has had an influence on our conception of American culture which is not equaled by that of any other writer of the last two decades," Trilling wrote. "His ideas are now the accepted ones wherever the college course in American literature is given by a teacher who conceives himself to be opposed to the genteel and the academic and in alliance with the vigorous and the actual."[6] Parrington had what Trilling called "the saving salt of the American mind, the lively sense of the practical, workaday world, of the welter of ordinary undistinguished things and people, of the tangible, quirky, unrefined elements of life." But he had no aesthetic sense: "Whenever he was confronted with a work of art that was complex, personal and not literal, that was not, as it were, a public document, Parrington was at a loss." The bloody crossroads, Trilling felt, was exemplified not just by Parrington but by the general "liberal" evaluation of Henry James and Theodore Dreiser, the former dismissed as an aristocratic aesthete and the latter celebrated as a man of the people who represented a larger swath of the actual than James. Trilling saw part of the problem as what he called an "impoverished" sense of reality, in which reality is reduced to a strict mimetic relation to materiality instead of including the reality of ideas. Dreiser, like James, has ideas, but they are bad ideas—chemism and the like—which are rightly ignored by his admirers. The problem, Trilling suggests, is that James's ideas smack too much of elitism for his leftist peers, and thus are wrongly ignored. This, he feels, is a critical miscarriage, a casualty of the crossroads.

By now, James's lapses from a full cosmopolitanism—his anti-Semitism, his distaste for immigrants—have been fully, or at least quite extensively, catalogued. But it should be equally clear that in his fiction James tended not to take sides, that he left in precarious balance the competing languages and claims of his Americans and Europeans, his men and women, his aristocrats, bohemians, and bourgeois. His cultural politics, despite, or perhaps it is better to say beyond, his blind spots, were, like those of the prairie artists, fundamentally noncommittal. Trilling is right to suggest that it is a mistake to see the mastery of language, the virtuoso display of literary writing in someone like James as at war with the egalitarian spirit. The original title of T. S. Eliot's *The Waste Land* was "He Do the Police in Different Voices," a line from Dickens's *Our Mutual Friend* describing Sloppy's virtuoso reading of the newspaper for his illiterate audience, and Eliot's virtuosity, like Sloppy's, is closely tied to his ability to speak in different voices.[7] Although Dreiser's ability along these lines is of a different order than James's, it is nonetheless the same basic procedure at work. Both James and Dreiser do the voices of people across an array of social positions, mimicking the speech of their several microclasses, and both offer their readers a kind of contested equilibrium or unresolved resolution in the storm of competing voices and values. The "effect of the real" they achieve, their wit (such as it is in Dreiser's case), their affective power, and many other elements of their literary art are enabled by this multiplicity, this openness. Dreiser and James justify through use the cosmopolitan value of the literary vista. Literature, whether with the bejeweled intricacy of a James or the sprawled fumbling of a Dreiser, enacts, in its cosmopolitanism, an advertisement for its own value.

Regionalism may seem an odd place to look for an ethos of cosmopolitan openness to difference and an odd place to stake a claim for the continued relevance of the literary for contemporary culture. Carey McWilliams wrote in 1930 that "in times so strenuous as ours, it is rather annoying to discover intelligent men devoting their talents to such tasks as listing the plants in Oklahoma folk-cures and noting, with infantile delight, the eroticisms in the folk speech of taxi-drivers," and the same kind of criticism could easily be leveled against some of the continued enthusiasm for local customs among writers and historians.[8] McWilliams was not reacting against literary regionalists, however, so much as academic folklorists who found in local folkways a bulwark against the degradations of modernity and who had a much more purely preservationist agenda than the literary writers. The latter assumed, almost without exception, that both the preservation of local culture and the integration of cultures were necessary, and they invariably found, in Oklahoma folk-cures or their equivalent, a source of both delight and shame. They tended to represent the local, as in the case of dialect, for instance, in ways that both preserve its distinctiveness and suggest its identity with other ways of speech: dialect is the "othering" of local speech even as it is a synecdochal sign of where some larger "we" came from and where "we" might be going. Literary regionalists and the majority of their critics and reviewers were attuned not to "infantile delight" but to social thought in these texts, and they assumed that what was important about representing local customs was their relation to other locales. As the historian Henry Steele Commager noted some years ago, "We have a regional literature, but it is rather a tribute to the passing of genuine regionalism than an expression of it."[9]

In this book I concentrate on regionalist writing for two reasons, then: first, regionalism was the most popular literary mode during the second half of the nineteenth century when this ethos was under construction, and as such was at the center of debates about the meaning, value, and purpose of literary art; second, regional literature, because it was responding to the radical transformation of American society preceding and following the Civil War, and because it took as its prime subject the conflicting interests of specific populations during these changes, is the most obvious literary enactment of the values I will be discussing. The later regionalisms I discuss—from the "revolt from the village" fiction of the 1920s through the more recent New Regionalism—continue this interest in conflicting populations and their values, and continue to demonstrate cosmopolitan investments, quite explicitly reacting against what they analyze as the provincialism of earlier representations. In all three periods, a central issue has been the relation of different groups to ongoing technological, economic, and social change, or, in other words, the relation of the region to the rest of the world.

Such local and global concerns were not opposed to, but completely enmeshed in, literary aesthetics. *Ur*–local colorist Hamlin Garland, whose *Crumbling Idols* (1893) was the first major manifesto of regionalist critical principles, insisted that what was central to literary art was not just that it was "at bottom sociologic," but that it "hasten the age of beauty."[10] These two projects come together, according to Garland, in the representation of a "broader Americanism" (129), in a "spacious, . . . democratic" (67) art that covers the "whole field of human experience" (68). And although William Carlos Williams, like many "localists" at mid-century, distances himself from the earlier regionalists, he does so using an analogous metaphor of inclusiveness. He claims for art the widest spectrum; the local colorists claimed for it the widest perspective, the largest prospect. Both argued, in their critical statements and their literary work, that true art consists of the fullest collection of colors.

Literary Progress

It might seem ironic, given this central critical and writerly push toward inclusion, that academic literary study has been pilloried in recent decades by the general culture (and by those in other academic fields) for various forms of exclusion: for the opacity of jargons that keep the uninitiated out of the conversation; for the stridency of its preaching-to-the-converted politics and its attempts to silence the masses to the right of the left-academic consensus; for what sometimes seems to be the paper-scissors-rock game of race, class, and gender one-upmanship; for its neglect of classic literary texts in favor of the study of cultural ephemera such as comic books, horror films, sitcoms, and women's magazines; and for other sins. In adopting the epistemological imperialism of cultural studies, according to these critiques, literature professors are not opening up the world, they are closing off the literary. Force-feeding students bad French theory and worse leftist litanies, say these critiques, does not broaden students' understanding of philosophy and politics, it reduces their full response to literature to a process of theoretical or political abstraction. In abandoning a commitment to literature as art, they suggest, literary scholars have lost their audience not just beyond the classroom but often inside it, and in failing to agree on, much less impart, some standard of cultural literacy, critics cut themselves off from a nonacademic literary public unafraid to evaluate texts on aesthetic grounds.

These debates have a complex relation to the continued decline of humanistic study, its waning cultural relevance and prestige, its slow fade from the center of college curricula, what John Guillory has described as its "decline in market value."[11] As faculties and budgets shrink, freshly minted PhDs continue to hop from adjunct job to adjunct job, flounder in technical writing positions, or start over in law school, and the surplus labor pool increases the publishing demands for new hires, tenure, and promotion, leading many professors, instructors, and graduate students into an upward spiral of "productivity" and increased anxieties not only about their own job security but about the profession itself and its value. Some scholars attempt to ensure the relevance of their work and their marketability by working in the newest, glitziest theoretical or topical subspecialties, those most often attacked as, among other things, glitzy or topical. Such attacks and the ensuing rebuttals produce a new mountain of journal articles and conference papers belittling, for instance, rearguard (or nonacademic) critics of neomarxist postcolonial criticism (or queer theory) for being apolitically complacent in the face of true injustice, say, or for general philistinism In this way, the profession works assiduously alongside its detractors to pave the road to irrelevance.

This seeming appetite for oblivion is sometimes attributed to "tenured radicals" who came of age in the 1960s, the very people who, while students themselves, began demanding more relevant curricula, which usually meant curricula that engaged contemporary realities and contemporary cultural politics. But the essential arguments in this debate have long been central to American literary culture—calls for a broader scope versus pleas for a renewed attention to traditional concerns, demands that literature and criticism represent life more comprehensively (i.e., represent more social groups) and respond to it more fully versus demands that art simply be art, and the insistence that criticism be more intellectually rigorous versus a plea for more widely accessible expressions of critical insight. Literary arguments in the second half of the nineteenth century, especially the various debates that led to the rise of realism and regionalism, and shortly thereafter of modernism, are full of such talk. Novelists, critics, and editors repeatedly announced that literature needed to include the experience of more and more people, especially (and here the echoes of recent forms of multiculturalism are clearest) those groups that had never been considered worthy of literary representation in the past. There were also regular demands for more "scientific" analysis and theory, for a more rigorous form of literary study than the gossip, chitchat, and claims to connoisseurship that, each generation continued to find, were impersonating true criticism in the magazines and journals. And there were regular calls from many quarters of the literary world for more political engagement on the part of literary writers and critics, both academic and independent.

William Dean Howells, the "dean of American letters," is as good a barometer of American literary values from the Civil War through the turn of the century as one could hope to find, responsible in his editorial work for publishing not only much of the old canon but most of what became the new post-1970s canon as well, and he regularly editorialized on exactly these points. He called for a more scientific, more rigorous criticism that was politically engaged and politically effective, and he never stopped harping on the necessity for literary texts and literary criticism to expand their purview and include more of the world. "I don't care for what people call 'art,'" Howells wrote to S. Weir Mitchell in 1885, "I like nearness to life, and this [Mitchell's new novel] is life, portrayed with conscience, with knowledge, both deep and quick, and with a most satisfying, self-respectful simplicity and clearness, which is the only 'art' worth having!"[12] The full representation of the real, "portrayed with conscience," was the mission of the literary, or as Howells had written in 1871: "Ah! poor Real Life, which I love. Can I make others share the delight I find in thy foolish and insipid face?"[13]

The complaints against Howells from the start tended to find in his novels not too much breadth but too little. Gertrude Atherton, already famous as a writer of California fictions, complained that Howellsian realism "is afraid of rough surfaces, of mountain peaks and deep valleys. It exalts the miniature and condemns the broad sweep of impressionism in art."[14] When Sinclair Lewis famously attacked Howells in his 1930 Nobel Prize acceptance speech ten years after Howells's death, he did so by recycling Howells's own arguments. He belittled Howells for not representing the full range of everyday life and for failing to tackle the tough political issues. Howells "had the code of a pious old maid whose greatest delight was to have tea at the vicarage," Lewis wrote, relegating him to the Puritan/Victorian/genteel dumping ground H. L. Mencken and others had prepared.[15] The true mark of his "timidity" was his failure to look the fullness of life in the face: "He abhorred not only profanity and obscenity but all of what H. G. Wells has called 'the jolly coarsenesses of life,'" Lewis wrote. "In his fantastic vision of life, which he innocently conceived to be realistic, farmers and seamen and factory hands might exist, but the farmer must never be covered with muck, the seaman must never roll out bawdy chanteys, the factory hand must be thankful to his good kind employer, and all of them must long for the opportunity to visit Florence and smile gently at the quaintness of the beggars." Lewis attacked the academic establishment for the same reasons: "Our American professors like their literature clear and cold and pure and very dead."

When Malcolm Cowley, in turn, reviewed a late Lewis novel, he accused Lewis himself of inadequate representation: "The characters in *World So Wide* (1951) talk almost exactly like those in *Main Street* and *Babbitt*," Cowley wrote. "The result is that they sound like survivors from a vanished world, like people just emerging from orphanages and prisons where they had spent thirty years conducting tape recordings of Lewis novels."[16] To claim that Lewis sounded the same in the 1950s as he did in the 1920s is another way of complaining that he had failed in the representation of social reality: his representation of that reality is undervoiced, missing the various ways of speaking that had emerged since the 1920s, when Lewis was correctly celebrated for his ability to represent, as Bakhtin would have it, the "stratified and heteroglot" languages—commercial, professional, artistic, generic, scientific, political, and so on—of the day.[17] Cowley was instead championing another writer from the 1920s, William Faulkner, who, by the time Cowley put together the *Portable Faulkner,* had been falling out of print, relegated to "regionalist" status, but whom Cowley was intent on establishing as a writer with a cosmopolitan thoroughness and appeal. Faulkner, Cowley wrote by way of introduction, writes the "richness of life" with "essential fidelity," and is cosmopolitan even as he describes the most detailed local peculiarities:

> He might have been thinking of his own novels when he described the ledgers, in *Go Down, Moses.* They recorded, he says, "that slow trickle of molasses and meal and meat, of shoes and straw hats and overalls, of plowlines and collars and heelbolts and clevises, which returned each fall as cotton"—in a sense they were local and limited; but they were also "the continuation of that record which two hundred years had not been enough to complete and another hundred would not be enough to discharge; that chronicle which was a whole land in miniature . . ." (xvi)

Faulkner, Cowley argued, succeeded where Lewis had come to fail, in achieving a significant cosmopolitan balance among the various contested versions of the miniature and of the "whole land." Faulkner has come under fire from many camps in the years since, of course, for his purportedly provincial inability to deal realistically and fully with race and gender, for not maintaining a wide enough purview.

In the history of regionalist literature a similar pattern emerges. Hamlin Garland lambasted the Easterners who tried to write about the West without ever having been west of New York, and who therefore produced anemic, partial portraits at best.[18] Garland also wrote to Sarah Orne Jewett (as did Elizabeth Stuart Phelps), chastising her in words much like those Lewis would turn against Howells for focusing on the smiling side of Maine life at the expense of the darker truths.[19] The "revolt from the village" writers of the 1920s (including Lewis) found fault with Garland's generation for its reluctance to represent the more sordid aspects of small town life. Some feminist critics since the 1970s, finding that local color writers such as Mary Wilkins Freeman had been unfairly shunted aside by the male canon, also found that Garland had underrepresented women, and that he had not adequately dealt with the actual lived experiences of the local populations he described.[20] And in the 1990s, Richard Brodhead and Amy Kaplan argued that regionalists such as Garland and Freeman were guilty of inadequate representation since they were writing not the fullness of the social life in their regions but fantasies constructed by urban, elite desire.[21]

And so on. In reviewing the current state of the discipline Michael Bérubé offers what he sees as "a modest proposal, which, like all modest proposals, is too radical for realization," according to which literary departments would attend to both aesthetics and politics, would embrace both canonical literary studies and contemporary cultural studies, both the word and the world.[22] This, I want to argue, radical or not, was already the project of American literary culture during the age of Howells, as it was during the age of Lewis and Faulkner. The current disciplinary relation to literature, always announced as new and improved, reiterates more than it revolts against the goals of our immediate and more distant professional forebears. Lewis had more in common with Howells (and Garland) than he cared to admit, Cowley had more in common with Lewis, and Brodhead and Kaplan with the authors they indict. Among the things we all share (along with the tendency to eat our old, to thoroughly reject as passé the last generation's efforts at increased relevance) is a continued insistence on evaluating texts based on their cultural politics and a continued belief in the social significance of literary art. And, as in the case of Howells and Lewis (again used simply as examples of general literary trends), the most egregious *literary* crime continues to be exclusion.

Indeed something very similar to Howells's and Lewis's principled dedication to full social awareness has led academic literary culture over the last several decades first to embrace feminism and African American studies, then to foment the multicultural revolution in syllabi, reading lists, and peer-reviewed publications, and more recently to insist on opening these same institutions to sexual difference and transnational literary and cultural production. And in developing over this same century and a half a poetics of complexity, ambiguity, and density, American literary criticism has made room for this literary and cultural politics of inclusion at the level of aesthetic theory. This is most obvious in the case of the New Criticism, as I will show, despite its reputation for being the enemy of difference.

A set of shared, if barely recognized values, then—the most important of which is an incorporative, inclusive, yet hierarchical cosmopolitanism—has remained at the center of literary culture as a whole and of its academic study. This almost contradictory literary cosmopolitanism, along with its ethos of inclusiveness, of wide, overdetermined perspective, is accompanied by an evaluative habit of cosmopolitan sophistication, the knowingness of the connoisseur, the implication, at the very least, of a cultivated and far-ranging aesthetic experience, of education and erudition. This too informs Howells and Lewis, Garland and the Agrarians, their predecessors and heirs—literary criticism requires eval-

uation, which requires comparison, which requires the widest possible knowledge of the field, but which also, finally, requires exclusion. Some texts are better than others, or what is a criticism for? This commitment to distinction has
obvious social grounds and consequences. Still, although many other forms of
evaluation were bought to bear on literary texts, such as stylistic or formalist criteria supposedly uncontaminated by external concerns, at the center of literary
assessment is the idea of multiplicity held in balance, contextualized by a claim
of broad, catholic, and finally social understanding. These two strands of literary cosmopolitanism, the first implicitly egalitarian and the second implicitly
hierarchical, the first inclusive, the second necessarily exclusive, continue to produce the essential tension of American literary studies.

Literary cosmopolitanism can be found on both sides of the century's central
literary debates. It not only underwrote the transformation of the discipline that
began in the 1960s but also the New Criticism taken as that revolution's old
regime. Versions of it were invoked by those who would rewrite the "traditional
canon" in the culture wars and by those who defended it. It has been central to
the rise of cultural studies and to its critiques. The more recent critical theories
that have been embraced (however partially) by the discipline over the last third
of a century also provide, I argue, a set of congenial analytic schemes for this incorporative logic: Bakhtinian polyvocality, Deleuzian schizopoetics and no-
madism, Foucauldian resistance, Derridean supplementarity, and so on, have
sprouted in well-prepared soil.

An ethos of cosmopolitan inclusivity necessarily finds, in its own past and
eventually in its present practice, evidence of ongoing, lurking provincialism,
since the cosmopolitan project is always by its very nature incomplete. Just as
each generation's attempts at fuller representation come to define the next's in-
adequacy, it will be easy for readers to identify, in each of the forms of literary
cosmopolitanism I outline, interested commitments and blind spots that give the
lie to their practitioners' implied claims. To do so, of course, would be to simply
repeat the procedures of the general project. As Henry David Thoreau wrote at
the beginning of this period, "We are," without a doubt, "essentially provincial
still," and our cosmopolitanism is always more of a desire than it is an accomplished fact.[23]

The politicization of criticism in recent decades, like the politicization in Parrington's generation, has been attacked on many fronts, from Stanley Fish's arguments about the disciplinary (as opposed to public) nature of such arguments
and their distance from the world of actual politics to the right-wing bewailing
of the destruction of the Great Tradition.[24] The problem is not that literary studies has become politicized, however; the tradition itself is similarly politicized.

The problem is that academic critics have half-forgotten the other half of their job. In off-hours professors do not avoid evaluation and are quite willing to trash the latest Spielberg film and praise the latest Coen brothers (or vice versa); scholars make evaluative decisions about stories, poems, plays, and novels all the time, at home, at parties, with friends. As Pierre Bourdieu puts it, "everyone knows, the confrontation over preferences plays an important part in daily conversations."[25] But literary evaluation of the twentieth-century, the nineteenth-century, or earlier canons is professionally suspect. Barbara Herrnstein Smith discussed the "exile of evaluation" in 1988 and argued for its return, but her arguments assumed that of utmost importance were, as her title suggested, the contingencies of value, and she offered an alternative "literary axiology" that would, she hoped,

> account for the features of literary and aesthetic judgments in relation to the multiple social, political, circumstantial, and other constraints and conditions to which they are responsive; it would chronicle "the history of taste" in relation to more general models of historical cultural dynamics and specific local conditions.[26]

A cultural studies project (or a theoretical justification for such a project), in other words, in which the history of taste remains in scare quotes.

The contingencies of value and our commitment to egalitarian openness have often left teachers and scholars unwilling to pronounce on the relative value of texts beyond adding them to the literary collection. Claims of aesthetic value are often mentioned in passing, as if it were negligible to the act of recovery, cataloguing, and explication. But critics do, in fact, continue to find one text more compelling than another, and while Nella Larsen and Jessie Redmon Fauset, Willa Cather and Mary Catherwood should all be in the canon, they might agree, most would also agree that Cather is a better writer than Catherwood, Larsen better than Fauset. One line of defense for these discriminations is itself political: Larsen and Cather produced texts with wider social sympathies, with a more inclusive sense of the social world than Fauset and Catherwood. This amounts to the same thing, I argue, as defending such distinctions on the grounds of "literary language": the textual attributes codified by the New Criticism, for instance—complexity, ambiguity, density, and paradox, what Brooks and Warren called the "resolution of diverse impulses" or "equilibrium of opposed forces"[27]—are descriptions at the level of language of what I have been describing in terms of representation. Such evaluative criteria are completely consonant with those that would judge a text on the thoroughness of its social representation, its ability to hold in "equilibrium" a series of "opposed forces."

But when the evaluative act is forgone, scholars fail to fulfill one of the prime functions of criticism, which is to manage the literary archive in such a way that nonprofessional readers might have some guidance in what to read. In this, it seems to me, literary scholars have indeed broken their implicit contract with the rest of the literary public.[28] Critics have 150 years of literary history from which to draw models for making an uneasy truce with the cultural politics of texts and their evaluation, and they should bite the bullet. The texts to which even the most historically- and socially-minded literary critics are continually drawn, and to which students respond, are those that are the opposite of the soapbox diatribe or the inadvertent confession, those in which the political consciousness and the political unconscious are complicated, to say the least. Locating that set of complications becomes impossible if the task is to identify the text's hegemonic or resistant force alone, and identifying a combination of these two forces in the text, only to conclude that the text has something like a political double consciousness, still misses the point. Bourgeois realism is ideologically messier than socialist realism, its aesthetic practices have more complicated relations to its themes, its politics are more convoluted, and, because of this, it is more literary. It is very Disney to conclude that it is a small world after all, and more literary to think, as Howells wrote, that "the world was once very little, and it is now very large."[29] It does not matter if one avoids the bloody crossroads in an attempt to ignore the aesthetic or in an attempt to steer clear of the political. Either way, one loses the literary. The literary lives at the crossroads.

Many, of course, will find this argument hopelessly naïve and inadequate. Cultural studies is what literature departments do now and many of its practitioners have claimed that they have a much more radical project than anything that has come before:

> [I]t must be remembered that the humanist rationale for the canon is based upon an hierarchical economy where cultural objects are ranked. Certain of those objects (Shakespeare's writing, for example) are assumed to be "the best" of western culture; they thus represent, synecdochally, the *essence* of the culture. It is exactly this symbolic view of culture against which Cultural Studies should fight. . . . This is to say that Cultural Studies look with suspicion upon any hierarchizing project through which culture is synecdochally delimited to certain of its parts, whether such parts represent the culture's essential "best" or even if they represent what has been predetermined as politically or ethically important and valuable. Cultural Studies should, in short, abandon the goal of giving students access to that which represents a culture. Instead, Cultural Studies has the possibility of investigating cul-

ture as a set of activities which is lived and developed within asymmetrical relations of power.[30]

I selected this passage almost at random, since it is of a piece with much of the writing in the field that takes as its opposite a version of "traditional literary study," which, to quote from the same piece, "has developed within formalistic parameters that set an almost impassable boundary between the study of a society and the study of a novel." This straw opponent has little relation to American literary history, which has always been a vigorously historical and social enterprise, even at the height of the New Criticism's influence. The description of the project that should replace traditional literary study is similarly untethered to real practice, despite its invocation of "praxis": "Only a counter-disciplinary praxis developed by intellectuals who resist disciplinary formation is likely to produce emancipatory social practices." Let us set aside any number of objections—for example, that, à la Fish, disciplinary formations determine what gets recognized as work, and therefore to resist them successfully is to do no recognizable work; that this statement cuts out of the picture all the emancipatory social practices of nonintellectuals; that it is ludicrous to suggest that literary scholars focus not on literary texts and contexts, not on their students and wider constituencies, but instead on the current organization of their disciplinary study in order to be emancipatory forces in the larger society; that to "produce emancipatory social practices" through literary criticism might be seen as a long way around; that the appeal to emancipation is a rhetorical move designed to gain assent without any warrant, without any description of the move from writing to producing practices. Putting all this aside, as I say, I will just note that in this very common sentiment about the necessity for "resisting" literary hierarchy we have a contemporary restatement of one of the main strands of literary criticism itself.[31]

In this kind of cultural studies formulation, literary political desire is much closer to the questions asked at the Iowa forum than it is to the artists' answers. Many of the dedicated prairie lovers and eco-activists at the symposium found in the artists' paintings a celebration of a landscape, an ecosystem, and a culture that they held dear, and which many felt to be embattled, threatened by what is called progress and its homogenizing culture, and they saw in such details as Jacobshagen's grain elevator and Easker's stop sign the signs of encroachment and destruction. Although these artists did not rise to the bait, artists often do agree that what is important about regionalism is its embattled region, which they are helping to preserve, as in the nonfiction from John Muir to Mary Austin to the Southern Agrarians to Aldo Leopold to Wendell Berry to Kathleen Norris, all of whom explicitly argue for a conservationist or preservationist relation to the land and cultures they describe. The "critical regionalists" in architecture would go even further, suggesting that architectural regionalism can be a form of active resistance to global capitalism itself, which is, after all, the real threat to local culture: "The fundamental strategy of Critical Regionalism," writes Kenneth Frampton, "is to mediate the impact of universal civilization with elements derived *indirectly* from the peculiarities of a particular place."[32] Several of the people at the symposium were devoted to re-creating the "original" environment of the Midwest by restoring "natural" prairies on preserves and through other ecological projects.[33] Industrial civilization is destroying localities, and the solution, they argue, is to reverse as much as possible the material effects of the invasion of global production systems in the region.

In literary studies, many critics have found exactly this kind of resistance in regionalism, arguing that because of regional authors' marginal position, their literary work "necessarily proceeds from a de-centered world-view" and that local color literature, or at least a reading of such literature, can help us recover what Foucault called "subjugated knowledges," a term he sometimes used interchangeably with "local, regional" knowledges.[34] The feminist recovery of local color literature starting in the 1970s included a good dose of similar talk, though somewhat less theoretically bulwarked: Josephine Donovan, Barbara Solomon, Marjorie Pryse, and others put regionalism back on the critical map with the argument that women local colorists were protofeminists, exercising power from the margins, and according to Kate McCullough, this is precisely why local color was taken off the critical map in the middle of the twentieth century, because these marginalized women's power was too evident and threatening.[35] What I call this antihegemonic strain of regionalist discourse can be found through the genre's entire history, explicitly in Garland's *Crumbling Idols* (1894), in which he condemns the literary imperialism of New York and Boston, and in the Agrarians' manifesto *I'll Take My Stand* (1930), where such arguments are central to both its cultural secessionist pronouncements and its antimodern rhetoric. Much more recently, David Jordan's postcolonial reading of regionalism and Judith Fetterley and Marjorie Pryse's introduction to *Norton Anthology of American Woman Regionalists* reprise this argument.[36]

Conversely, the literary regionalists have also been accused, again since the 1880s, of being in league with the enemy, of strip-mining their regions' cultures, selling a mythic vision of rural and marginal cultures to jaded city folk interested in buying images of the quaint or degraded. Regionalism, from this perspective, is urban elite fantasy in which literary authors purvey a patronizing pastiche of parochialisms to an audience that finds pleasure in its own superiority to the quaint backwaterish provincials represented in their magazines and books. This argument too finds full expression in *Crumbling Idols* (in its warn-

ings against literary tourism) and *I'll Take My Stand* (in its denunciation of earlier forms of regionalism), and its latest proponents are Brodhead and Kaplan,
who argue that regionalist literature in America has always been an urban elite
consumable, a collective pandering of quaint rural caricature by former provincials to readers in the urban social groups to which they sought entry.[37] According to Stephanie Foote, to take a more recent example, regional fiction is
not interested in its region; instead it tries "to transform . . . the meaning of the
social and economic developments of late-nineteenth-century urban life."[38]
Regionalism constructs a fantasy national past, an image of "an earlier, genera-
tive community" (6) against the backdrop of increased immigration and great
anxiety about the strangers in our urban midst. The "self-estrangement" Foote
attributes to nonimmigrant, urban Americans in the face of immigration is what
she assumes motivates regional fiction: "The solidity of the simple 'primitive'
folk of the region is . . . an alibi for [urban] alienation and self-estrangement"
(15). There are many other debates in the history of criticism, of course, having
to do with local color's "minor status" (pro and con), the genre's relation to gender (it's women's province; no, it isn't), to ethnic literature (ethnic lit is also local color; no, it's something else), to political progressivism (local color is fer it,
it's agin it), to realism (it is a degraded popular offshoot, it is where true realism
begins and develops), and to regional identity.[39] But the central debate over the
last couple of decades has been the one I outlined just now, concerning regionalism's hegemonic or counterhegemonic force.[40]

   Brodhead describes Jewett's writing about Maine, for instance, as something
akin to a travel brochure; Jewett played to an upper class, he writes, "by re-
hearsing the leisured outlook that differentiated it as a social group," and by creating "a world realized in a vacationer's mental image."[41] Kaplan too finds in
local color writing "allegories of desire generated by urban centers."[42] Fetterley and Pryse, by contrast, find the opposite of urban elite desire: what distin-
guishes writers such as Jewett, they say, is the "desire not to hold up regional
characters to potential ridicule by eastern urban readers but rather to present
regional experience from within, so as to engage the reader's sympathy and identification."[43] And Nancy Glazener (though she agrees with Brodhead about
Jewett) has recently argued that we should see Garland not as the urbanized
turncoat from the Middle Border recent critics have made him, but as the prairie
populist he said he was.[44] June Howard is virtually alone in arguing that the
"celebratory" arguments of feminist recovery critics and the historicizing critiques of the ideological critics both need to be addressed in any comprehensive account.[45]

   As I have been suggesting, it is no accident that these two opposing arguments can be found coexisting in contemporary critical discourse and in the regionalist manifestos of seventy and a hundred years ago. At one level, the literary

regionalists, like the three painters at the Iowa conference, have been more interested in art and its values than in the regions they represent and those regions' specific cultural values. And they have been more interested in art and its values than the cultural values, other than literary values, espoused in urban centers. The region in literary regionalism is at most of secondary importance— the morals of the stories that were told in literary forums, from the end of our regional conflict in the 1860s into the globalized 2000s, have been remarkably similar, whether they were set in Iowa, Georgia, Maine, or California. They use very similar techniques and motifs, and all share one central conviction: that literary sensibility, literary culture, is better than, of more value than, either the local cultures in which these dramatizations of literary value were staged or the larger urban cultures across the country within which the texts were produced and where they found their largest audience. The literary culture to which literary regionalists subscribed and which they helped create was based on cosmopolitan ideals of cultural inclusiveness, ideals embedded in regionalism's narrative conventions. These stories represented, through character, theme, event, direct address, and implied author and reader, both urban and rural, both powerful and powerless, both local and more global concerns, both hegemony and antihegemony.

Joni Kinsey, in her exhibition catalog for *Plain Pictures,* uses the word "prospects" to signal the confluence in prairie paintings of the aesthetic—the prospect that is the organizing point of view in landscape aesthetics—and the actual social and economic prospects of the place represented.[46] Like Kinsey's use of "prospects," I intend "cosmopolitanism" as a term that collapses the distinctions between the economic, ideological, and artistic realms and thereby helps to demonstrate their interconnectedness in local color and other literatures for artists and audiences. This is not, I want to stress, simply a question of the privileged class status of many interested in literary production. Cosmopolitanism, as some of its most recent theorists have stressed, is a quality that can be acquired accidentally or purposely by people in or out of power, in or out of the money.

The hegemonic and antihegemonic approaches are not very satisfying, in part because both smack of hubris, though in different ways. The hegemonic reading assumes that the writers we study were bigger numskulls than we are, less capable of multiple commitments, less able to understand the ideological forces at work in their cultures, less politically savvy, less empathetic, more likely to be the unwilling dupes of power, less cosmopolitan than ourselves. And the antihegemonic reading seems to maintain the equally arrogant (and ahistorical) assumption that the regionalist authors' politics mirror critics' own. As explanations they fall short not because both are wrong, but because both are equally incomplete. Either can be supported quite easily with textual

evidence because each gets at precisely half the full picture. Both sets of understandings and attitudes are represented in the texts, in fact, and played off
each other. Regionalist literary texts represent both sides of the major cultural
debates of their time. They dramatize the differences between and within
classes, regions, sexes, and communities, but not with the intention of resolving them. Instead of settling these debates, they opt for an oscillation between
the sides, a kind of contrapuntal, unresolved Bakhtinian symphony of cultural
voices and positions.[47]

Both the hegemonic and antihegemonic readings themselves, I would argue,
are based on fundamentally cosmopolitan assumptions. That is, both are motivated in part by their analyses of social exclusion from a perspective that
embraces inclusion. The idea that urban elites quaintified rural people and exploited them for literary fun and profit gains its power, as an analysis, from the
assumption that such lack of respect for Others is wrong, that it silences those
outside privileged circles, that its orchestration of cultural discourses is undervoiced. Otherwise the analysis is not worth making except perhaps as an attack
on authenticity, which in most cases is not the point: when Judith Fetterley and
Marjorie Pryse celebrate Jewett as a respecter of Maine persons and denigrate
Garland as a creator of marginalizing grotesques there is no argument that one
or the other author is in fact more authentically local, more legitimately a
native member of the group represented. Theirs is a perspectival argument:
Garland writes from "outside" and Jewett from "inside" their characters' perspectives, they claim, and thus Jewett gives them true voice while Garland silences them. The unspoken ethic is one of inclusion, in both social and critical
terms; the very rediscovery, or recovery, of local color is predicated on an argument about critical exclusion.[48] And in this sense the hegemonic reading is, of
course, the same: local color writers ventriloquize rural voices, and the voice of
the people supposedly represented cannot be heard. Here lies the critique's
force: local color fiction (from this perspective) is exclusive.

The hegemonic and counterhegemonic readings necessarily miss half of what
local color authors understood as their task. Irvin Cobb, a largely forgotten
writer of Kentucky local color stories, published in 1914 what was clearly a fable of regionalism and authenticity. Titled "Local Color," the story concerns a
writer who has penned and sold short stories and novelettes about prison life
for years but who felt like a fraud, since he had never been inside a jail. "The
truth about [prison life] has never been told in the form of fiction," he decides,
and "fiction is the most convincing form of telling truth. Always the trouble had
been that the people who have been to prison could not write about it and the
people who could write about it have not been to prison."[49] He hatches a plan
to have himself arrested and sent to jail. During the arrest the policeman checks
his hands and, finding them smooth, sees them as proof that he is a pickpocket,

when in fact they simply prove he is a writer, not a manual laborer. This is one of the many moments in the story problematizing authenticity, showing that even the material signs of the way one lives in one's local life are not easy to read. On the day he enters prison, all the other prisoners are miserable, but he is ecstatic. The other prisoners enter the prison grounds already dreaming of their freedom, but the writer enters savoring his imprisonment as a vocation. He is living the life, looking forward to each new day and each new prison event as a rich mine of material and experience. He greedily jots down surreptitious notes, hiding them in his cell.

This lasts for almost a year, after which he loses interest in his notes and becomes more and more like the other prisoners. By the time he gets out after three years, any distinction he felt in relation to the other prisoners has been erased. Upon his release, he walks the streets for a day and then mugs a man, recklessly, as if wanting to get caught. He is sent back to prison, fully hopeless. The obvious point is that if the writer lives the life he is writing about authentically enough, he ceases to be a writer. It is the writer's distance from his subject that allows him to write.

But Cobb does not suggest that regionalist stories are therefore, as Kaplan and others have argued, simply "urban" folk tales, or as Brodhead suggests, the literary equivalent of middle-class tourism. Cobb writes the story of his writer's imprisonment, he writes of the bad air, the hard cots, the "padding tread of the guards" (31), the violence, the contraband. He, unlike his imprisoned protagonist, manages to write prison fiction. The literary purview includes the authentic and the inauthentic, and Cobb's writing, like regionalist and literary fiction generally, constructs this sense of panoramic thoroughness by exposing little by little the limits of subliterary understandings. His protagonist does not lack the proper experience, he lacks literariness—he is not the writer Cobb himself is. The protagonist is right to think that writing about prison without knowing it is wrong, but wrong to think that living in prison will magically transform him into a better writer. He does not manage to stay both within and outside his subject at the same time.

Kate Chopin's "A Gentleman of the Bayou Têche" (1894) provides a slightly more complex but equally obvious argument along the same lines. Mr. Sublet, a rich outsider, wants to photograph Evariste, a poor local man, as a bit of "local color" for a magazine. Evariste, understanding the conventions of the portrait, wants to wear his finest clothes, but Sublet tells him, no, he wants him in his everyday rags, and he pays him in advance for posing. When Evariste is told that the caption will probably describe him as one of the "low-down" Cajuns of the Bayou Têche, he has his daughter give the money back and explain why he won't pose. Evariste, coincidentally, then rescues Sublet's son from drowning, and Sublet suggests that they caption his picture "A hero of Bayou Têche."

Evariste insists that his was not a heroic act, just what anyone would do; what he wants as a caption is "a gent'man of de Bayou Têche." And Sublet agrees. Chopin is writing about the ethics of representation within the context of the competing desires of the magazine audience for "picturesque" depictions of everyday life and the desire of the people represented to be seen in some way that jives with their own self-image. Evariste does not want false representations of himself, whether they are hurtful or romantically overblown. He was willing to be photographed in his "low-down" clothes rather than his Sunday best; what he really objected to was the kind of reading the picture would be given. And finally, of course, Chopin's story shows him to be a bit of both, one of the low-down Cajuns and a gentleman, a gentleman who says "de" instead of "the." This story, like Cobb's, is about art more than it is about Cajuns, and about literary art in particular. Anyone can come down to the bayou on a quick hunting vacation like Mr. Sublet and take a picture of a local character. But only the literary artist has the kind of perspective necessary to represent what is lost and gained, by all concerned, in the cross-cultural encounter. Only the literary artist can write from both the inside and the outside.

The hallmark of local color and later regionalist writing, then, is its attention to both local and more global concerns, most often achieved through a careful balancing of different groups' perspectives. This can be seen in the trope, extremely common in regionalist fiction, of the visitor who frames, interprets, and/or invades the scene, as in Jewett's narrators, Garland's returning emigrants, Charles Chesnutt's Northerners, Edith Wharton's narrator in *Ethan Frome,* Jim Burden in Cather's *My Antonia,* and so on. In these texts the urban visitor's perspective is represented as in some ways clearly superior to the rural ones, but that perspective is far from stable and rarely reliable. The visitor does not, in the end, determine our reading, but helps give these texts their cosmopolitan flavor, since the competing cultural views voiced by visitors and visitees mirror and contend with one another. Even when the distance between visitor and implied author is slight, the implied author and the implied reader meet in an understanding broader than, more cosmopolitan than, that of the characters or the narrator. Jewett's narrator in *Country of the Pointed Firs* clearly does not understand some of what she sees, for instance a deficiency we as readers note. The narrator depicts the retired whaling captains she visits as quaint, provincial, out of touch; but we cannot help noticing that these men have been to China, to ports all over the world, and in some ways have a broader purview than either the other locals or our urban visitor. The rural people and the urban people in these texts have discrepant forms of cosmopolitanism, and only we, the implied readers and the implied author, who meet in a cosmopolitan compact of literary vision, comprehend them all.

These texts abound with images of failed, partial, incomplete cosmopolitan-isms, prompting us to larger and larger overviews. Jewett's visiting writer's cos-mopolitan vista is figured when she needs to leave Mrs. Todd's house, where she has been boarding, and move into a schoolhouse on the hill, which gives her the commanding overview she feels she needs as a writer. In Mary Hartwell Catherwood's "Pontiac's Lookout" (1894), the protagonist stands on a "grassy open cliff" above her village where, forty years earlier, the great Ottawa chief Pontiac had gazed across the land in "hope of the union of his people."[50] This is related to what the Southwestern regionalist Mary Austin called regionalism's "proverbial bird's-eye view of the American scene."[51] We as readers are prompted to the bird's-eye view by these represented vistas, but we are also prompted by the oscillation between interested perspectives (between urbanites and villagers, villagers and farmers, Norwegian and French settlers, Northerners and South-erners, and so on) to the kind of sweeping view of the cultural scene that these interested parties either cannot or will not take.

This dynamic of alternating cultural visions structuring a reading that exceeds them all occurs in all the great regionalist writing, and any text that fails this test is without exception considered subliterary. Regionalist texts represent the ar-guments alive in the culture about city and country, nature and culture, center and periphery, tradition and modernity, high and low, masculinity and feminin-ity, the costs and benefits of progress, and any number of other issues; but in-stead of resolving these debates, they oscillate between the sides, producing, finally, a complex symphony of cultural voices and positions whose only reso-lution lies in the reader-writer compact to survey the fullness of the scene. It is significant, too, that Garland's urbanite in "Up the Coulee" is an actor, that Jim Burden is an attorney, that Eggleston's Hoosier is a teacher, and that the narra-tor of *Ethan Frome* works for an engineering firm. These professional types con-sider themselves cosmopolitan, but they all fall short. The *philosophes* from whom Howellsian cosmopolitanism descended made little distinction between litera-ture, science, and politics, but the nineteenth-century writers understood these as conflicting forms of knowledge, competing for cultural authority. What made for local color fiction was the newly expanded magazine market, which was not a phenomenon the Eastern metropolis, but a national one. What made for the expanded magazine world was—in a word—industrialism, which cre-ated the rise of a middle class with some discretionary cultural spending power on the one hand, and the professionalization of all kinds of cultural and scien-tific work on the other.[52] Pierre Bourdieu has outlined a similar set of changes in France in the nineteenth century, although the full opposition to the bour-geois world he takes to be central to the structure of the literary field in France is not as important in America, any more than Howells is as antibourgeois as

Flaubert.[53] This is at least in part because of the nature of the struggle for cultural authority in America, which was not so much a struggle between classes as one within the middle class.

In this scramble for cultural authority, the ministers, the physicians, the businessmen, the politicians, the scientists, the journalists, and the social scientists were all making their pitches, and in that melee, the literary writers, along with their editors and reviewers, staked out a specific place in the cultural landscape by making specific claims. They could not very well, in the face of science, claim to have final say about objective reality (although some tried); they did not do a very good job battling the ministers and doctors for primacy in the cure of souls (although again, some tried); and so on. What they did do quite successfully was claim, in a world of increasing specialization and fragmentation, that they maintained the broadest, most inclusive view. The businessmen were as parochial as the Brahmins (as, for instance, in Howells's story of the local culture of Boston in *The Rise of Silas Lapham,* or for that matter his more explicit discussion in "The Man of Letters as a Man of Business"), the scientists were as parochial as the divines; only literary writers, they claimed, could see it all. Their cosmopolitanism was announced as their stock in trade.

The local color writers' first commitment was to this new ethic of the evolving literary market. In *Crumbling Idols,* Garland makes clear who he is battling against in his constant digs at the "academics" who have arrogated literary culture to themselves on the one hand, and his disdain for popular fictions on the other. His literary culture is locked in a battle with competitors, and the only things holding back the new flowering he foresees are "first, lack of a market; and, second, lack of perception" (16). At times he casts the materialist sciences as the competitor and then argues that literature does more than relay sociological facts; it can "touch, and lift, and exalt men" (133). At other times the competitors are the schools, and then he is willing to claim that "literary power . . . is at bottom sociologic" (140).

The academics make two basic errors, according to Garland. First, they do not want new literature: "'We have books and paintings enough in the market,'" he has them say. "'When we want a book, we buy a classic, and know what we are getting'" (132). In so protecting their control of the literary market, they are making a fundamental error, since only by representing the fullness of evolving contemporary life can literature fulfill its "sociologic" function. And second, they have too provincial an outlook. "From your library, or car-window, you look upon our life; that is the extent of your knowledge of our conditions" (133), he chides them. "All over America, in towns and cities, there are groups of readers who . . . have not only all the substantial acquirements . . . but possess . . . a more intimate knowledge of American life than the aristocrat who prides himself on never having been farther west than Buffalo" (129). The liter-

ary arbiters' purported disdain for readers is, among other things, undemocrat-
ic and a sign of their limited view of the American scene. Garland also claims
that what has made for the new literature (which the "academics" ignore) is the
"splendid light" of Darwin and Herbert Spencer, and just as these scientists have
shown the path of physical development, so will literary writers provide our social development with a "search light" (38–39). The past is feudalistic, the future
democratic, he writes, and if the past ignored women and children, the future
will include them, "and fiction will embody these facts" (39). The academics are
stuck in the past, but the new literary sensibility sees both past and future. The
biologists see only the physical, but literature comprehends the physical and the
spiritual. The sociologists understand types, but the literary "veritists" understand
both types and individuals. The academics are absolutists, while Garland and his
gang are the avenging "relativists in art" (64).

A negative review of *Crumbling Idols* in the *Atlantic Monthly* suggests the ubiq-
uity of arguments about inclusiveness. "The book should have been printed on
birch bark and bound in butternut home-spun," the reviewer writes, ridiculing
its earthy pretensions. But more important, the reviewer suggests that it "should
have had for cover design a dynamite bomb, say, with sputtering fire-tipped fuse:
for the essays which it contained were so many explosions of literary Jingoism
and anarchy."[54] Jingoism is closed-mindedness and exclusion, even as anarchy is
inclusion gone wild, a fear of unregulated openness to difference, of hierarchy
abandoned. Reviews of local color fiction commonly praised authors' aesthetic
inclusiveness. An 1884 review in the *Nation* of *Where the Battle Was Fought* by
Charles Egbert Craddock (Mary Noailles Murfree) claims that a close reading
of the text will show "how rich and varied a material can be found in a dull,
deserted country neighborhood by an imagination keen in detecting the poetic
value" there. The reviewer praises Craddock's earlier *In the Tennessee Mountains*
for its "exquisite balance" and "fine harmony," and claims that while Craddock
is not yet writing *King Lear*, "the highest places are open to him."[55] Almost thirty
years later, the *New York Times* reviewed Craddock's *Raid of the Guerrilla*: "In her
latest work, she gives some admirable stories of these mountains and their picturesque people, all presented with the true artistic idealization, which is truer
than the realism of actuality."[56] William Baskervill in 1897 claimed that her
"real power . . . rests upon a sympathetic understanding of human life"; she realizes that "untutored souls are perplexed with the same questions and shaken
by the same doubts that baffle the learned . . . in any environment."[57] Her literary "power" is the result of her egalitarianism.

Similar reviews were given to all the local colorists. Henry C. Vedder finds in
George Washington Cable's *Old Creole Days* "a natural aptitude for literature . . .
a style of limpid clearness; a style of pure English, instinct with life and passion,
sometimes reaching the borderland of poetry."[58] A review of Bret Harte in the

Nation in 1883 claims that Harte does for Western characters what Dickens does for Londoners: "That is, he has idealized them, made us like them, think well of them, and feel our common humanity in them."[59] In the *Atlantic Monthly* in 1894 we are told in a review of *Bayou Folk* that Kate Chopin is not a writer who is "afflicted with a purpose to add to our stock of knowledge concerning obscure varieties of the human race. Mrs. Chopin simply deals with what is familiar to her, and happens to be somewhat new in literature. She deals with it as an artist."[60] Willa Cather famously called *The Awakening* a Creole Bovary, and in her review produces a somewhat defensive reversal of the standard procedure: "I shall not attempt to say why Miss Chopin has devoted so exquisite and sensitive, well-governed a style to so trite and sordid a theme. She writes much better than it is ever given to most people to write, and hers is a genuinely literary style."[61] Another local color writer, Alice Brown, reviewing the *Country of the Pointed Firs*, wrote that the "pointed firs have their roots in the ground of national being" and that Jewett represents Maine with "Miltonic grandeur";[62] but Horace Scudder worries whether "Miss Jewett will ever attain the constructive power which holds in the grasp a variety of complex activities."[63] Another critic, after discussing the local characters in Mary Wilkins Freeman's work, concluded that "the center of [Freeman's] art . . . is humanity, the individual soul. . . . Her backgrounds are incidental."[64] William Dean Howells, reviewing Garland's *Main-Travelled Roads,* praises its thorough verisimilitude, "full of the bitter and burning dust, the foul and trampled slush of the common avenues of life," but claims that it is first and foremost "a work of art, and we think of fine art."[65] Writers were praised for their literary accomplishment in aesthetic terms— style, interest, clarity, balance, harmony, and so on—which necessarily shade into assessments of cosmopolitan comprehensiveness in their depiction of "life," especially the life of specific local populations. These populations, in turn, are important not for their specificity, which becomes "incidental," but for their "humanity." And this, in turn, is essential to what makes these works "fine art."

Howells hoped one day to see such literary critical procedures become fully scientific. The literary critic's job, he wrote, was:

> to classify and analyze the fruits of the human mind very much as the naturalist classifies the objects of his study, rather than to praise or blame them. . . . There is a measure of the same absurdity in his trampling on a poem, or novel, or an essay that does not please him as in a botanist's grinding a plant underfoot because he does not find it pretty. He does not conceive it is his business rather to identify the species and then explain how and where the specimen is imperfect and irregular. If he could once acquire this simple idea of his duty, he would be much more agreeable company than he is now, and a more useful member of society.[66]

Grace Isabel Colbron, writing in the *Bookman* in 1898, used similar arguments. "Specialization in art is not merely a matter of business," she writes. "It mirrors the great economic and scientific tendency, which is but a logical evolution in the growth of the world, mental and physical." Literature's specialization, nonetheless comprehends "the immensity of the field of the world's work."[67] Reviewers often praised writers for their achievements by comparing their works to that of scientists and other professionals. A 1904 review of Garland's latest novel praises the book's power to compel "the reader in spite of himself to feel that the novelist is in reality a historian" and claims that although "it does not claim to be a scientific treatment . . . as a study in the field of experimental psychic it is one of the most thought-stimulating works that has appeared in America in years."[68] In 1911 Harry Aubrey Toulmin compared Craddock to a social psychologist who had "served an apprenticeship in a stupendous human laboratory"; she thus had made a "genuine contribution to the science of social organization as well as to the creation of an artistic and literary success."[69] A reviewer in the *Overland Monthly* in 1886 praises Jewett as a social historian: since she is depicting events from a decade earlier within a disappearing group, a reader realizes "how great is the mere historic importance, apart from the purely humane or artistic value, of these stories."[70] Vedder notes George Washington Cable's religious thought, William Malone Baskervill notes his abilities in logic and moral philosophy, Randolph Bourne his ability to blend "romance and sociology."[71]

Critics did not necessarily believe that these were actual contributions to other sciences—such talk was at least in part critical hyperbole asserting literary value. And such claims always also included a suggestion that literature stood above and encompassed the sciences. Literature is as good as any science, critics suggested, but this did not mean that science was as good as literature. Norman Foerster, in his *Toward Standards* (1930), dedicated to regionalists Robert Frost and Willa Cather, makes this point in his discussion of the relation between naturalism and humanism: "Naturalism has prided itself upon its humble devotion of science, presumed to be the only respectable authority in modern thought, forgetting that, whatever science may do for us it cannot give us standards. Science gives us natural knowledge, not human objectives."[72] In the "picture of reality that science offers there are no values, but only quantitative measurements," Foerster writes, and literature, which is "skeptical of all such speculation based upon assumption of an underlying unity," is concerned with values (160–61).

And in asserting such literary values, local colorists developed a set of generic conventions for addressing the sociological, political, and philosophical issues of their day, the hallmark of which was to display both sides of pressing cultural debates without promoting either side, without suggesting "an underlying unity," but instead giving us "a greater sense of the complexity of life."[73] Whether the lines of cultural division are farmer-townsman, Eastern-Western, capital-labor, urban-rural, Anglo-Other, poverty-wealth, progress-tradition, or marriage-spinsterhood, what these narratives offer again and again is a third space, a vantage point from which to watch "the gliding panorama"[74] in which distinctions represented are erased in favor of a cosmopolitan ethic, an ethic that usually respects and disrespects both poles, "true to the broad exhibition of nature."[75] These texts promote a superior cultural position that comprehends all difference, and though not quite dismissing difference as atavistic, they suggest that a literary overview will make cultural differences not so much the basis for different identities, as the many elements of a larger, *literary* identity based precisely on such accumulated representations. Every text becomes thereby, whatever else it is, a parable of the value of the cosmopolitan literary sensibility. This ethic of cosmopolitanism has remained the central tenet of the literary class from the 1870s to the present, and membership in the supposedly exclusive club of the broad-minded and artistic is what these texts offered, and continue to offer, their readers.

Democratic Vistas and the Cosmopolitan Charge

W alt Whitman, the "Great Enumerator" whose lists of peoples, occupations, and possibilities in his poetry provide one model for American literary inclusiveness (and from whom I have cribbed my title), made some of the earliest arguments for literary cosmopolitanism in *Democratic Vistas* (1871):

> Like our huge earth itself, which, to ordinary scansion, is full of vulgar contradictions and offence, man, viewed in the lump, displeases, and is a constant puzzle and affront to the merely educated classes. The rare, cosmical, artist-mind, lit with the Infinite, alone constructs his manifold and oceanic qualities—but taste, intelligence, culture, (so-called,) have been against the masses, and remain so.[76]

Ordinary perspectives make the fullness of life look contradictory, and only artists are not puzzled by its manifold nature; they in fact "construct" it as such. Whitman follows this passage by calling for a fuller representation of the "rude rank spirit of the democracies," but not in the way later realists would defend representing the people. Rather Whitman always reaches toward the cosmic— "Far, far, indeed, stretch, in distance, our Vistas!" (956), he declaims, and likens the literary geniuses of world culture to "orbs and systems of orbs, moving in free paths in the spaces of that other heaven, the kosmic intellect, the soul" (973).

William Dean Howells was not exactly a fan of the rude and rank, and was certainly less "kosmically" inclined. But in his capacity as editor of the *Atlantic* and *Harper's* he was instrumental in publishing the first wave of local color writing as well as what we might call the second wave, ethnic literature, and he, too, understood the literary as that which comprehends seeming contradiction. Like many in his day, Howells believed that American literature ought to be representative. Celebrating regional writing as "our decentralized literature," he claimed that like the House of Representatives, hundreds of writers, each with his or her own regional sensibilities and interests, would collectively author the bills of an American literature. And the hallmark of our literature and of our politics was attention to both local and national interests. Howells's calls for realism, his famous argument about the timidity of art, the call to represent what is not conventionally represented, to survey more of the scene—all of this is part of an argument for comprehensiveness, an argument about literature's responsibility to provide a full overview. He wants novels that are "spacious," he writes, because "art must become democratic."[77]

Other novelist-critics made similar statements. John De Forest, in an essay in 1868, said that the "great American novel" would appear in sections, because we are a "nation of provinces."[78] Others thought that the multiplicity was not just national, but global; Julian Hawthorne, writing in the *North American Review* in 1884, claimed that America is not a "petty nationality, like France, England Germany," in part because we had inherited all of their cultures and more.[79] Others saw literary breadth in terms of fields of knowledge rather than locations of culture. Edward Eggleston explained his own career in terms of his openness to science, literature, and experience:

> There was nothing like specialization in my tastes or pursuits, and this accursed versatility has been one of the unlucky elements of my life. My fondness for languages was diversified and diluted by a rage for such mathematics as I had a chance to study . . . and my literary pursuits were interrupted by a dabbling in geology, favored by the exposure of fossiliferous strata near Madison, where I lived during my geological period. With my limited powers of nervous endurance it was not well to spread my exertions over so many acres of endeavor; but the error was not so bad as the opposite one of a narrow specialization at an early age might have been.[80]

Breadth of knowledge makes possible "that exhilaration and exaltation which the liberated mind feels in the rebound from constraint," Eggleston claims, "and which carries it for a time to a higher level than it might otherwise have attained" (285). His clumsily false humility (his "accursed versatility") is part of his general argument for literary breadth of perspective. The Southern regionalist James Lane Allen in 1886 sounds much like Howells:

> To relate nature to life in literature as they are related in reality requires that one be more than a mere novelist—more than a novelist and an artist combined. It requires that he shall also be in some measure a scientist: he must comprehend the significance of the natural pictorial environment of humanity in its manifold effects

upon humanity, and he must make this knowledge available for literary presentation.[81]

Frank Norris made these same arguments in his magazine essays, collected in
Responsibilities of the Novelist (1903), and enacted them in his fiction, especially
The Octopus (1901), with its Eastern visitor protagonist and last-minute rush to
spread blame and credit across the entire social landscape.

In many cases, along with the social inclusiveness came explicit social distinction. The editors of the *Overland Monthly* explained their mission in 1883
as: "to make a bond between the various castes and clans and cliques of people
now pulling in different ways or forgetting each other's existence, in the various branches of the struggle toward the highest civilization." But they often
mixed this progressive egalitarianism with statements more clearly elitist: "In all
great literature the humanity is larger than the provincialism, and intelligible to
all whose opinion is worth having." One reviewer claimed that Mary Wilkins
Freeman "knows how these village people live within themselves. The slug-
gishness of their intellectual processes. The almost bovine placidity"; because of
this she manages "delicately drawn, sympathetic" portraits. Again, openness to
difference is merged with cultural snobbery.[82]

Academic criticism has from the start been infused with both the elitist and
the inclusive parts of this complex. "Our association is a representative body in
the fullest sense of the word," MLA President James Taft Hatfield wrote in 1901,

its members show a growing interest in each other's work, and in the progress of
science as a whole. . . . I hold then that the first duty and highest function, even as
an organization of linguistic specialists, is in relation to the total life of the commonwealth, is political, and that this deep note should be the first sounded at every
gathering: we must place enlightened, trained intellect at the direct service of the
state, as the only solvent of the problems of municipal government, corporate
greed, and the tyranny of manual labor.[83]

Hatfield's call to arms should give the lie to the idea that a politicized version
of the discipline is of recent mint: the "first duty and highest function" of criticism is political and cosmopolitan. In 1894 Professor Henry C. Vedder praised
Edmund Clarence Steadman's poetry for its "cosmopolitan spirit," and Frances
Hodgson Burnett for "the breadth of her knowledge, her sympathy, her humanity." In explaining his general aesthetic principles he takes a more clearly
Kantian cosmopolitan line: "A truth, to be beautiful, must be a whole truth. This
principle excludes from poetry all didacticism, which is essentially half-
truths."[84] Professor Bliss Perry writes in 1902 that "our choices, in the selection
of fiction," or our evaluations, "turn upon the more or less unconscious desire
to enlarge the range of our experience."[85] As if bringing the argument up to

the postcolonial present, Professor George Woodberry claimed in 1905 that "the language of literature is the language of all the world."[86]

Two decades later the same arguments endured. William McFee, writing in *Harper's Magazine* in 1926, went so far as to claim that "more than in any other calling, has the teacher of English need of a colossal general knowledge. He should be a master of allusion. He must take all knowledge for his province."[87] When Mencken, in inimitable style, attacked J. E. Spingarn's nascent new critical theory in 1919, he did not blame him for having a theory, "for a professor must have a theory, as a dog must have fleas," but for a particular kind of overreaching.[88] Spingarn's theory, he argued,

> throws a heavy burden upon the critic. It presupposes that he is a civilized and tolerant man, hospitable to all intelligible ideas and capable of reading them as he runs. This is a demand that at once rules out nine-tenths of the grown-up sophomores who carry on the business of criticism in America. Their trouble is simply that they lack the intellectual resilience necessary for taking in ideas, and in particular new ideas. (14)

As Trilling would argue thirty years later, Mencken also suggests that professors' political beliefs constitute a trained incapacity to read openly.

> As practiced by all such learned and diligent but essentially ignorant and unimaginative men, criticism is little more than a branch of homiletics. They judge a work of art . . . simply and solely by [the artist's] orthodoxy. If he is what is called a "right thinker," if he devotes himself to advocating the transient platitudes in a sonorous manner, then he is worthy of respect. But if he lets fall the slightest hint that he is in doubt about any of them, or worse still, that he is indifferent, then he is a scoundrel, and hence, by their theory, a bad artist. Such pious piffle is horribly familiar among us. (15)

Although Trilling is complaining about leftist intellectuals and Mencken about conservative Christians, the impulse is the same. "We are in fact a nation of evangelists," Mencken writes on one of his favorite themes. "Every third American devotes himself to improving and lifting up his fellow citizens, usually by force; the messianic delusion is our national disease. Thus the moral Privatdozenten have the crowd on their side, and it is difficult to shake their authority" (15–16). And so Mencken likes Spingarn's theory for its cosmopolitan demands: Spingarn insists that "the critic be a man of intelligence, of toleration, of wide information, of genuine hospitality to ideas," writes Mencken, all of which is good. But then, "once he has stated his doctrine, the ingenious ex-professor, professor-like, immediately begins to corrupt it" (17).

Spingarn, in insisting on reading the text on its own terms, on not subjecting it to contextual readings, is, Mencken feels, ridiculous. "Having laid and hatched, so to speak, his somewhat stale but still highly nourishing egg, he begins to argue fatuously that the resultant flamingo is the whole mustering of the critical Aves" (17). Spingarn tries to close down criticism, but critics should in fact think about everything—politics, biography, morality—if for no other reason than that artists do. Neither Spingarn nor Mencken was writing directly about cosmopolitanism, but both base their central claims on cosmopolitan assumptions and assume that their audience agrees. Spingarn, in his seminal essay on the New Criticism, objects to "sociological" forms of criticism because they are not inclusive enough, since literary art at its best transcends its represented objects and therefore reaches beyond sociological facts into ideals and possibilities.[89] When Mencken attacks Spingarn he does so by claiming, in turn, that Spingarn is not inclusive enough, that a full criticism should tackle a broader range of human topics than Spingarn allows.

The Southern Agrarians, often taken to be the opposite of open-minded cosmopolitans, nonetheless used very similar arguments in the early 1930s. In their introductory "Statement of Principles" in *I'll Take My Stand* the Twelve Southerners argue that "we cannot recover our native humanism by adopting some standard of taste that is critical enough to question the contemporary arts but not critical enough to question the social and economic life which is their ground" (xliv). Donald Davidson in his essay in that volume and elsewhere commends the "broad sense of the world which comes, paradoxically, from a comparative retirement from the world."[90] Allen Tate claims that while provincialism may not assume a relation both to history and to the rest of the world, regionalism always does.[91] John Crowe Ransom, like the earlier regionalists, thought that the "important benefit" of the regional way of life is that it "feels right, it has aesthetic quality."[92] In these writings, as in John T. Frederick's Midwestern regionalist version in the same years (which encouraged the Agrarians' efforts), classic New Critical denials of the relation of literature to life were often followed by an equally classic statement of literary cosmopolitanism. Frederick, who founded the *Midland* in 1915 in a Garland-like rejection of Eastern dominance in favor of local, provincial self-determination, also wrote that "regionalism is an incident and a condition, not a purpose or motive"; the regionalists' work "has literary importance only in so far as it meets the standard of good writing at all times and in all places."[93] And although the Agrarians made many political arguments, Ransom also wrote that "true poetry has no great interest in improving or idealizing the world, which does well enough. It only wants to realize the world, to see it better."[94] The Agrarians and other regionalists of the 1920s and 1930s claimed to present larger, wider, more thorough sets of representations than their predecessors, helping readers to "realize the world."

As new groups of literary authors made their stands, they regularly employed parallel arguments and were answered in kind, each claiming it was the first group of writers not too timid to represent all of life. Ezra Pound made the argument explicitly in "Provincialism the Enemy," in which he defines provincialism as simply "ignorance of the manners, customs, and nature of people living outside one's own village, parish, or nation."[95] Gertrude Stein came close to fulfilling the ideal of full representation *ad absurdum* in *The Making of Americans* (1925), where her goal, she said, was to represent not just every kind of person, but every person in the world; she only stopped when she realized it was possible, she said, and so lost interest. Many others—the proletarian writers, the noir writers, the Beats, the multiculturalists—argued in turn that previous literature had excluded important aspects of the full social life, which they, with their broader vista, would correct.

Three encyclopedic histories of American literature appeared in the twentieth century that demonstrate the durability and versatility of this literary ethos: the 1988 *Columbia Literary History of the United States,* edited by Emory Elliott et al.; the 1948 *Literary History of the United States,* edited by Robert E. Spiller, Willard Thorp, Thomas H. Johnson, and Henry Seidel Canby; and the 1917–1921 *Cambridge History of American Literature,* edited by William P. Trent, John Erskine, Stuart P. Sherman, and Carl Van Doren. The 1988 *Columbia History* stakes its claims on the dual grounds of representing critical diversity rather than consensus and reflecting the "significantly broadened scope" of literary studies since the 1948 *Literary History.*[96] This broadened scope is the result of the discipline's necessary involvement in the social changes of the 1960s and 1970s, Elliott writes, especially those surrounding the Vietnam War and the civil rights and women's movements. The preface consciously "acknowledges diversity, complexity, and contradiction" (xiii) and apologizes that it "could not be exhaustive," settling for an "attempt to establish an overview" of the various literatures, histories, and critical perspectives in America (xiii). It makes a case for its own scientific basis through reference to changing epistemological theories since Spiller's time, which necessitate and account for multiplicity in both literary and critical terms.

The 1988 *History,* while it does indeed add some African American authors that Spiller ignored, also has considerably less coverage in other areas. Spiller includes much more discussion of non-English writings in the seventeenth century, for instance, more on philosophical writing in all periods, and, notably, more on regionalist writing. The 1988 *History* ignores many of the women who were "rediscovered" beginning in the 1970s but were already part of the discussion in 1948. Rose Terry Cooke, Annie Trumbull Slosson, Celia Thaxter, and

Ruth McEnery Stuart are all discussed in Spiller et al. and not mentioned in Elliott et al.; the only regionalist briefly mentioned in 1988 and not in 1948 is Alice Brown.

Spiller's *History* is, in fact, a monument of inclusiveness. Just as Elliott explains the need for a new history in relation to social change, Spiller et al. refer, if somewhat obliquely, to World War II and the beginning of the Cold War: "The values as well as the facts of modern civilization must be examined if man is to escape self-destruction," they write, and therefore, as Garland and Mencken and post-1960s critics would suggest, they need to be less academic and more engaged in the world.[97] "Scholars can no longer be content to write for scholars; they must make their knowledge meaningful and applicable to humanity" (vii). They assure readers that they, the editors and writers, unlike the contributors to the 1917–1921 *Cambridge History*, "are historians and critics rather than specialists in a narrow sense" (vii).

The *Cambridge History*, however, had this same sense of itself: the editors of 1917 disparage their immediate predecessor, Charles F. Richardson, because his *American Literature 1607–1885* (1886–1888) too exclusively focused on a single set of aesthetic criteria. Rather than being narrow aesthetic specialists, Trent et al. worked at what has come to be called "recovery," to wit: "to restore the memory of writers who are neglected because they are forgotten and because they are no longer sympathetically understood."[98] To understand these writers is to abandon ideas of "art for art" and attend to the full expressive culture of Americans in relation to their "exploration, settlement, labour for subsistence, religion, and statecraft," including attention to "a prose competently recording their practical activities and expressing their moral, religious, and political ideas" (xii). Like the cultural studies radicals of the 1990s and the official encyclopedists of the New Critical era, they argue that broad "acquaintance with the written record of these two centuries should enlarge the spirit of American literary criticism" for anyone with "a taste and judgment unperverted by the current finical and transitory definitions of literature" (xiii).

Rather than arguing, as the two later histories would, that their approach was sui generis, the *Cambridge History* editors praise a number of earlier works, including the 1855 *Cyclopaedia of American Literature,* by Evert A. and George L. Duyckinck, because it attempted "to bring together as far as possible in one book convenient for perusal and reference, memorials and records of the writers of the country and their works, from the earliest period to the present day" (xv). The Duyckincks's sense of comprehensiveness was based on the idea (again very congenial to today's multicultural cultural studies), that "it is important to know what books have been produced, and by whom; whatever the books may have been or whoever the men" (xv). The editors of the *Cambridge History* applaud this openness and that of Moses Coit Tyler, whose *History of American Literature, 1607–1765* (1878) they feel was animated by "similar breadth of historical interest" (xv).

It was "breadth" that they felt justified their own project, both in terms of the material covered and in terms of the contributors:

> It was a hard saying of a Spanish aphorist of the seventeenth century that "to equal a predecessor one must have twice his worth." We should deprecate the application of that standard to *The Cambridge History of American Literature*, yet we are not without hope that the work, of which we here present the first volume, will be found to mark some progress in the right direction. We would call attention to the following as perhaps its chief distinctive features: (1) It is on a larger scale than any of its predecessors which have carried the story from colonial times to the present generation; (2) It is the first history of American literature composed with the collaboration of a numerous body of scholars from every section of the United States and from Canada; (3) It will provide for the first time an extensive bibliography for all periods and subjects treated; (4) It will be a survey of the life of the American people as expressed in their writings rather than a history of *belles-lettres* alone. (vi)

The four main editors of the *Cambridge History* as well as the contributors were chosen because of their geographic representativeness, and it is arguably the most comprehensive of these three major projects, with its essays on Yiddish newspapers, magazines, economic and political writing, "Amerind" literature, and American writing in French and German. The missing figures in each of these earlier histories (there are very few women in Spiller's representation of the Harlem Renaissance, for instance) seem obviously egregious to our own sense of the field, but the desire for representational breadth in each case is demonstrably the same. Likewise, if the *Heath Anthology of American Literature* (1990) is the most ethnically inclusive of any literary anthology to date, in other ways it pales in comparison to the wildly comprehensive nineteenth-century anthologies by Rufus Griswold and others, with their hundreds and hundreds of poets. As in the case of the histories, Paul Lauter's preface to the *Heath Anthology* repeats its predecessors' claims to "the widest sampling," including many texts that were "lost, forgotten or suppressed," and claims anew to "reconnect literature and its study with the society and culture."[99] (Lauter sometimes makes his case somewhat unfairly, it should be said, mistakenly claiming, for instance, that Spiller does not mention Frederick Douglass, when in fact Spiller discusses Douglass, his books, his magazine work, and two biographies of him.) Lauter makes a case for the diversity of his slate of academics, which is unlike the "small homogenous editorial board—of the sort that had up to then characterized *every* anthology" (xxxviii), just as the editors of the 1917 and 1948 histories advertised the diversity of their boards. The literary cosmopolitanism that is our current ethos has been alive and well for 150 years.

Literary cosmopolitanism's ethic of inclusiveness can take many different shapes, informing literary manifestos by realists and antirealists, modernists and antimodernists, hypertexters and literary Luddites alike. It explains why multiculturalism, and before it feminism and ethnic studies, found their most congenial home and some of their most forceful articulations and elaborations in literature departments: not because of changes in literary values, but because of consistency in them. In the deconstructive insistence on incommensurability and indeterminacy, as in New Criticism's enthroning of ambiguity and complexity, psychoanalytic arguments for overdetermination, Marxian insistence on considering structure as well as superstructure, and, as I mentioned before, Bakhtinian and Deleuzian theories, over and over again literary culture redefines itself primarily by taking a wider, more inclusive swath, by finding texts to be more complex, by finding more kinds of writing by more kinds of people, by finding more ways of reading, by finding more uses for our methods, by finding theories that reinvent or reinvigorate this ethos. As this quick survey of major histories suggests, there is often a Derridean supplementarity at work, with groups of authors and texts quietly forgotten amid the fanfare of new additions. But the advertisement is most often for an addition, a complication, a widening. Partisans of one critical school counter others by attacking them with the term "illiberal" or "elitist" or some other synonym for exclusionary bias. Critics of all stripes end their articles with claims that the text under study "disturbs basic social categories," suggests "the impossibility of resolution," "explodes cultural dichotomies," "illuminates paradox," "recasts crippling oppositions," produces "productive incommensurability."[100]

These last phrases are all culled from the writings of the faculty of a single institution and can be found in profusion everywhere. For instance, take a recent issue of *Profession*: Mary Louise Pratt applauds "efforts of alterity" and suggests that rather than translation, we should think of "doubling," of "multiplying"; Sherry Simon ends her essay validating a view that is "with and against," "aligned and adverse," and "multifocal"; Doris Sommer ends her introduction embracing differences "that make both natives and newcomers uncomfortable and self-conscious"; Dianna Taylor writes that we "do not simply or unproblematically understand one another. Let us recognize that every effort toward understanding needs to work against notions of easy access, decipherability, and translatability"; James F. Slevin claims that the aim of higher education is "not how to solve problems but how to problematize, not how to fix but how to make more complex, even difficult, one's understanding."[101]

Of course the counterurge that would find a clear political unconscious in literary art has been very important to literary criticism in recent decades as well, leading to a serial debunking of canonical authors and a rousing or hollow-sounding (depending on one's perspective) call to political action. In a recent piece on immigrant fiction, Nancy K. Harris worries about what she sees as Abraham Cahan's "ambivalence" about ethnic politics, claiming that "Cahan's stories often tend to deconstruct all possible values, so that no position is finally presented as preferable, although almost all are viable."[102] (I of course see this not as Cahan's ambivalence but his method.) But often even the most politicized critics rely in their arguments on the cosmopolitan ethos. Lisa Lowe's recent *Immigrant Acts: Asian American Cultural Politics* (1996), to take just one example, is a catalog of crimes of exclusion that regularly exhorts its audience to attempt "dialectical unification across difference."[103] Lowe castigates the forces of canonicity for ignoring Asian American cultural production, but exhorts us to "diversify our practices to include a more heterogeneous group . . . in the ongoing work of transforming hegemony" (83). Although it represents itself as a radical break from the past, obviously this critique of the literary takes as its ground what I am arguing is already the foundation of literary culture.

When I argue that the mainstream of literary criticism continues to privilege both rather than either/or, continues to be additive rather than reductive, to be and celebrate the inclusive, I do not mean to suggest any Platonist universality, in which the best literature or the best criticism is that which sees the full truth rather than the shadows on the wall. The hegemonic reading of regionalism is correct in arguing that regionalist authors' worldviews are contingent, partial, and the cosmopolitan perspective, especially as I have represented it here, does smack of privilege and imperialism, after all. The class status of the majority of those who consider themselves literary readers and writers has always been preponderantly above the middle. Literary inclusiveness is not political inclusiveness or economic justice. And the price of admission to this cultural compact exceeds the ability to pay of many of the very people being called to its characterological shores. Literary history is full of and driven by what we continually find are inadequate cosmopolitanisms. But the history of literary production and reception since the 1850s, as in the case of the revision of the canon over the last several decades, is a history of attempts at coming closer to the cosmopolitan ideal of inclusion. The local colorists and their critical supporters were among the first to articulate this cosmopolitan defense of and standard for literary art, and it lives on throughout our wildly diverse discipline.

The artists at the Iowa conference, it seems to me, were right to resist the politico-disciplinary desires of their academic critics. Their paintings should not be reduced to one political reading. The academics, conversely, are perfectly right to point out that such a reading is possible and worthwhile. They would only be wrong if they denied what was also palpably present in the artists' work: a suggestion of the represented land's ability to absorb not just its ravages but its readings. These artists, as Susan Gillman has suggested about local color writers, manage to "look away from and toward the disturbing present" at the same time.[104] They, like the regionalist literary artists, are not apolitical, they are multiply political. In Richard Ford's *Independence Day* (1995), a veteran real estate salesman explains to an apprentice that the three laws governing real estate sales are "locution, locution, locution," but the Iowa artists and the local color writers are not selling the land they represent, at least not in the way realtors do. Regional writers' and artists' locutions are saturated by economic interests, yes, but their primary interest, their region, is art. That is what they want to produce, and that is what they would like to sell.

And in artists' talk, art is therefore what they insist on. When Patrick refers to Greenberg, she is, among other things, legitimating her work through reference to a prime theorist of the artistic. When Easker talks about his lines, he declares, likewise, that it is the formal nature of his painting that is its best guarantor of artistic status. Jacobshagen resists mimesis and politics in favor of a modernist/romantic version of the naïve expressive artist. In each case their descriptions of their paintings correspond to a basic formal, aesthetic framework; each reading is also a reference to a legitimating theoretical tradition. Literary writers in America, I argue, though they sometimes also justify their work in formal terms, have most often, over the last 150 years, legitimated their work, argued for its literariness, through reference to their texts' cosmopolitanism. Even when referencing notions of literary language, for instance, they point to larger cosmopolitan justifications.

In the strongest recent arguments for cosmopolitanism—including those by the likes of Julia Kristeva, Arnold Krupat, Hollinger, Ross Posnock, and Martha Nussbaum discussed below—cosmopolitanism is taken as the highest moral ground in a world beset by violent tribalism. In other arguments, notably Bruce Robbins's, Homi Bhabha's and James Clifford's, cosmopolitanism is taken to be the necessary effect of a global world, while writers from Christopher Lasch to Robert Reich have recycled the Marxian critique, claiming that the perfect cosmopolitans in our world are the corporate consultants in Park Avenue offices, manipulating the world system and beholden to no group, a critique that has roots in the eighteenth century and whose literary embodiment, if it can be called that, is Melville's Confidence Man. I mean to keep all these connotations alive, along with another: the colloquial meaning of "cosmopolitanism" as up-to-date connoisseurship, of not so much knowing everything the world has to offer as knowing the best the world has to offer. Because, as I say, cosmopolitanism in literary culture involves not just a politicized openness to experience, but an evaluation of literary texts as well, and herein lies its ongoing tension.

Our judgments of literature have been bounded by our sense of their cosmopolitanism, our cosmopolitanism the standard by which we judge both pos-
itively and negatively, the way we hierarchize, the way we have historically
decided whether, in fact, something is literary in the honorific sense or not. This
has put literary artists and critics from the 1870s to the present in the awkward
position of continually arguing that their distinction should rest on their refusal
to embrace distinction, that theirs is the best, most comprehensive view, even
though no view is inherently better than any other.

Cosmopolitanism

"Cosmopolitanism" is, of course, a word of extreme semiotic vagrancy, one that has become increasingly prevalent after the few lean decades when it languished in political exile. Marxists were not the first, but were certainly the most influential, to use the word as an insult, as a synonym for an elite intellectual lack of commitment to progressive, or indeed any community principles. The negative critique of the Enlightenment gave the tainting of cosmopolitanism a philosophical pedigree, and the lingering whiff of Stalinist anti-Semitism further contaminated a word that came to signify elite, effete taste-cultures. Amanda Anderson, in her excellent brief history of the term, also outlines more recent arguments against cosmopolitanism, including the charge that it overemphasizes "a heroicized individual cultivating its relation to otherness and to global diversity," and thus substituting "an art of virtue" for an actual political program.[105] The word was rarely if ever used as an honorific by American intellectuals from the 1960s through the 1980s.

The word's first meaning in most dictionaries still refers to the basic universalizing ethic of the Enlightenment, in which the *philosophes* declared themselves citizens of the world rather than subjects of a sovereign or state. It is this meaning that Julia Kristeva invokes, for instance, when she claims that she "is a representative of what is today a rare species, perhaps even on the verge of extinction in a time of renewed nationalism: I am a cosmopolitan."[106] But the species is not as rare as Kristeva suggests, since, as cultural critics, historians, and others have rethought their relation to ethnicity and globalism over the last decade, the word has been widely revived, to the point where David Harvey says, simply, "Cosmopolitanism is back," and Paul Rabinow can declare, "We are all cosmopolitans now."[107] The MLA Bibliography, to cite one index, shows a steady increase in uses of the term as a keyword, from one citation a year to al-most twenty; for all of the 1970s there are eleven recorded uses of the word, in the 1980s, twenty-five, in the 1990s, over a hundred, two-thirds of them in the second half of the decade.

Like Kant in "Idea for a Universal History from a Cosmopolitan Point of View" (1784) and "Perpetual Peace" (1796), many have turned to cosmopoli-tanism as an alternative to tribal or nationalist violence. Kant's essays are gov-erned by two assumptions—first, that the best society is one that maximizes personal freedom and minimizes the conflicts inherent to the "unsocial socia-bility" of human beings; and second, that the world had progressed to the point where "a violation of rights in one place is felt throughout the world."[108] Martha Nussbaum, writing in the *Boston Review* in 1994, though she traces her use of cosmopolitanism back to Diogenes, the Stoics, Seneca, and Plutarch, uses "Kantian morality" as the center of her proffered program of cosmopolitan ed-ucation.[109] Nussbaum, in what Richard Sennett criticizes as "Kantian opti-mism," urges us to teach children not that they are Americans first and human beings second, but the other way around. Diogenes's "invitation to think as a world citizen" is for Nussbaum the necessary basis of ethical relations.

> The accident of where one is born is just that, an accident; any human being might have been born in any nation. Recognizing this, [Diogenes's] Stoic successors held, we should not allow differences of nationality or class or ethnic membership or even gender to erect barriers between us and our fellow human beings. We should recognize humanity wherever it occurs, and give its fundamental ingredients, rea-son and moral capacity, our first allegiance and respect. . . . One should always be-have so as to treat with equal respect the dignity of reason and moral choice in every human being. (7–8)

This cosmopolitanism, Nussbaum suggests, is the road to peace and justice.

The *Boston Review,* which published Nussbaum's piece, also published a se-ries of replies and rejoinders, and I will devote some time to them and other re-cent arguments about cosmopolitanism in order to tease out those complex meanings of the word I would like to retain in what follows. Some of those who responded found Nussbaum's distinction between patriotism and cosmopoli-tanism too strongly drawn, and as such, invidious. "There is nothing wrong with encouraging children fully to explore their most local existence in order to reach beyond it in degrees," Sissela Bok wrote. "Nor need there be anything wrong with lasting pride in, love for, or identification through particular bonds, com-munities, and cultures." Kwame Anthony Appiah, taking his Ghanian patriot fa-ther as an example, also disputed the idea that the two terms are mutually exclusive. Some people think of national culture in terms of what Appiah calls a *tribal fantasy,* in which nations are ideal societies of face-to-face communication and shared values, and in which a common culture is at the heart of every family and individual. This common culture, of course, does not exist anywhere, and certainly not in any large modern nation. Thus patriotism in the US is never about that common culture, it is about shared (liberal) principles that, Appiah writes, are worth supporting and fighting for. This requires a kind of internal cosmopolitanism, in which diverse cultures within a state agree on shared principles, such as respect for human dignity and personal autonomy. These are as much Asante ideals as they are Western, Appiah notes, and are in both cultures often honored in the breach.[110]

Others saw the ideal itself as fundamentally flawed. Robert Pinsky condemned the "arrogance that would correct *your* provinciality with the cosmopolitanism of *my* terms," and rejected what he sees as a bloodless, rationalized refusal to feel the passions of local, communal, regional, and even national affiliation:

> In short, Nussbaum falls into the formulation of one particular province, the village of the liberal managerial class. I do not mean to be excessively scornful toward this conceptual village, a realm where the folk arts are UN institute reports and curriculum reform committees and enlightened social administration: like other villages it has within it valuable customs and individuals. But its inhabitants characteristically fail, as Nussbaum so spectacularly fails, to achieve precisely what she calls for—understanding others, comprehending the eros of what is different from home through the eros of home.

Gertrude Himmelfarb agreed with Pinsky's assessment of bloodless rationality: "To pledge one's 'fundamental allegiance' to cosmopolitanism is to try to transcend not only nationality but all actualities, and realities of life that constitute one's natural identity. Cosmopolitanism has a nice, high-minded ring to it, but it is an illusion, and like all illusions, perilous." Justice, rule of law, rights of minorities, reason, and humane treatment are all fine ideals, Himmelfarb writes, but "not even the most ardent cosmopolitan would claim that these are the values of 'humanity as a whole.'" Benjamin Barber thinks Nussbaum "underestimates the thinness of cosmopolitanism and the crucial humanizing role played by identity politics in a deracinating world of contracts, markets, and legal personhood" and at the same time underestimates the "pathologies" of cosmopolitanism, such as imperialism.[111]

Some of the criticisms of Nussbaum's piece are based in general discomfort with the Enlightenment heritage Nussbaum embraces. The reigning stereotype of the Enlightenment, especially in talk about postmodernism, links it to "rationalism, instrumentalism, scientism, logocentrism, universalism, abstract rights, eurocentrism, humanism, masculinism," and other ills, as Keith Michael Baker and Peter Hans Reill have pointed out in their recent collection.[112] David A. Hollinger further characterizes this critique:

> We are told that the Enlightenment project apotheosized individuality and has left us without means of acting on the elementary communitarian truth that selves are the product of social groups. The Enlightenment project denied the constraints and the enabling consequences of history by assigning to human reason the role of building life anew from a slate wiped clean of tradition. This project tyrannized a host of particular cultural initiatives and tried to make everyone alike by advancing universal rules for identifying goodness, justice, and truth. Politically, the Enlightenment promoted absolutist and imperialist initiatives. Above all, the Enlightenment project blinded us to the uncertainties of knowledge by promoting an ideal of absolute scientific certainty.[113]

Cosmopolitanism, exactly to the extent that it carries Enlightenment baggage, is open to similar criticisms. Judith Butler, in her response to Nussbaum, struggles with this legacy in noting that the universal is always a culturally contingent idea, and yet at the same time a powerful and useful ideal. She, like others, wants to endorse "a universality that is yet to be articulated" even as she critiques the limits of existing notions of universality.[114] Absolutist relativism is obviously a contradiction in terms, and so postcolonial theorists trying to work out a middle ground between universalism and relativism have come up with a series of bridging concepts, like Gayatri Spivak's "strategic essentialism" or Homi Bhabha's "hybridity." According to Dipesh Chakrabarty "cosmopolitanism" is the latest term to serve this function, in what Scott Malcomson has called (playing off Spivak) a "strategic bargain with universalism."[115] Arnold Krupat uses cosmopolitanism to describe an ethnocritical perspective that "is consistent with a recognition and legitimation of heterogeneity," and Bhabha, less clearly, says something quite similar.[116] Ross Posnock follows Nussbaum in seeing a direct line leading from the Greco-Roman Stoics to Kant and later critics, such as W. E. B. DuBois's and Alain Locke's "democratic challenge" and "cosmopolitan . . . communalism."[117] Appiah has summed up this strand of thinking, albeit too neatly: "Cosmopolitanism is, to reach a formula, universalism plus difference."[118]

For others, Nussbaum's faith in reason and ideals is itself misplaced, given the world's actual political and economic state, and therefore tweaking the theory, or even revamping it, won't help. As Richard Falk writes, "structural factors overwhelm value preferences," and like many he sees neoliberal globalism as the evil twin of Nussbaum's Kantian ideal.[119] Kant's arguments, which are based on notions of individual states with competing interests, no longer adequately account for the world's situation, Falk points out, in which states are not the only or even the most central powers. Others stress the importance of socioeconomic position to the individual holders of such ideas; Immanuel Wallerstein writes, also in response to Nussbaum, "We live in a deeply unequal world, . . . and the consequences of acting as a 'world citizen' are very different depending on time and space."[120] The people who have access to the world's cultures as a series of imported products and tourist packages will necessarily have a different relation to an imagined world community, in other words, than a Palestinian refugee or a dump-picking orphan in Manila, even if both are wearing Nike swooshes. And still others suggest that one's national relation to this system also determines the value of cosmopolitan ideas. Pheng Cheah, in his introduction to *Cosmopolitics* (1998), argues that "the ethico-political work that nationalism and cosmopolitanism can do at any given moment depends on how either formation emerges from or is inscribed within the shifting material linkages and interconnections created by global capitalism at a particular historical juncture."[121] Cheah quotes as an example Sun Yat-sen in the 1920s, who said that although Westerners are advocating cosmopolitanism, "'It is not a doctrine which wronged races should talk about. We . . . must first recover our position of national freedom and equality before we are fit to discuss cosmopolitanism'" (30).

From this perspective, again, cosmopolitanism is an ideological effect of social position. The consuming bourgeoisie, Karl Marx suggested, are natural cosmopolitans. In the *Communist Manifesto*, Marx and Friedrich Engels famously argued that cosmopolitanism necessarily follows the march of capitalism: "The need of a constantly expanding market for its products chases the bourgeoisie over the whole surface of the globe. It must nestle everywhere, settle everywhere, establish connections everywhere."[122] This gives a "cosmopolitan character to production and consumption in every country. To the great chagrin of reactionists, it has drawn from under the feet of industry the national ground on which it stood" (476). And the same, they argued, is true for intellectual and literary production:

> In place of the old local and national seclusion and self-sufficiency, we have intercourse in every direction, universal interdependence of nations. And as in material, so also in intellectual production. The intellectual creations of individual nations become common property. National one-sidedness and narrow-mindedness become more and more impossible, and from numerous national and local literatures, there arises a world literature. (476–77)

For Marx, this is a good thing, one of the ways capitalism contains the seeds of its own destruction, preparing for the global consciousness of the proletariat.

But others have been less sanguine. Antonio Gramsci and Frantz Fanon, in part authorized by a particular reading of these passages from Marx, assumed that cosmopolitans were always reactionary. Gramsci used the word to denote a form of blinkered relativism to which uncommitted intellectuals subscribed. In Gramsci's case, as in Sun Yat-Sen's, cosmopolitanism is seen as the enemy of a "national culture" that might resist imperialism; the Roman Empire is Gramsci's example of a society in which cosmopolitan culture served the imperial ruling class over and against more local cultures. Cosmopolitanism was an enemy of the local commitments necessary for class solidarity, or any solidarity. Gramsci blames the cosmopolitanism of intellectuals, in fact, for the "disintegration" of Italy from the fall of the Roman Empire until 1870.[123] Fanon sees cosmopolitanism as a form of "intellectual laziness" and "spiritual penury" on the part of the middle class, a kind of narcissism in which the national middle class of former colonies identify with the international bourgeoisie instead of their own nation, the end result being that they are simply "stupidly, contemptibly, cynically bourgeois."[124]

This later Marxist condemnation of cosmopolitanism is complicated by the anti-Semitic use of the term in Soviet Russia, culminating in Stalin's "anti-cosmopolitan" purges of 1949 to 1953. The charge was that Jews had commitments to other Diasporic Jews that superseded any allegiance to communism or to Russia, and were therefore "rootless cosmopolitans" and reactionary traitors, exactly as Gramsci and Fanon argued regarding their bourgeois and imperial counterparts. Stalin's arguments have sometimes been dismissed as a simple cover for power struggles within the party, and Howard Fast, writing in the *Daily Worker* just a few years after the death of Stalin, pointed out the obvious, that not only was Stalin's use of the term anti-Semitic and paranoid, but anti-Marxist, since Marx's internationalism was itself a form of the cosmopolitan. Cosmopolitanism, Fast wrote, has no necessary politics; it is the basis of every internationalism, Marxist or capitalist, and of every humanism, bourgeois or progressive.[125]

The Gramscian critique continues to appear among American progressives, as, for instance in the case of Timothy Brennan, who recapitulates the work of Gramsci and Fanon, and in a more interesting way in the work of Sheldon Pollock, who takes cosmopolitanism to be an effect of empire; Latin and Sanskrit were imperial cosmopolitan languages, he argues, contrasting them to the vernacular. These imperial languages "underwrote . . . a new vision of power," and demonstrate the way the cosmopolitan (once again) is the enemy, culturally, of the local and the destroyer of autonomy. Brennan too sees a connection to empire: "To understand the history of cosmopolitanism is to learn something about the elusiveness of imperial attitudes themselves, which are . . . always more or less painfully obvious in the historical record."[126]

These Gramscian readings find odd bedfellows in the likes of former labor secretary Robert Reich, who, in *The Work of Nations* (1991), also points out the "darker side of cosmopolitanism."[127] The true cosmopolitans of our day,

Reich argues, are the multinational corporate consultants who wheel and deal across the globe, not beholden to any nation, much less any local group. "Citizen[s] of the world," such multicorporate types "feel no particular bond with any society." Christopher Lasch agrees, and claims that cosmopolitanism cannot, as Nussbaum would suggest, counteract tribalism. "The cosmopolitanism of the favored few, because it is uninformed by the practice of citizenship, turns out to be a higher form of parochialism," Lasch writes, and one that is itself adopted in reaction to the increase of tribalism, which in turn is a reaction to elite concentrations of wealth and power, and so on.[128] Friedrich Nietzsche too had argued that "cosmopolitanism in foods, literatures, newspapers, forms, tastes, even landscapes" was related to the will to power, and he also found it reactive, though he connected it to cultural exhaustion and pessimism.[129] In these cases cosmopolitanism is not an ethical ideal or a philosophical idea but the description of a cultural attitude that is superstructural, contingent, socioeconomically determined, and not too pretty.

Theorists interested in salvaging the term have thrown any number of qualifiers in front of it in an attempt to deflect the various forms of criticism. Bruce Ackerman and Mitchell Cohen have both opted for "rooted cosmopolitanism" in order to counteract the problems of rootlessness identified by Gramsci et al.[130] Homi Bhabha has suggested "vernacular cosmopolitanism," Bruce Robbins proposes that we think in terms of "already existing cosmopolitanisms," and James Clifford that those be thought of as "discrepant cosmopolitanisms."[131] What David Harvey calls these "countercosmopolitanisms" are themselves sometimes received as positive models (comparative, strong, feminist, ecological, socialist, postcolonial, inclusive), sometimes as negative (Christian, Western, bourgeois, imperial, liberal-managerial-globalist-capitalist, exclusive).[132] Many who argue against cosmopolitanism or these new countercosmopolitanisms do so only to invoke, finally, a solution that sounds very much like cosmopolitanism itself. Pollock, for instance, calls for a cultural practice that is neither vernacular nor cosmopolitan but both: "The future must somehow become one of *And* rather than *Either/Or*. . . . To know that some people in the past have been able to be universal and particular, without making either their particularity ineluctable or their universalism compulsory, is to know that better cosmopolitan and vernacular practices are at least conceivable—and perhaps . . . eventually reconcilable" (625). To those who would dismiss cosmopolitan ideals as utopian, Jacques Derrida suggests that this is precisely our mission, to think of cosmopolitanism as "forms of solidarity yet to be invented. This invention is our task; the theoretical or critical reflection it involves is indissociable from the practical initiatives we have already, out of a sense of urgency, initiated and implemented."[133]

This impulse toward reconciling the cosmopolitan and the vernacular, and toward imagining beyond current forms of solidarity, is at the center of regionalism as a literary practice. The regionalists, from the early local color writers through the regionalists of the 1920s and 1930s, are cosmopolitans in Amanda Anderson's sense: they "cultivated detachment from restrictive forms of identity, . . . manifest[ed] a complex tension between elitism and egalitarianism" at a time "when the world . . . suddenly seemed to expand in unassimilable ways," and unlike universalists required "at least limited self-reflexivity" within "cultural multiplicity." They are cosmopolitans, in other words, for many of the same reasons that we are. In a recent article Ross Posnock has suggested that cosmopolitanism is "less an identity than a practice," and, as I am also suggesting here, finds that it is both a way to "elude disciplinary social demands for legibility and to appropriate cultural goods."[134] Although he links the resurgence of cosmopolitanism to the waning of the regime of multiculturalism, he defends the long historical connection between cosmopolitanism and egalitarianism, part of which he has himself outlined in *Color and Culture: Black Writers and the Making of the Modern Intellectual* (1998), where he identifies the cosmopolitan ethos at the center of African American intellectual production in the late nineteenth and early twentieth centuries. "To recover the intellectual," Posnock writes, "is to recover a cosmopolitan universalism that has been held under suspicion during the reign of postmodernism."[135] And this cosmopolitan ethos predates the rise of the modern intellectual Posnock describes; it is under formation in the regionalist writing of the mid-nineteenth century.

And there are other connections between the cosmopolitan localists of the second half of the nineteenth century and our own cosmopolitan theorists. The regionalists were obviously interested in the relationship between geography and the rest of culture, in much the same way that many contemporary cultural studies of cosmopolitanism are. Celia Thaxter's *Among the Isles of the Shoals* (1873), to take just one brief example, gives geographical information about the islands' location, topography, geology, climate, flora, fauna, and currents with great scientific precision: "At Smutty-nose alone certain plants of the wicked-looking henbane (*Hyoscyamus niger*) flourish, and, on Londoner's only, there spreads at the top of the beach a large sea-lungwort (*Mertensia maritima*)."[136] And Thaxter regularly balanced her descriptions of the enforced solitude of winter on the isles with a dose of literary cosmopolitanism: "Nowhere does one follow a play of Shakespeare's with greater zest, for it brings the whole world, which you need, about you" (101). She uses the same basic procedures as David Harvey, linking the specificity of geographical study to cosmopolitan literary and philosophical thought. "Cosmopolitanism bereft of geographical specificity," Harvey writes, "remains abstracted and alienated reason, liable, when it comes to earth, to produce all manner of unintended and sometimes explosively evil consequences. Geography uninspired by any cosmopolitan vision is mere het-erotopic description or a passive tool of power for dominating the weak."[137]

The word, then, has no simple or necessary relation to philosophical univer-salism, to political beliefs, to economic developments, or to cultural work. Pre-cisely because it is a location of dense, overlapping, overdetermined arguments, convictions, and confusions, I find it the right word for my purposes. I do not want to side with one or another of these various perspectives; instead, like a good cosmopolitan, I want to stay alive to the multiplicity of meaning and the array of cultural possibilities evoked by the term. From the far edges of un-committed aestheticism to the most practical or most utopian political argu-ments, the term is a synecdoche for Trilling's bloody crossroads, and rather than attempt to cleanse it of any elite, exclusive connotations, I mean my use of the term to suggest them; rather than belittle the term's progressive, egalitarian po-litical force, I mean to endorse it. American literary culture is animated by ex-actly these multiple loyalties. It lives and thrives at the crossroads where aesthetics and politics meet, and therefore cannot be described in aesthetic or political terms alone.

There are many repercussions that follow from this argument. One is that the original impetus that led to the inclusion of "minority" or "marginal" texts or literatures in the canon is at odds with their strategic use in what is broadly known as "identity politics," since the cosmopolitan perspective that literary texts produce is completely at odds with readings that find virtuous eligible identities in them. Readers are prompted to both identify and *not identify* with characters in the text—since no character, no political position, no side of any cultural debate is represented as having ultimate value in the literary text, no character can provide, for literary readers, a model for being in the world. When Flaubert says "Madame Bovary, c'est moi," he doesn't really mean it—like the authors I discuss he means that he identifies with her, and wants his readers to identify with her, but obviously only up to a point and certainly not exclusively. It is our constant recourse to a larger overview than any characters in the text possess that makes them unavailable to readers as identity models. If we think of those African American or Asian American texts most widely considered great literary texts, for instance, like Ellison's *Invisible Man* or Kingston's *Woman War-rior,* we find in them not models for identification but catalogs of incomplete, inconsequential, uninhabitable, or at best significantly flawed identities. Any text that *does* champion a particular position or population or recipe for authentic-ity is necessarily didactic, and on such grounds roundly pronounced subliterary by all except partisans more interested in their politics than in the literary.

This may sound to some like the New Critics of the mid-twentieth century who would have us read without reference to social and political realities. But I am suggesting the opposite—that the regionalists' involvement in the political and cultural debates of their day is necessary to their texts' literary quality. Without displaying the competing claims of cultural partisans these texts cannot display their own literariness. Nevertheless, any attempts to find in the texts we study literary allies in cultural or economic insurrections, be they left, right, or center, are doomed. Like that of the regionalists, the politics of the literary text is, in the main, an engaged politics that does not take sides, except on literary matters. These texts are, in a word, cosmopolitan.

1850 — 1900

Representative Fiction

Two anthologies of local color fiction published in the 1990s can function as a working canon of the genre: Elizabeth Ammons's *American Local Color Writing* and Judith Fetterley and Marjorie Pryse's *American Women Regionalists.* The latter is obviously incomplete, since it selects only women authors, but it includes six pieces not in Ammons's collection: three antebellum texts (by Harriet Beecher Stowe, Alice Cary, and Rose Terry Cooke) and stories by Celia Thaxter, Grace King, and Willa Cather. Both anthologies have pieces by Jewett, Murfree, Mary Wilkins Freeman, Kate Chopin, Alice Dunbar-Nelson, Sui Sin Far (Edith Maud Eaton), Zitkala-Sä (Gertrude Simmons Bonnin), and Mary Austin. Ammons also includes Joel Chandler Harris, Charles Chesnutt, Garland, Mary Hartwell Catherwood, Alexander Posey, Finley Peter Dunne, Sherwood Anderson, Abraham Cahan, Pauline Hopkins, W. E. B. DuBois, Bret Harte, Jack London, and María Cristina Mena. These lists do not differ significantly from the local color canon of thirty or fifty years ago except in their inclusion of writers of different races and ethnicities.

American Local-Color Stories, for instance, an anthology compiled by Henry R. Warfel and G. Harrison Orians in 1941, has stories by thirty-eight authors published between 1829 and 1907. The two recent anthologies contain a total of twenty-seven, twelve of which are in the 1941 anthology. Of the fifteen that are not, eleven are from beyond the Warfel and Orians's 1907 cutoff date or are nonfiction writers (several discussed in their introduction) excluded for generic reasons. Of the twenty-six stories collected by Warfel and Orians but not by the later anthologists, sixteen are by men, ten by women, and eight (six men and two women) are before the period covered by Ammons. If we correct for the period covered, then, the ratio of male to female writers in the two anthologies is very similar, slightly over 50 percent women in the Ammons anthology, slightly under in Warfel and Orians. Unlike Warfel and Orians, the later editors understand their work as "recovery"; Gertrude Dorsey Brown[e], for instance, had published only a handful of stories in the limited-circulation *Colored American Magazine* and had never been reprinted until the Ammons anthology, and Pauline Hopkins wrote primarily for the same small audience. The only writers from the period with national reputations whom Warfel and Orians ignored and the later anthologists include, then, are Alice-Dunbar Nelson and Abraham Cahan. And this is not because the earlier editors were hostile to difference: they conclude their introduction by apologizing for not including Native American literature: "A comprehensive collection alone would afford adequate space for the part the Indian has played in our literature."[1]

Many of the writers included in the Warfel and Orians anthology but not in the later collections are still in print and/or under critical discussion, including Caroline Kirkland, Constance Fenimore Woolson, George Washington Cable, Alice French (Octave Thanet), Ruth McEnery Stuart, Margaret Deland, Mary Hallock Foote, Alice Brown, and Zona Gale. Others are primarily known for work in other genres, such as Frank Norris, William Allen White, and Stephen Crane. Hence, in terms of the incorporative principles involved and the dedication to what Warfel and Orians call "cultural diversity," to differences of "racial heritage," "community and family traditions" (including ethnic and religious traditions), "occupations," and "environment" (ix–x), the anthologies separated by half a century are quite similar.[2] They are also similar in that the editors looked for stories that were willing to "front some of the unpleasant facts of life" (x) and that bring attention to the fact that "amazing differences in the modes of thought, in traditions, in dialect set apart the New Englander and the Southerner from the Westerner, the city dweller from the farmer, the old English stock from the more recent immigrants. Small cultural islands retaining Old World folkways exist within the busiest metropolis and in open rural areas" (ix). These differences, which "slip the tether of uniformity," shape the "cultural responses" (xi) of groups and thus their literatures.

Fetterley and Pryse agree that different cultural backgrounds (they include "women's sphere" as such a background) shape literary production and that this is a particularly significant fact for regionalist writing. Their grouping of regionalist writers into those who represent their cultures from "inside" and those who do so from "outside," apart from the comico-feminist coincidence that, in their estimation, all the highly valued insiders are women and most of the outsiders men, can better be thought of as a distinction between more or less balanced arrays of cultural conflict. Ammons uses Mary Pratt's "autoethnography" to combine a notion of insiderism with a contextual reading of cultural conflict, but, like Fetterley and Pryse, Ammons still relies on an identity between the author and the region.[3] This distinction between insider and outsider is, of course, notably fraught. How many years must one reside in a place before one can legitimately go native? How many years in New York's mainstream or bohemian class of cultural producers would it take to delegitimate one's auto-ethnographic representations of a former home? In the end, readers must necessarily rely on the text and on their sense of adequate balance between the demands of the geographic or cultural region and the demands of translation.

The literary fortunes of the various writers associated with regionalism can instead be measured by how successful readers judge them to be in maintaining a balance in their orchestrations of contemporary debates about that region. From the 1890s to the present, those critics who found Garland too much a populist pedagogue have found him less than literary, as did more recently those who have seen him as too Bostonian. Those who saw Jewett's representations as too soft and genteel found her subliterary. In both cases, the author's perceived inability to hold conflicting viewpoints in vivid abeyance is the essence of their artistic failure. Those who find that Garland is both a populist and a critic of populism, and those who find Jewett to be a brave and subtle chronicler of the real depth hiding behind a mask of unruffable gentility, are also sure of these writers' literary merit. The other stories in the current canon also succeed in literary terms whenever they manage to outline the important issues of their day and resist resolving them, and when they represent their culture from both inside and outside, wherever they may in fact live, or however deeply they identify with the population they write about.

What follows has two sections, the first on Hamlin Garland and the second on other writers from the nineteenth century. I begin with Garland, who wrote at the end of the period, because his methods, his issues, and his reception were typical, and because the critical debates about his work in recent years have been the most instructive for a discussion of the relation between literature and politics. I also chose him because so much critical work over the last quarter century has focused on regionalism as a women's genre. I have made little distinction between men's and women's local color in what follows because I think both men and women were working with the same fundamental issues and with the same basic techniques. The ethnic fictions are not, for the most part, as interested in questions of rural geography as the "sectional" texts, but otherwise they engage the issues of place, culture, and class in very similar ways. Many of the basic elements of the genre that I note in the case of Garland are found throughout the history of the genre, from the earliest examples through the 1920s and beyond. These include the invocation of classic literary scenes and foreign locales as a standard opening or aside, the use of urban or foreign interlopers and

frame narrators, the oscillation between natural and civilized and other antinomies, and the direct appeal to cosmopolitanism by narrators. What the male and
female, native and immigrant, Anglo, Hispanic, and African American texts and
their anthologizers share, finally, is their investment in and enactment of literary
cosmopolitanism.

Hamlin Garland's
Provincial Literature

arland's critical stock might seem to have reached an all-time low. He was not exactly a New-Critical darling ("a sensitive observer and chronicler rather than a great artist" is a typical assessment),[4] but he was always featured on graduate syllabi and reading lists until he became one of the white male casualties of the canon revisions of the 1980s and 1990s. Even in the revived discussion of regionalism Garland does not have the place he once had as the premier local color writer, since much of the recent talk about regionalism has focused on women's writing, on African American and ethnic writing, and much of the writing that discusses Garland is not particularly kind.[5] Garland is just barely in print—amazon.com has a number of library-bound, library-priced volumes, including the collected works for $3,643, but only two volumes in paper. One of these is *The Captain of the Gray-Horse Troop*, which is marketed as a pop Western, with a Louis Lamour-like cover painting of a cowboy on a horse (very *Bonanza!* even though the novel's hero is not a cowboy but a military man running an Indian reservation), overheated blurbs ("The battles are over . . . but the war has just begun!"), and no mention anywhere of the original publication date or of the fact that Garland might have written anything else. The other book in print is his acknowledged masterpiece, his first collection of stories, *Main-Travelled Roads*.

The original volume in 1891 had six stories. (Three more were added in 1899, and in 1922 two other stories, originally published in magazines in the 1890s, were added as well; this eleven-story edition has been reprinted ever since.) Of the six original stories, four were first published in journals and two were written for the collection. In each of those two, "Up the Coulee" and "A Branch Road," the central character is a cosmopolitan outsider in the local world. "Up

65

the Coulee" opens as Howard, having left Wisconsin for New York and become a wealthy and famous actor, comes home for his first visit in many years. From the train he appreciates the bucolic "panorama of delight" out his window, "full of delicious surprises" and "a certain mysterious glamour," and he identifies with this land: "It was *his* West. He still took pride in being a Western man."[6] He is stirred by the scenery and approaches his old hometown "like a lover as he nears his sweetheart" (54). But when he arrives, right away he finds something else altogether, starting with the "grimy little station" with its "broiling hot splintery planks" and "few idlers lounging about" (55). The town he finds "dull and sleepy and squalid . . . unrelieved by a tree or a touch of beauty. An unpaved street, drab-colored, miserable, rotting wooden buildings" (55). These two perspectives—one distanced and aestheticizing, one close and unremitting—combine to give us our first sense of place, and the story continues to oscillate between the two, with quaint images of small-town life alternating with images of wasted lives, rural beauty alternating with rural idiocy.

Immediately after assessing the town ("the same, only worse"), he lifts his eyes to the "majestic amphitheater of green wooded hills that circled the horizon":

> He thrilled at the sight.
> "Glorious!" he cried involuntarily. . . .
> Richly wooded, with gently sloping green sides, rising to massive square or rounded tops with dim vistas, they glowed down upon the squalid town, gracious, lofty in their greeting, immortal in their vivid and delicate beauty. (55)

And this is not just a case of natural beauty contrasted to a degraded culture. As the story goes on and the rain starts to fall, everything begins to look "dreary," and even "the chickens seemed depressed" in "a horrible mixture of mud and mire" (91). Nature becomes a battleground as Howard watches his brother Grant milk the cow, "on whose legs the flies and mosquitoes swarmed, bloated with blood"; she "lashed with her tail as she tried frantically to keep the savage insects from eating her raw" (78–79).

As we meet the persnickety and morose country folk, the narrative at first remains on the actor's side, encouraging readers to feel, as Howard does, the poverty of their minds and imaginations. The loafers at the station, the card-players in the town, as they make idle arguments and threats, spit tobacco and "jaw," look like the young men he used to know, except dirtier, grayer, more bent, and "degenerated" (56). But then we meet William McTurg, a "soft-voiced giant" who "stood as erect as an Indian" even though his "leonine" hair and beard were white, and who had a sense of the beauty of nature. As the sun sets, William and Howard, riding in a buggy, silently watch:

The heart of the young man swelled with pleasure, and the eyes of the older man took on a far-off, dreaming look, as he gazed at the scene which had repeated itself a thousand times in his life, but of whose beauty he never spoke. . . . It was a genuine pleasure to ride with one who could feel that silence was the only speech amid such splendors. (58)

At such moments, the degenerate, infantile loafers are forgotten, and rather than inarticulate and uncomprehending, the locals are strong, silent, sympathetic, and contemplative.

When we meet the actor's family, especially his brooding, angry brother, we again get a double view. The actor finds out on his way from the station that his mother and brother had been forced to sell the family farm and become tenants on a poorer one. As he sees their new place, he is struck by "all its sordidness, dullness, triviality, and its endless drudgeries" (61). His brother Grant does not recognize him, and as they stand looking at each other for the first time in ten years, "Howard's cuffs, collar, and shirt, alien in their elegance, showed through the dusk, and a glint of light shot out from the jewel in his necktie" (61). Howard intuits the "hard, bitter feeling which came into Grant's heart as he stood there, ragged, ankle-deep in muck," and soon thereafter Grant verbalizes, at first indirectly, and then very much on the nose, his sense of the injustice. For much of the rest of the story, Grant's anger is unabated. The narrative moves in and out of each brother's perspective, oscillating between condemnation of the actor's selfishness—he has been yachting and buying diamond stick pins while his mother and brother were forced off the family farm—and disapproval of Grant's childish inability to rise above his own peevish envy, or even to see it as such. As the actor blithely talks to his early-rising, hard-working family about how hard acting is and complains that the thousand-dollar nights do not come along very often, we see the validity of his brother's anger. The actor's narcissistic lack of empathy becomes palpable before it too oscillates into self-pitying guilt. But then, when the actor does his best to bridge the gap, admitting his negligence and asking what he can do to help, only to be sulkily repulsed, Grant appears not so much wronged and justifiably angry as spiteful and small-minded. At each turn we are shown the strengths and weaknesses of the urban actor's view and the strengths and weaknesses of his rural brother's outlook.

This oscillation is the standard technique of local color fiction. Its effect is to suggest an implied author who stands above the fray, who sees both sides of the argument and can thus move back and forth, first empathizing here and then there, never finally taking sides. Through this oscillation a cosmopolitan overview is offered to readers, since only the implied author and the reader can see both sides: neither the actor nor his brother is capable of the full overview of the situation they share. The story's melancholy appeal, in fact, stems in part from these characters' inability to escape their limited perspectives. Grant never manages, as far as we can tell, to get the full view of Howard that the text gives us, and Howard never sees Grant or himself with the fullness we as readers are allowed.

The story ends in irresolution, even though the brothers manage to shake hands at last. In the final scenes, Howard decides to buy back the family farm and give it to Grant. Grant, predictably, refuses the offer. Howard apologizes for his neglect and begs to be forgiven, offering his hand and his financial help. Grant finally takes the hand, and Howard is overjoyed. But Grant suggests that it is too late for financial help. "Money ain't worth very much to me," he says, "I'm too old to make a new start. I've come to the conclusion that life's a failure for ninety-five per cent of us. You can't help me now. It's too late" (97).

I have taught this book several times and students often have the same experience I had reading it the first time; in the New American Library edition that has been available in paper since 1962, the last line of the story falls at the very bottom of the recto page, and the ending is so unresolved that readers are surprised when they turn to find the next story beginning. This is the final one-sentence paragraph:

> The two men stood there, face to face, hands clasped, the one fair-skinned, full-lipped, handsome in his neat suit; the other tragic, somber in his softened mood, his large, long, rugged Scotch face bronzed with sun and scarred with wrinkles that had histories, like saber cuts on a veteran, the record of his battles. (97)

The story ends, in other words, as it might just as well have begun, with a physical description of the two men that encodes their different economic and social lives of the previous decade, balanced by a semicolon. Does Howard agree that Grant cannot be helped? Does Grant mean it? Are we supposed to agree? Should Howard, then, buy the farm back or not? And what does all this mean for the question of rural poverty, for the relation of the country to the city more generally? The story leaves all such questions in abeyance, working carefully to array the options without choosing any of them.

Richard Brodhead reads "Up the Coulee" as a story of Garland's identification with Howard's social position and corresponding guilt toward people like Grant.[7] But the implied author of this text keeps such distance from Howard, swooping in and out of his perspective and demonstrating the partiality of it so convincingly, that reading such an identification simply does not account for the whole text. One of Howard's least attractive qualities, in fact, is his recurring and momentary spasms of guilt. His guilt, just as much as his sense of superiority, shows his lack of cosmopolitan understanding, and is one of the ways readers are encouraged *not* to identify with him. Bill Brown has come closest to the argument I am making here when he writes that *Main-Travelled Roads* "operates according to a double logic: the cosmopolitan must save the struggling people, but 'the people' must save the cosmopolitan."[8] By cosmopolitan Brown means the urban outsider; and although he recognizes that "cultural production and reception" is the arena of the text's politics, he finds this to be a failure of political imagination, an "incoherence" (103). Garland's "refusal to aestheticize the Midwest," on the other hand, is central to Stephanie Foote's reevaluation of Garland and she suggests that Howard's romanticization of the landscape is a representation of misrepresentation. Here I would agree that Howard's romantic appreciation of the landscape is shown by Garland to be inadequate to full representation.[9] But it is also necessary to full representation. Nancy Glazener, in her comparison of the *Atlantic*-based regionalists such as Jewett and those such as Garland, who wrote for the *Arena* and other magazines, suggests that they served very different interests:

> Insofar as regionalist fiction could be read as attesting to the inferiority of rural life, or insofar as it led urban readers to believe that they had a cognitive purchase on rural society . . . regionalism was part of the ideological apparatus of the nation's urban and northeastern-identified center. But insofar as regionalist fiction could be read as testifying to the exploitative consequences that certain national policies had for rural Americans, and to the injustice of a system that gave meager or unpredictable rewards to agricultural producers . . . regionalism had the potential to swivel in its orientation and serve the periphery.[10]

I am arguing that this "swivel" was integral to the way literary regionalism was written and read, and that it happened not in different stories or different venues but within a given story.

Further evidence for this is the discourse about art that runs through this and many other local color stories. Howard the actor works in a rival art, one that takes "a lot of machinery and paint and canvas" (89) but is not, at least in the work Howard does, an adequately literary form. Garland praises Ibsen's realism in *Crumbling Idols,* but when Howard talks about theater all he can relate is his "success," and almost every mention of the theater devolves into a question of the money he makes from it (97); he wonders if it has any real worth, likening the struggle for theatrical success to Darwinian strife (74) and plain "business" (74). Just as Howard is the most cosmopolitan character in the book, so is he the most artistic, but in both cases he falls radically short. This too is typical of regionalist fiction, as we shall see—it is often the figure of a failed cosmopolitan who is also a failed artist that constructs and highlights the cosmopolitan compact between reader and writer. The inadequate cosmopolitanism of the represented artist demonstrates, through implied contrast, the virtues of literary art. In different fictions Cather, for instance, uses the limitations of painters, sculptors, musicians, and singers to advertise the breadth of the literary perspective.

The local characters' relations to art often show them to be less cosmopolitan than the urban interlopers in these stories. The walls of Grant's house are adorned with "a few soap-advertising lithographs" (68), another image of art degraded by commerce. The wallpaper is, Howard thinks, a very meager concession to the "Spirit of Beauty" (91). In Howard's city home he has hanging, "between a landscape by Enneking and an Indian in a canoe in a canyon, by Brush, . . . a somber landscape by a master greater than Millet, a melancholy subject, treated with pitiless fidelity" (67). Unlike the lithographs, these paintings are legitimated by the names and ranks of their artists, but at the same time, the fact that the "somber landscape" that is the prize of the collection is a painting of a farm in a valley, that the "Indian in canoe" is likewise a "natural" cliché, and that Howard is lying in bed, imagining these paintings as a source of comfort he needs because real rural life is too upsetting, all suggest that his relation to art is not all it should be. He thinks of a sentence of Millet's that marks the combination of rural beauty and tragedy, and it prompts him to go to his room and write a long letter to "Margaret" (a woman not otherwise identified) unburdening himself, after which he feels better. This is not, the text suggests, any different from his other mood swings; he is writing, but his writing is not art and not a proper response to art, since it does not involve a better understanding but is rather a continuation of his emotional weakness (90–91). And Garland makes it clear that it is not just these painters but painting itself that is inadequate. As the sun sets one night, Howard finds it beautiful. He "looked at [it] through his half-shut eyes as painters do, and turned away with a sigh" from the sounds of the daily battle between men and cows (79). Painting requires half-shut eyes, rather than, as in the case of literary art, fully open ones, requires turning away from, rather than surveying, the daily battle.

Two performances bring us close to real art in the story, both of which occur at the house party thrown for Howard's homecoming. Grant is moved to speak at one point on the plight of the farmer, and Howard is thrilled "with emotion like some great tragic poem" at Grant's public oration of his discontent (86). By this point in the narrative any change of heart Howard might have cannot be trusted to indicate a change of mind, and although Grant's oration is important to the reader's understanding of the scene, Howard's aestheticized response is suspect. Immediately after this, William, the elderly fiddler, plays the old tunes that Howard knew from his youth, such as "Honest John," and people get up to dance. Under the spell of the music, Howard feels "closer to them all than he had been able to do before" (87). In this case it is not just Howard's fantasy of community, the narrator suggests. When the dancing stops and William plays the "unconscious expression of his unsatisfied desires," it silences the entire party. "The magic of music sobered every face; the women looked older and more careworn, the men slouched sullenly," while other distinctions were erased in the communal response. There is no question that this is a kind of art. It is as if, the narrator tells us, "the spirit of tragedy had entered the house" (87).

But there remains a noticeable disjunction between the enlivening dance music and the evocation of unsatisfied desire; although we are told that William is never melancholy except when he plays, it is his music that, moments before, had had people up smiling, dancing, flushed, and looking younger. In *Son of the Middle Border*, the first of a number of autobiographical volumes, Garland recounts listening to an old fiddler, "as quaint a character as ever entered fiction," who played "Honest John" and got people dancing. "I suspect that his fiddlin' was not even middlin'," Garland writes, suggesting that the artistic accomplishment of William in "Up the Coulee" is serving narrative themes rather than verisimilitude.[11] The music William plays has a similar oscillation to that of the text and approaches its artistic quality. But literary art goes one step further, and requires, in addition to our momentary emotional responses, a comprehension of their relation to each other. William's dance music stirs happy memories in Howard and fills his eyes with "a tender, luminous light" (87). The more somber music also stirs him, and as he walks in the night he ponders "the tragedy he had rediscovered in these people's lives" (88), bringing on a "deep distaste" (88) for his own life. It leads him to consider for a moment chucking it all, but "he knew that this was a mood, and that in a few hours the love and the habit of life would come back upon him" (88). The music and Grant's politicized oratory change his mood, but neither can move him to a comprehensive understanding. Only literature, the story suggests, has this power.

Garland recounts his own provincial youth in *A Son of the Middle Border*, a story of his gradually increasing cosmopolitanism, and hence of his movement toward the literary.

All of this universe known to me in the year 1864 was bounded by the wooded hills of a little Wisconsin coulee, and its center was the cottage in which my mother was living alone—my father was in the war. As I project myself back into that mystical age, half lights cover most of the valley. The road before our doorstone begins and ends in vague obscurity—and Granma Green's house at the fork of the trail stands on the very edge of the world in a sinister region peopled with bears and other menacing creatures. Beyond this point all is darkness and terror. (1)

His relatives lived beyond these hills to the east, in a place significantly named Salem, and Garland "was eager to visit them, for in that direction my universe died away in a luminous mist of unexplored distance. I had some notion of its nearby loveliness for I had once viewed it from the top of a tall bluff which stood like a warder at the gate of our valley" (14). The vista of the Hawthornian east provides a glimpse of the larger world. The provincials themselves were not entirely devoid of the literary spirit: "A deep vein of poetry, of sub-conscious celtic sadness, ran through them all" (23), and his mother was "a wordless poet, a sensitive singer of sad romantic songs" (24), his father "by nature an orator and a lover of drama" (24). But this is not enough, and every movement out into the world is a movement toward the literary, enlightenment, and cosmopolitanism. "Month by month the universe in which I lived lightened and widened. In my visits to Onalaska [which also has a commanding view], I discovered the great Mississippi River and the Minnesota bluffs. The light of knowledge grew stronger." He dreams of "distant countries and the sea" (31).

But his true cosmopolitan education is the result of an inborn "hunger for print" (35). He devoured whatever writing came his way, such as the serial stories in the county newspaper and *Harper's Weekly*. And then, "suddenly, unexpectedly, miraculously, I came into possession of two books, one called *Beauty and the Beast,* and the other *Aladdin and His Wonderful Lamp.* These volumes mark a distinct epoch in my life" (68). Aladdin, he writes, took him to Persia. His grandmother had already taught him to "love the poems of Whittier and Longfellow" (29). And a series of other books and journals— *The Female Spy, Cast Ashore,* McGuffey Readers, *New York Weekly,* Beadle's Dime Novels, *Hearth and Home,* and in culmination, *The Hoosier Schoolmaster*—continues his education (80, 112–14). This last Garland calls "a milestone in my literary progress as it is in the development of distinctive western fiction" (114). Garland does not seem to be particularly interested in the internal coherence of this narrative of his own education. The "only books" in the house change in identity and number several times in his recounting (see 120–22). And likewise, the attitude toward rural life ranges from "we loved every day for the color it brought, each season for the wealth of its experience, and we welcomed the thought of spending all our years in this beautiful home where the wood and the prairie of our song did actually meet and mingle," (78) to "we all hated it. We saw no poetry in it" (129).

This self-contradiction does not work the way oscillation works in the fiction. The implied author is Garland, the character Garland, and there is no readerly space constructed by the text outside the consciousness of the author-subject. This text and the other autobiographies do not have the literary qualities I have been describing and that might have kept them in print. Garland describes the growth of his own literary education—"a page or two" into *Mosses from an Old*

Manse, he claims, his "mental horizon widened" (219); "Whitman's *Leaves of Grass*
. . . changed the world for me" (323)—but his own account is a chronicle, not
a literary text. In his fiction, at least in *Main-Travelled Roads,* he managed to offer
readers cosmopolitan literary perspectives; but not here. He tells many of the
same basic stories, and plot elements and epiphanies that are central to the stories in *Main-Travelled Roads* are sprinkled throughout, but the literary effect is
missing.

"A Branch Road," for instance, clearly derives from Garland's experience in
the seminary that provided his secondary education and that he describes in the
autobiography as the place that, since "it placed the rigorous, filthy drudgery of
the farm-yard in contrast with the care-free companionable existence led by my
friends in the village," gave him his "first set of comparative ideas, and with them
an unrest." In the story, the main effect of seminary training for the protagonist
is that it submits him to the jealous taunts of his farm neighbors when he is
home for the summer. The story's main relation to the autobiography does not
lie in any realistic portrayal of class issues in the Midwest but in its allegory of
literary vision. Will, because he has spent a year at the seminary, sees the world
differently from the other farmhands. He appreciates "the interest, picturesque-
ness of it all" (15), but he is no slouch. "He wanted them to understand that he
could do as much pitching as any of them and read Caesar's *Commentaries* besides" (25). He has more empathy than the other characters, though perhaps not
enough; he resolves that next time he will not be so selfish and let his sister-in-
law go to the fair in his place, for instance, since he sees, a bit late, how little freedom from care she has. Still, he has the ability to comprehend existence in
Darwinian terms and to entertain "a vague feeling of the mystery and elusiveness of human life" (34). He condemns the small-mindedness of those who can
only believe in "petty utility" (40). These are attributes of a man, the text suggests, who has read more widely than his neighbors.

The story is in two parts, the second taking place seven years after the first.
The first half is a finely told story of a young man's first love, and the little fits
of jealousy, miscommunication, and despair that he feels. It ends with him writing her a nasty note and leaving town. In the second half, he returns a somewhat wealthy man, sees the horrible conditions she lives in and decides to take
her and her son away from her abusive husband (his former rival) and in-laws
for an out-of-state divorce and remarriage. When he decides to rescue her from
the fate to which he had left her seven years before, his eloquence opens the
world for her. "She rose flushed, wide-eyed, breathing hard with the emotion
his voice called up. . . . Then she heard the words beneath his voice somehow,
and they produced pictures that dazzled her" (49–50). She worries, of course,
about what people will say, about her responsibilities, but he keeps at her. Garland makes it clear that it is not passion that moves her, but vision. "Flesh had

ceased to stir in her; but there was vast power in the new and thrilling words
her deliverer spoke. He seemed to open a door for her, and through it turrets
shone and great ships crossed on dim blue seas" (51). This language is similar to
that which Garland uses for each moment in his literary education, from the
sudden miraculous opening of the world in *Aladdin* to the way *Leaves of Grass*
"changed the world" and Hawthorne widened his horizon. The last line of the
story, as the two set off, the sun shining on the waving wheat, the blue sky like
a wide sea above them, is "—and the world lay before them" (53).

    In this story, too, Will is not an ideal character. For all the world-opening he
does in yanking Agnes out of her confinement, yank he does, and the impetu-
ous cruelty of which he is capable in the first half has real echoes in the second.
His empathy throughout is mingled with a series of other emotions and selfish
motives. He gives no thought, for instance, to her son until the last minute, and
then decides it is okay to bring him along because he has blue eyes. These moments, when we see the limits of Will's empathetic understanding, reveal the literary vision we share with the implied author, the breadth of understanding we,
unlike Will, are cosmopolitan enough to grasp.

    Other stories in the collection work this same vein. "God's Ravens" is an-
other homecoming story, in which a Chicago editor, sick of the rat race, goes
back to the Wisconsin coulee of his youth for a better life and to recover from
the nervous debility brought on by life in the city. Robert Bloom is another
typical almost-literary local color protagonist. He has published a story or two
in the Eastern magazines and plans to write about his new neighbors, "their
queer ways, so quaint and good" (210). His coworker gives us the first turn of
the screw: "Oh, bosh, Bloom! . . . You'll find men and women just as hard and
selfish in their small way. It'll be harder to bear, because it will all be so petty
and pusillanimous" (211). When Bloom arrives he, like Howard in "Up the
Coulee," immediately appreciates the "splendid" and "magnificent" countryside.
But "first contact with people disappointed Robert" (213). He treats the people like servants rather than neighbors, is imperious and obtuse; "he could be
generous toward them in general; it was in special cases where he failed to know
them" (214–15). His wife finds them all vulgar and offensive, and he encour-
ages her to reach out, but cannot himself. As we meet his neighbors we find
them attractive and repulsive by turns, and scenes oscillate between those that
represent the Blooms's complaints as justified and those that do not. When
Robert falls ill, his opinion of the town gets worse: "They are caricatures," he
complains to his wife. "They don't read or write or think about anything in
which I'm interested. This life is nerve-destroying. Talk about the health of the
village life! It destroys body and soul. It debilitates me. It will warp us both down
to the level of these people" (218). As this attitude becomes more pronounced,
the townspeople, rather than turning further against him, excuse him because

he is clearly "failin' fast" (218). When he finally collapses, the people rally and help nurse him back to health. He wakens from his fever to find them taking care of him, and then it is they who broaden his view, literally as well as figuratively. When a man helps turn him over in his bed, "a new part of the good old world burst on his sight" (219). They have brought him back to life, and again the change is represented in terms of widened vistas: "O God, it was so beautiful! It was a lover's joy only to live, to look into these radiant vistas again" (220).

The story ends with two final flips of perspective. As Robert regains his health with the help of the neighbors he had cursed, he is overcome with gratitude. He tries to thank them, and they brush it off—it's nothing, you would do the same, they say. On his first walk out of the house after his illness, when everyone greets him kindly, he is again overcome. He turns to William, the man who had helped the most, and, grateful, trembling, says:

> "Oh, I understand you now. I know you all now."
> But William did not understand him.
> "There! There!" he said soothingly. "I guess you're getting' tired."
> . . . "Matie," the alien cried, when William had gone, "we know our neighbors now, don't we? We never can hate or ridicule them again."
> "Yes, Robert. They will never be caricatures again—to me." (221–22)

This last interchange may seem to resolve the basic dialectic, as Robert's over-romanticized view of the village swings to contempt and back to respect. But the understanding that Robert claims to have is qualified by his inability to communicate with William, and his wife's last words suggest that even she doubts that the understanding he claims to have is actually achieved. Readers, once again, are offered a range of interpretive options greater than that commanded by any of the characters. The local characters give Robert his larger perspective on the world, but not at all in the romantic way he first thought they might and the readers' perspective is meant to be larger still.

"Among the Cornrows" is an ill-shaped story, in which the second half of the frame seems to be missing. It opens with a conversation between Rob, a farmer, and Seagraves, the editor of the local paper, the *Boomtown Spike*. Seagraves's name suggests one fate of wanderers, and Seagraves is our figure of the near-cosmopolitan, near-artist. He thinks the big, wide thoughts, and when Rob expresses a democratic sentiment, Seagraves sees in it cosmico-historic wisdom: "This atom of humanity (how infinitesimal this drop in the ocean of humanity!) was feeling the nameless longing of expanding personality" (103), he thinks, and decides to write an editorial on the subject.[12] The conversation turns to their bachelor status and Rob reveals that he plans to go back East, to Wisconsin, to get a wife.

The rest of the story follows Rob on his quest, in which he courts and proposes to a Norwegian girl, all in an afternoon. Here the social divide is no longer
farm worker/brain worker, but native/immigrant. Julyie, the girl Rob courts,
is under the thumb of an immigrant father who wants her free labor, and Rob
the enlightened American finds such exploitation inexcusable, "a d———n
shame" (116). Julyie already has some sense of Rob's perspective on her plight;
because of her contact with the other children in town, she "no longer found
pleasure in her own home. She didn't believe in keeping up the old-fashioned
customs" (114), and felt like a hired hand. The text moves in and out of Rob's
perspective here, showing him to be gallant but clumsy, and the proposal far
short of Julyie's dreams. But the offer of freedom wins the day, and she meets
him to elope that night.

That meeting is the end of the story, as if the conventional marriage plot had
narratively trumped the story's other themes. But even here, there is an allegory
of local color literature at work, since the editor had claimed to find Rob's ideas
worthy of print and dissemination. Rob's ideas "plunged [Seagraves] deep into
thought" and "astonishment" (102–3), even though Rob does not recognize
them as such: "My ideas! Why, I didn't know I had any" (102). In the end, Rob's
"ideas" persuade Julyie as well, and do so because the picture of their future he
draws was charged with "a sort of romance such as her hard life had known little of" (118); it allows her to live imaginatively "that free life in a far-off wonderful country" (120). But readers of course go farther, and see the limits not
just of Rob's articulateness, but of his understanding; he does not, for one thing,
understand much about the girl he is marrying. And Julyie's "far-off wonderful
country," we know she will shortly find, is simply Rob's mouse-ridden shanty
with its rickety stools and table crudely fashioned from a box.

"Under the Lion's Paw" is the most "partisan" of these stories, the one often
pointed to as the paradigmatic case of politically committed fiction. William
Dean Howells wrote that "'Under the Lion's Paw' is a lesson in political economy, as well as a tragedy of the darkest cast."[13] But Howells takes these social
themes ("the upper dog and the under dog are everywhere, and the under dog
nowhere likes it") to be Garland's "allegorical effects," and claims "they are not
the primary interest of Mr. Garland's work: it is a work of art, first of all, and we
think of fine art" (16–17). Howells feels that Garland's work is not yet perfectly
balanced—"he has still to learn that though the thistle is full of an unrecognized
poetry, the rose has a poetry, too"—but he praises him for raising moral issues
and leaving it to readers to decide their morality (17). A reviewer in the New
York Tribune in 1891 found a better balance, and claimed, in a clear exposition of
this form of literary evaluation, that Garland "is a realist, and he offers views of
life such as present themselves actually to the observer; fragmentary views, that
is to say, having neither beginning nor end, full of perplexities and unsolved

problems. That is how the world panorama passes under our eyes, and that is how Mr. Garland paints what he sees."[14]

Many critics, from the publication in 1891 on, criticized Garland for too much rose or too much thistle. Arthur Inkersley, in an 1895 review, concludes: "Precisely because he is an enthusiast and a rebel, his spirit of revolt blinds him to much that may fairly be considered on the other side. . . . We think, as he himself says of Ibsen, that the swing of the pendulum has carried him too far in the opposite direction."[15] C. M. Thompson, writing in the *Atlantic* in 1895, similarly condemns him for a lack of balance:

> The reader has an uneasy, ever-present feeling that they are written not so much for him as at him. "Here is a pretty state of affairs," they seem to say between all their lines, "for which our author holds you personally responsible. What are you going to do about it?" When an argument is thus suggested, the reader loses faith a little. Instinctively he puts himself on his guard, and warns himself that these are the adduced examples of a controversialist, and may accordingly be overcolored.[16]

H. L. Mencken, writing in 1919, also sees the preachiness, which Garland approaches most closely in "Under the Lion's Paw," as the death of art: "He was a moralist endeavoring ineptly to translate his messianic passion into esthetic terms, and always failing."[17]

But in story after story, the verve with which Garland attacks Eastern capital can be seen to be matched by that with which he condemns rural ignorance. He praises the beauty of the West as often as he belittles romantic illusions about it. He is, sentence by sentence, paragraph by paragraph, proselytizing for this position or that. But finally, he proselytizes—just as he did in his lectures in Boston before he wrote his Western stories, and just as he did in his late screeds against "pornography" in fiction—for cosmopolitan literary art. It is easy for us to see where he fails in this balancing act. His best stories, however, are those in which he is successful not at making a political point, but in making it and its opposite, which is why "Up the Coulee," not "Under the Lion's Paw," is the story most regularly anthologized. The former is the only story of Garland's in the *Heath Anthology* and in Elizabeth Ammons's *American Local Color Writing, 1880–1920,* for instance. And even "Under the Lion's Paw" is far from a simple didactic indictment of capitalism, especially in the context of the rest of *Main-Travelled Roads.* The landlord's crime in "Under the Lion's Paw" is to double the asking price for a farm he owns based on improvements done by his tenant. But we are shown early in the story that there is a smart way and a dumb way to do business, and the tenant has not been smart. His despair, in the end, is at the fact that his own landowning days are farther off than he thought, that he will not become a landlord in turn as soon as he thought. "There is no despair so deep as the despair of the homeless man or woman," the narrator declares, but the angry tenant is not homeless; he has a home, in fact, because the landlord had given him credit and reasonable terms when he was homeless. The story, although it is more thistle than rose, contains both. The balance seems to be tipped in the end, more than in "Up the Coulee," and it has, for that reason, a less literary, slightly more didactic feel, as readers since Howells have noted, especially since the ending, as readers who appreciate its supposed politics point out, so clearly condemns the capitalistic exploitation of the working farmer. But the ending is not the whole story, and it is the tenant farmer in the end who chases the landowner off the land. The farm the tenant had before this one he lost to a plague of grasshoppers, which chased him into this new life. And that new life was made possible by the landowner, a man, we are told in being introduced to him, who rarely foreclosed and "had the name of being one of the 'easiest' of men in the town. He let the debtor off again and again, extending the time whenever possible." And our tenant farmer, although the story ends with him in the guise of the populist downtrodden abused hero, is introduced to us as a whining pessimist without any real gumption or vision. To read the end of the story as its point is to highlight the text's didactic possibilities at the cost of recognizing its literary qualities.

Local Color

The earliest story most anthologists or critics have included in the genre, Stowe's "Uncle Lot" (1834), begins with an aporia that is a riot of cosmopolitan references:

> And so I am to write a story—but of what, and where? Shall it be radiant of the sky of Italy? or eloquent with the beau ideal of Greece? Shall it breathe odor and languor from the orient, or chivalry from the occident? or gayety from France? or vigor from England? No, no; these are too old—too romance-like—too obviously picturesque for me.[18]

Celia Thaxter similarly, opens *Among the Isles of Shoals* (1873) with Tennyson, Melville, the Galapagos, Homer's lotus-eaters, Swiss mountains, Hawthorne's Italian tales, and Socrates sprinkled throughout her detailed local geography and history. The title of Rose Terry Cooke's "Freedom Wheeler's Controversy with Providence" (1877) plays on Michael Wigglesworth's 1662 "God's Controversy with New England," and in the story she alludes to Emerson, medical discourse on the nerves, Fra Angelico, Darwin, the Westminster Assembly of Divines, and Spenser's *Faerie Queen*. Constance Fenimore Woolson, to establish her cosmopolitan cultural authority, opens *Anne* (1882) with quotations from Wordsworth and Emerson, and in the early pages invokes Diana and ancient Greek maidens, German chorals, the Greek alphabet, Damascus blades, Irish soldiers, French fishermen, *Arabian Nights*, and Persian rugs, as well as local dialects and "a whole vocabulary of roughest fisherman's terms." In one story, Bret Harte cites Ali Baba, Frankenstein, and the difference between a priori and a posteriori reasoning; he sprinkles the text with other Latin words, and justifies his own authorial intrusion by referring to the tragedies of TsienTsiang and "the old Greek comedies, whose parabasis permits the poet to mingle with the *dramatis personae*, to address the audience and descant at length in regard to himself, his play, and his own merits."[19] Such moments demonstrate and reinforce the implied author's cosmopolitan purview and are an invitation to readers to adopt or confirm a similar cosmopolitanism. Such references are most often in the narrator's direct address to readers, suggesting an imagined community that separates the implied author and reader from the less cosmopolitan characters. They thus offer readers a cultural perch to share with this implied author and from which to survey the local scene being represented.

In some cases, these references are supplied not by the narrator but by an interloper from outside the local community. Like Howard in Garland's "Up the Coulee," these interlopers are at first glance more cosmopolitan than the locals, and provide a model of significant but inadequate cosmopolitanism. James Benton, the handsome stranger in "Uncle Lot," knows how to do everything, from teach Greek and Latin to perform farm chores, forming a bridge between the local and the larger world. The well-to-do hunters who come to the mountain villages of Kentucky in Murfree's stories, the college friends on a hunting trip in Mary Hallock Foote's "Maverick" (1895), Jewett's urban narrator in *The Country of the Pointed Firs* or the ornithologist in her "White Heron" (1886), John Fox Jr.'s German-educated Easterner in "A Mountain Europa" (1895), the New England schoolteacher in the South from Constance Fenimore Woolson's "King David" (1899), Norris's Eastern protagonist Presley, who refracts the "story of California" in *The Octopus* (1901), the Northern narrator of the frame tales of Charles Chesnutt's Uncle Julius stories—these protagonists, characters, and narrators all serve the same function, representing a nonlocal, usually (but not always) urban perspective. Often, as in the case of Garland and Norris, or in Lucy S. Furman's "The Scarborough Spoons" (1912), the interloper is a relative whose urban background forms a clear contrast. Occasionally, the interloper is even a ghost, as in Mary Catherwood's "Pontiac's Lookout" (1894). But in all cases the interloper's more worldly perspective and the locals' more provincial one are allowed to clash, as in Howard and Grant, and in the most literary of these texts neither wins the contest.

In many other local color stories, this balancing function is served not by an interloper per se but by an institutionalized representative of the outside world. In Gertrude Atherton's stories, such as "The Vengeance of Padre Arroyo" (1894), it is the missionaries; in Catherwood's "Pontiac's Lookout" it is the Fur Company's officers. As these examples suggest, often the fault line between classes has to do with the relations between the "original" inhabitants and more recent colonizers, which historically and thematically parallel the class issues under debate. In many other texts the established powers of the town function as outsiders for the rural people, just as the native, established inhabitants are the outsiders for the immigrant communities in urban regionalist narratives. In others, such as Woolson's "Peter, the Parson" (1875), there is only a marginally important voice of an outside institution, in this case a virtually flockless Anglican minister. In Alice Dunbar-Nelson's "Sister Josepha" (1899), the institution, a convent, is the scene of the story of a young novitiate's frustrated desire for a larger world. A similar mechanism, albeit a clumsier version, is at work in Bret Harte's use of the garrison commandant in "Princess Bob and Her Friends" (1870). In Paul Laurence Dunbar's reverse-regionalist tale, "Mr. Cornelius Johnson, Office Seeker" (1899), the Alabaman protagonist comes up against the U.S. Congress in the person of his congressman. The claims of these personified institutions never quite win, and never quite lose, the ideological contest of the text.

In each case, the text's cosmopolitanism is defined and delimited by the full collection of perspectives represented by these different individuals and groups. In María Amparo Ruiz de Burton's *The Squatter and the Don* (1885), for instance, which Carrie Tirado Bramen has called "pan-patrician regionalism," the outsiders are the new Anglo landowners, the insiders the landowning *Californios*, the upper 5 percent of the Mexican population who are the economic equals but feel themselves to be the cultural superiors of the Anglo colonizers.[20] The very limited cosmopolitanism of the text tries to survey the competing claims of these two elite groups. The novel is unsatisfying to current audiences in its very limited purview of the various populations we know to have existed in the region—the Native Americans, the itinerant and settled laborers, the smaller homesteaders and their families, the servants—populations that are barely mentioned, much less given their place in the cultural world of the text. But each of the two elite groups is cosmopolitan in its own way—the *Californios* sing peasant ballads by day and go to the opera by night; the Anglos carry Eastern and urban values into the countryside along with Western, rancher attitudes—and each lacks whatever fullness of perspective the text provides.

In some of these tales the arguments about the "cultivated" characters' lack of full perspective is made baldly by the narrator. In Mary Noailles Murfree's "The Star in the Valley" (1898), Chevis, Varney, and a local guide are camping in the mountains. Chevis fancies himself a particularly sensitive and "susceptible" character, while Varney was a "man of this world; his mental and moral conclusions had been adopted in a calm, mercantile spirit, as giving the best return for the outlay."[21] Chevis thinks that "infinite as was the difference between" Varney and the guide, "they were alike incapable of appreciating and comprehending his delicate and dainty musings" (257), setting off the play of identity and difference in the text. This statement has a notably satiric edge, as does the telling fact that Chevis is in the habit of lifting his hat "with that punctilious courtesy which he made a point of according to persons of low degree" (258). Chevis becomes infatuated with a young woman, and yet cannot muster the gumption to talk to her: "The gulf between his station and hers—so undreamed of by her (for the differences of caste are absolutely unknown to the independent moun-taineers), so patent to him—could be bridged by few ideas" (261). This passage is closely followed by another that I will quote at some length, since it is a clas-sic instance of a character's inadequate cosmopolitanism:

> [Chevis] piqued himself on the readiness with which he became interested in these people, entered into their thoughts and feelings, obtained a comprehensive idea of the machinery of life in this wilderness. . . . They appealed to him from the basis of their common humanity, he thought, and the pleasure of watching the devel-opment of the common human attributes in this peculiar and primitive state of society never palled on him. He regarded with contempt Varney's frivolous dis-pleasure and annoyance [with] . . . their mental poverty, their idle shiftlessness, their uncouth dress and appearance. Chevis flattered himself he entertained a broader view. (262)

Chevis's cosmopolitan open-mindedness is commendable when compared to Varney's lack of it, but the narrator is quick to remind us of its all-too-obvious limits. Chevis is proud of his abstract understanding, but practically he is at a loss; he finds "few ideas" with which to build even a conversational bridge.

And often local color authors make their cosmopolitan argument as a direct exhortation. "There is a noble saying of Plato that the best thing that can be done for the people of a state is to make them acquainted with one another," Jewett writes in the introduction to *Deephaven,* and she credits her own cos-mopolitan education to Stowe. "It was, happily, in the writer's childhood that Mrs. Stowe had written of those who dwelt along the wooded seacoast and by the decaying, shipless harbors of Maine." *The Pearl of Orr's Island,* Jewett writes, allowed her "to see with new eyes, and to follow eagerly the old shore paths from one gray, weather-beaten house to another where Genius pointed her the way."[22] In Rose Terry Cooke's "Miss Lucinda" (1861), the narrator tells us, "I have the same quick sympathy for Biddy's sorrows with Patrick [her local char-acters] that I have for the Empress of France" (161). And Murfree, in "The Star in the Valley," feels the need to make her point explicitly as well. Chevis, the nar-rator relates, "had not even a subacute idea that he looked upon these people and their inner life as only picturesque bits of the mental and moral landscape; that it is an aesthetic and theoretical pleasure their contemplation afforded him; that he was as far as ever from the basis of common humanity" (262). The girl he cannot bring himself to talk to, however, is closer; when she risks her own life to stop a blood feud, the narrator again announces the moral: "Perhaps, without any philosophy, she stood upon the basis of a common humanity" (269). Chevis, when he realizes her fine moral character, experiences "a sense of deep humiliation" and a "glimmering perception" of his own shortcomings. Even as he has his moment of explicit realization, we are ahead of him, with the narrator cheerleading.

Sarah Orne Jewett's "Miss Peck's Promotion" (1888) uses most of the same techniques. Miss Peck's home, "high on a long Vermont hillside," gives her a commanding view of the village below.[23] The plot moves her from the hill, from which she has in both senses looked down on the village, to a recently widowed minister's house in the village, and from there she looks back at the farm with "dread" (239) at the dark and lonely existence she now feels she led there. She relishes the new, wider world of the minister and the town, but this is just the first oscillation. It is not long before village life makes her feel "too much shut in" (242) and the minister appears to her full of faults. Then, within a paragraph, she reflects on the "most rewarding condition" of her new life, "the feast of books, which were new and bewilderingly delightful" to her, and she basks in the minister's ability to read sonorously to her: "Many an evening went joyfully by in the presence of the great English writers" (242). She cares for the minister and his daughter and waits for a proposal of marriage. When the minister marries someone else, she keeps her great disappointment to herself, and returns to the farm, happy to be in that environment again, happy not to have wasted the year just doing farm chores, and happy to have her new relation to books. The conclusion combines a cake-and-eat-it-too logic with a sense that she has not quite had either the cake or the eating.

Jewett's *Country of the Pointed Firs* (1896), more a series of sketches than a novel, in which an unnamed narrator has come from Boston to Dunnet Landing, Maine, for the summer, begins with a slightly occluded form of address. The first chapter of the novel is in the third person, and the second chapter begins evasively, with passive constructions, and then briefly stays in the second person, giving a slight objective frame to the narrator's presentation and productively confusing the address until, several paragraphs later, the first person intervenes. The narrator, who had been in Dunnet Landing briefly a few years before, returns to find "all that mixture of remoteness, and childish certainty of being the centre of civilization of which her affectionate dreams had told,"[24] one of the many times the sympathetically patronizing narrator suggests the superiority of her own view. As I mentioned in the introduction, Jewett literalizes the cosmopolitan vista by moving her writing desk from Mrs. Almira Todd's house to the schoolhouse on the hill, which overlooks the town, the adjoining farms, and the sea. The move to the schoolhouse takes the narrator away from too close a

proximity to everyday life, which makes writing impossible, giving her the prospective distance she needs. Jewett keeps the equation from being too neat, however, with a series of quick images: first, an infantilizing one of the narrator
hanging her lunch box on the wall like a "small scholar"; then a falsely aggran-
dizing one of her sitting at the teacher's desk "as if I were a great authority, with
all the timid empty benches in rows before me"; and finally, a defamiliarizing
one of the occasional "idle sheep" stopping to take a long look at her (53). All
these images keep us from settling on any sense of her authority. She attends a
funeral with the rest of the community, but then, instead of walking to the graveyard, she returns to the schoolhouse to watch from the heights and write about
it, and she realizes that this "made myself and my friends remember that I did
not really belong to Dunnet Landing. I sighed, and turned to the half-written
page again" (56). The literary act is not local.

In the funeral procession she notices a man she had not met before, Captain
Littlepage, who soon comes to visit her at the schoolhouse. His first words are
a line from *Paradise Lost*—"a happy, rural seat of various views"—establishing
his cosmopolitan credentials, which are then undercut by the narrator's thinking he looks "as pleased as a child" at his performance, and by his comment about
Milton's greatness—"Shakespeare was a great poet; he copied life, but you have
to put up with a great deal of low talk"—which show him to be less cosmopolitan than the realists (57). Mrs. Todd thinks that Littlepage has "overset his
mind with too much reading" (57–58), but the narrator finds him refined and
elegantly dressed. He then quotes Darwin's saying that "there is no such king as
a sea-captain; he is greater than a king or a schoolmaster," and he waves his hand
gesturing at the houses below, saying, "in that handful of houses they fancy that
they comprehend the universe" (58–59). The interchange between the two
continues, the narrator implying her own superior view, Littlepage declaring his
own, and although the portrait of Littlepage, like his name, tends to diminish
him, we cannot help but notice that his range of references at least equals the
narrator's, and his firsthand knowledge of the world—he has sailed all around
it—is far greater. "A community narrows down and grows dreadful ignorant
when it is shut up to its affairs, and gets no knowledge of the outside world except from a cheap, unprincipled newspaper," Littlepage declares, and claims that
the seagoing men and their families had a sense of "proportion" that was lacking now that the great age of seafaring was over (60). Ship captains also tended
"to get the habit of reading," which further broadened their perspective. "There's
no large-minded way of thinking now," he laments (60). They sit for a moment
in silence contemplating this, and the narrator hears the water on the beach below. "It sounded like the strange warning wave that gives notice of the turn of
the tide," she believes, and through the rest of the book the tide will turn in sim-

ilar ways, first asserting and then undermining the narrator's "large-minded way of thinking."

Some chapters later we have another literalization of the overview, this time on a walk the narrator takes with Mrs. Todd's brother, William. They mount a promontory on the island where he lives, from the top of which they can see the entirety of that island, the islands around it, and the mainland. "It gave a sudden sense of space, for nothing stopped the eye or hedged one in—that sense of liberty in space and time which great prospects always give" (81). But when William suggests that "there ain't no such view in the world, I expect," his dialect speech and lack of experience make the narrator feel "as if an untraveled boy had spoken" (81). William is already past middle age, and the disparaging comment suggests the lack of perspective of the narrator even as she announces his.

Most of *Country of the Pointed Firs* describes the narrator accompanying Mrs. Todd, the village herbalist with whom the narrator boards, as she makes her visits. When they visit a certain Mrs. Fosdick, a woman who has outlived most of a large brood of sailors and sailors' wives, the narrator describes her as a woman "not without a touch of dignity and elegance" (92). The double negative insists on the distance the narrator feels, and Mrs. Fosdick is further distanced by a comparison to Mrs. Todd. "In a wider sphere one might have called [Mrs. Fosdick] a woman of the world, with her unexpected bits of modern knowledge, but Mrs. Todd's wisdom was an intimation of truth itself. She might belong to any age, like an idyl of Theocritus; but while she always understood Mrs. Fosdick, that entertaining pilgrim could not always understand Mrs. Todd" (92). Understanding is the yardstick, and of course one thing Mrs. Todd would not understand, at least without some explanation, is the reference to Theocritus, author of the oldest extant pastoral poetry and not exactly a household name. When Mrs. Fosdick bemoans the loss of the old days—"What a lot o' queer folks there used to be about here, anyway, when we was young Almiry. Everybody's just like everybody else"—the narrator silently demurs: "It seemed to me there were peculiarities of character in the region of Dunnet Landing yet, but I did not like to interrupt" (96). The joke is on Mrs. Fosdick, from the narrator's perspective, and we in part agree, since the series of portraits seem drawn to accent regional peculiarities. But the various stories we hear about Dunnet Landing's past, its harbor teeming with ships arriving from every port in the world, and the Fosdicks and Littlepages of the town exercising their peculiarities with all the energy of youth, suggest that Mrs. Fosdick is probably right as well, that the town has lost some of its particular character. Mrs. Todd meditates a moment on Mrs. Fosdick's statement, and then agrees. Captain Littlepage had already reflected on the decline of civilization in general and its practice in Dunnet Landing in particular, and the narrator, with her blithe dismissal of such ideas, loses her authority and leaves us alone with the implied author, surveying not just Dunnet Landing, but Bostonian attitudes as well.

The big social event in the book is the Bowden family reunion, an annual gathering of Mrs. Todd's clan. The pies had been prepared with writing in frosting and strips of pastry—dates and names and one with "Bowden Reunion" written across it—and a large gingerbread construction of the Bowden family house, complete with windows and doors and lilac plants in front. The family consumes images of itself in the same way that readers consume the images of them in the text, suggesting that local culture is something made and consumed not just by local color writers but by the people themselves. "There was a general sigh" when the gingerbread house collapses at the end of the meal, "and it was shared by a great part of the assembly, not without seriousness, and as if it were a pledge and a token of loyalty" (132). The baker says that it might have stood longer if she had made it all of frosted cake, but "'t wouldn't have been the right shade; the old house, as you observe, was never painted, and I concluded that plain gingerbread would represent it best" (132). The accuracy of representation and the seriousness of consumption are like those of literature, but something else is missing. Immediately after dessert come speeches and then a poetry reading by the poetess in the family, and when the "long faded garland of verses came to an appealing end," even Mrs. Todd, generous as she is, recognizes that the poetess "harps too much" on the recently departed (133). Like the gingerbread house, these creations are not meant to last very long. Unlike lesser expressive forms, literature lasts.

"The Queen's Twin," a Dunnet Landing story written after *Country of the Pointed Firs* but in later editions included with it, opens with "the beautiful prospect which is halfway between Dunnet's Landing and the Twin's home" (226). The narrator reminds us that there are "all sorts of folly in the country, just as there is in the city" (234–35) and comments favorably on those who are "high above makin' mean complaints of other folks" (235). The narrator goes with Mrs. Todd to visit the title character, a woman who feels she is the queen of England's twin. She understands, however, that there are some differences: "I ain't like the Queen's majesty," she explains to her new visitor, "for this is the only palace I've got" (239). The Twin had been to England in her youth and had been in a crowd when the queen passed by. The queen, she explains, when she saw her twin in the crowd, looked at her "just as if she knew there was something different between us from other folks" (239). This moment of recognition was the transformative event in her life, and she has had "no friend I've felt so near to me ever since" (239). The narrator, rather than finding this pathetic self-delusion, sees it as "a lovely gift of imagination and true affection" (239). Mrs.

Todd too finds in it a kind of wisdom: "Such beautiful dreams is the real part of life," she says (242). Readers, of course, are not so sure—we are meant to appreciate these sentiments, but, in part with the help of the nonstandard grammar, also to retain some distance from them. There is a freak show quality to the successive visits of the narrator, and the characters' eccentricities, while they should occasion no "mean complaints," are not simply beautiful dreams, they are instances of "all kinds of folly" as well.

Although Jewett's work has been used as prime evidence for both the hegemonic and the antihegemonic readings of regionalism, the best recent criticism recognizes the complexity of her work. Sandra Zagarell identifies different registers in *Country of the Pointed Firs*—one womanist, one Nordicist, and one localist—which, though each fundamentally reducible to an ideological position, partially conflict with one another and certainly do not line up neatly with our contemporary cultural-political categories.[25] June Howard has written that Jewett's work gives "a sense that the center of the world is not the site of social dominance but the site of consciousness; it is potentially everywhere and anywhere."[26] She should be read, Howard suggests, not just alongside regionalists, but with writers who tell "the story of civilization" (378). Howard also edited *New Essays on The Country of the Pointed Firs,* and three of the four other essays in that volume are similarly cosmopolitan.[27] One, by Zagarell, is another run at the way the text invokes and "call[s] into question" nationalism and Nordicism, arguing that the text is "both inclusive *and* restrictive."[28] Another is a piece by Michael Davitt Bell that concludes: "The truth is that Jewett's women in *The Country of the Pointed Firs* are at the same time rooted *and* restless, enriched *and* impoverished, sustained by domestic routine *and* frustrated by it. . . . We should resist the impulse to reimpose these bifurcations on *The Country of the Pointed Firs.*"[29] Elizabeth Ammons's article argues that the text is nationalist and imperialist, but it is followed by one by Susan Gillman that finds *Country* to be an example of "Janus-faced" regionalism, "separate from and engaged with the nation," in "dialogue" with empire.[30] Howard in her introduction to the essays concludes that the novel is "one of the most rewardingly complex American narratives we have."[31] These essays also offer scolding admonitions against the text's inadequate cosmopolitanism. Zagarell suggests that the use of racial slurs by Jewett's characters "probably makes other readers as uncomfortable as it makes me" (39). Ammons, though she has resisted such a reading in the past, she writes, finds "subtle but clear protofascist implications" in the text, and Gillman reproaches Jewett for the nativist, anti-immigrant sentiments in the text. Even Howard, whose argument is most clearly focused on Jewett's achievement in balancing the competing cultural claims the text addresses, feels it necessary, in her final paragraph, to apologize that *Country* is "not a timeless masterpiece," that it cannot completely "disengage from the historical conditions of possibility in which it emerges" (30). The praise and the admonishments are alike cosmopolitan.

Charles Chesnutt's "The Goophered Grapevine" (1899) has a classic local color frame tale, in which a Northerner, John, has come south for his wife's health and, he hopes, his own profit. He is a cosmopolitan fellow, knowledgeable about life in regions from California to Europe, and his cosmopolitanism increases as he gets to know his new region. The town he settles near at first seems "almost sabbatic in its restfulness," but he soon learns that "underneath its somnolent exterior the deeper currents of life—love and hatred, joy and despair, ambition and avarice, faith and friendship—flowed not less steadily than in livelier latitudes."[32] Looking over a ruined plantation and vineyard he is considering buying, he meets Uncle Julius, who tries to dissuade him and his wife, Mary, with a long involved tale of a deadly hex on the grapevines. It becomes clear, however slowly, that Julius is selling the grapes himself and would like the estate to remain in receivership. In the other stories in the collection, Uncle Julius tells folktales to get his way—in "Po' Sandy," for instance, Julius tell a story whose moral is that a certain shed is made of "hanted" wood and therefore should not be torn down for use in building an addition onto John's kitchen; Mary convinces John to buy new wood; Julius starts a church in the supposedly haunted shed. The stories each move from the genteel white perspective of the frames and interludes to the folk culture of the tales, and on to the struggles between these two views. Deciding the validity of either side is never really an issue. John, who has since bought the plantation, is not always convinced by Julius's stories and remains skeptical, and although his wife often seems to believe, she may in fact simply be pretending in order to give Julius what he wants.

Chesnutt is the man of the hour in American literary studies these days: Eric Sundquist devotes 185 pages of his *To Wake the Nations: Race and the Making of American Literature* (1993) to Chesnutt, for instance; Brodhead devotes his fifth and final chapter of *Cultures of Letters* to him; and Ross Posnock awards him a central role in *Color and Culture* (1998). Brodhead argues that Chesnutt wrote local color stories by trading on his cultural capital as a marginal person, but that when he tried to write stories that were less "colorful"—including the stories in *The Wife of His Youth and Other Stories* (1899) and the novels *The House behind the Cedars* (1900) and *The Marrow of Tradition* (1901)—publishers and critics were less enthusiastic.[33] I think it would be easier to explain the relative difference in interest by the fact that social and cultural judgments in the novels and most of the stories in *The Wife of His Youth* are less ambiguous—to read them is to read fairly specific condemnations of racism and injustice, alongside occasional applause for virtue. The dialect stories, on the other hand, can be read in several ways—as Uncle Tom-ish on the one hand, or as polyvocal, balanced, resistant, or preservationist on the other.

Kenneth M. Price argues for the polyvocal reading, saying that the stories could appeal to those who saw themselves in John's position or to those who identified with Uncle Julius.[34] My argument, of course, is that we are meant to read both sides in dialogue and all these possibilities. Sundquist opts for the last two—the resistant and preservationist readings. He argues that the grape culture in "The Goophered Grapevine," for instance, is a trope for culture in general and that, just as the Northerner comes down and all but destroys the vineyard, so does the invasion of the South by the forces of the industrializing North all but destroy Southern African American culture. The writing of these stories, many of which are based on well-known oral tales (though in one collected version of this tale the slave gets an enormous penis instead of working strength; as Sundquist notes, Chesnutt's versions are a bit bowdlerized) is an attempt to preserve the culture that is being pruned too close to the branch. This preservationist move is not simply antiquarian or curatorial, according to Sundquist: Chesnutt "reached into the vibrant world of slave culture to find the origins of modern African American cultural resistance to racism."[35]

Certainly this seems to be a fairly straightforward part of the narrative structure of *The Conjure Woman:* Julius gets what he wants by telling folk tales; he gets rewarded economically, thereby successfully resisting (to a point) the dominance of the whites. But the stories can also be read as the opposite, an instance of the longstanding relegation of African Americans to roles as either marginal workers or entertainers. In moving from his supposed role as agricultural laborer to that of an entertainer of whites, Uncle Julius subverts nothing, still steppin' and fetchin' to get by. Sundquist argues that we should see Chesnutt as producing a kind of cakewalk, since the cakewalk, Sundquist writes, occupies "a liminal territory with a significant potential for resistance, . . . an African American reversal of the stereotype" (277). Chesnutt makes Uncle Julius perform in stereotypically Negro ways, in this reading, in order to expose the facts (and logical, cultural weaknesses) of Northerners' racism.

Brodhead argues something very similar. Although "nineteenth-century regionalism is among other things a work of ethnic imagining, a literary form performing the larger cultural service of imaging Americas different in habits, speech, and appearance from a norm this form helps render normative" (177), Chesnutt's work is an exception. Chesnutt, unlike Jewett, "understands that the parties to the regionalist dialogue [are] antagonists, not friends" and he "unfolds a contest between them, a contest of domination and indigenous resistance played out on several planes" (200). The conjure stories show that "there is no such thing as total domination" (200). But if we can make this argument for

Chesnutt's critique of racism, can we not do the same for Mary Wilkins Freeman's paleo-feminist claims, Garland's agrarian populism, and Jewett's dialogues
on nativism and cosmopolitanism? The argument for Chesnutt's stealthy resistance to the normative seriously undermines Brodhead's general argument for
the normative force of regionalism, at least as he constructs it. The norm espoused by Chesnutt's texts is that of literary cosmopolitanism, just as it is for
Garland, Freeman, and Jewett. It is impossible to read the conjure stories and
not see the value of Julius's perspective as a refusal of racist ideology, just as it is
impossible to miss the validity of rural complaint in Garland or the validity of
antipatriarchal sentiment in Freeman. At the same time it is impossible to read
the conjure stories and not see the value of the landlord's perspective; in case we
doubt it, Chesnutt gives us the contrast between the landlord and his wife, with
their very different levels of openness to Julius's seduction, empathy toward him,
resistance to his wiles, respect for his intelligence, and pity for his lack of "advantages." The exposure of racism requires only a very small part of the fictional
machinery Chesnutt puts into motion, and this machinery has larger ambitions,
the largest of which is comprehensively to survey the social scene. Uncle Julius
is, in the end, far from a simple font of wisdom or ameliorative settler of scores,
and however much we might identify with him and his cause, we still, despite
it all, exist as readers within the frame; that is, Chesnutt, the implied author, has
chosen not to give us a collection of Uncle Julius stories but a collection of stories narrated by a white man, within each of which is embedded an Uncle Julius
story. We begin and end with a narrator who, however much we may give ourselves over to the voice of Uncle Julius, brings us back to the realm of the au-
thored text, a text much more akin, culturally, logically, and linguistically, to the
narration of the landlord than it is to that of Uncle Julius. We, the readers, are
offered the facts of resistance within a broader array of cultural attitudes and understandings. Only some of those understandings do we share with Uncle Julius,
only some with the narrator, and only some with his wife. We share them all
with the implied author.

    In Mary Wilkins Freeman's "A Mistaken Charity," Harriet and Charlotte
Shattuck are impoverished old women cared for by the community, and they
have a fear of ending up in the poorhouse. One sister is blind, the other rheu-
matic, and two philanthropic townswomen decide to send them to a "Home."
The poor women hate it and want to get back to their farm; eventually they
run away.

> The "Home" was comfortable, and in some respects even luxurious; but nothing
> suited those two unhappy, unreasonable old women. The fare was of a finer, more

delicately served variety than they had been accustomed to; those finely flavored nourishing soups for which the "Home" took great credit to itself failed to please palates used to common, coarser food.[36]

On the one hand, this is a simple story celebrating the simple life. The narrator calls them "unhappy, unreasonable old women" with a ladle of irony, and the Home appears ridiculous in its pretensions, not the least of which are its name and its pridefulness about its soups. On the other hand, the simple life is one of near starvation and fear, and the Home is a haven in an otherwise heartless world.

At times, the philanthropic women, one of whom is the moneybags and the other the busybody, do not come off particularly well. They are officious, only structurally rather than interpersonally empathetic, and provincially incapable of understanding the sisters' resistance to their charity. But the poor sisters do not make a very good impression either much of the time. They are in fact a tad unreasonable, and the narrator's opinion of them is very mixed. "The Shattucks had always been poor people and common people; they had always been poor and coarse and common. The father and his father before him had simply lived in the poor little house, grubbed for their living, and then unquestioningly died. The mother had been of no rarer stamp, and the two daughters were cast in the same mould" (302). Again, a certain amount of irony and a certain level of true disdain animate these sentences, with the irony producing the oscillatory effect.

As the sisters are escaping from the "Home" hidden in a covered wagon, the matron and "one of the gentlemen in charge of the home" pass them in a buggy, "truly alarmed and anxious for the safety of the old women, who were chuckling maliciously in the wagon they soon left far behind" (311). The narrative stays with the poor sisters' perspective throughout the story, and when they escape we are with them. The matron and gentlemen mean to thwart the sisters' desires, so they are the oppressive police, and they never even think to look in the covered wagon, suggesting they are also anxious fools. But the last clause turns against the sisters again, the single word "maliciously" pulling us out of a simple reading.

Throughout the text the oscillations come fast and often. The philanthropists are invasive, insensitive, and oppressive, but the sisters do live in a house that is falling down and that cannot keep out the rain or the wind. One sister is blind and the other seriously arthritic and they are living on what are essentially weeds picked from their yard. The philanthropists' intervention is thus wonderful and their intentions perfectly admirable. The sisters are the salt of the earth, but one is inexcusably bitchy and the other not "any too strong in her mind" (303). The question of how a community should care for its elderly was urgent, obviously, in a society with no welfare system to speak of and a semi-migrant population, and Freeman's text displays the issues involved. The title, "A Mistaken Charity," can mean that the philanthropists were in the wrong, or that the sisters simply did not take it correctly. The story remains open.

This openness, as I have suggested, is exactly what critics of the time used as a prime criterion for judging artistic success. The critic E. C. Steadman wrote that the difference between Constance Fenimore Woolson and the "ordinary realists" is that "she liked the beer gardens and the concert halls . . . and was accustomed to study nature in its commoner as well as its finer phases."[37] J. H. Morse wrote that Woolson has "the chance of becoming our best novelist" because she has both the "power of passion" and "the analytic touch," because she has clearly absorbed "what is best in the new school, without altogether sinking the old nobility of the virtues in the vulgar realities of the day," and because she shows us both sides of her characters: "The author gives us the materials for judging the man, but paints love so strongly that the argument of the heart almost overpowers that of the head"—almost, but not quite.[38] This is what the "great dramatist says to himself," according to Morse:

> Here is a remarkable event. Let us see if we can trace the gathering passions that brought it about. Let us place ourselves at the beginning, and come up to it by every road, private or public, and see if we can gather into a selected number of persons the representative forces, showing how they acted on one another, as well as how they combined to bring about the event. Let us give the local color, and revive the times as well as the men, and so make the reader an actor, and not alone a critical spectator. (372)

What we need, Morse argues, is the writer "who can grasp all these details. . . . Is the new novelist to take his stand with the healthy livers, or with the dyspeptic? Is he only to analyze down to the dissolution, and deny us our dreams?" (375). The answer, for Morse, is always that we need both. Analyzing dissolution is part of what the new school has to offer, but we cannot have only that, we need the dreams as well.

Not all critics agreed that both were represented in local color literature. An anonymous critic in the *Nation* wrote in 1907 that "we all know to our sorrow what local color is. The novel of to-day reeks with it—dialect so carefully spelled as to be unintelligible, passages of precise description of persons and places, meticulous attention to costumes, forms, and customs. It is realism run mad."[39] Many critics agreed that local details were only valuable if they were in the service of a larger cultural and literary project. The *Overland Monthly* in 1884 maintained that Bret Harte was no good when he wrote anything but his Western stories, and "this fact in itself shows how small the proportion of fundamental truth and human interest in Mr. Harte's stories has always been, and how much of their worth depends upon the picturesque setting which he constructed with so much skill."[40] These critiques use the same cosmopolitan criteria, of course; they simply do not find adequate literary quality in the texts they are evaluating.

Literary cosmopolitanism was central to the evaluation of ethnic literature as well. The Cincinnati *American Israelite* attacked Abraham Cahan and Israel Zangwill, claiming that each "intentionally exaggerated what is worst among his own class of people," supposedly for sensationalist purposes. "A man who is capable of painting the people from whom he comes in such vile colors would be enough of a scoundrel to lie about them for the sake of a few dollars."[41] Other critics, uninterested in the politics of Jewish American life, nonetheless condemn Cahan for too much sordidness, because it demonstrates a lack of balance. "From the beginning to the end," writes Nancy Huston Banks, for example, "throughout the work there is not a gleam of spirituality, unselfishness, or nobility," and this is not "truly representative."[42] But Banks, commenting on the *American Israelite*'s attack, claims that anyone can see that "within the Ghetto, with all its limitations, its antiquated observances, its dirt, its pitiful and oft-times sordid poverty, Mr. Cahan finds the best material for a finer and loftier interpretation of the dreams and aspirations, the ancient spirit of the race" (429).

Related to these arguments are those that congratulate writers from underrepresented groups or warn against celebrating writers simply because they are from such groups. The following excerpt from an 1897 issue of *Poet Lore* is a perfect example of the latter:

> The democratic enlargement of vision has set up in certain quarters a hunt for geniuses, especially among the ranks of women and the laboring classes, which is itself a most excellent tendency, provided the hunters do not in their enthusiasm lose their better judgment and hold up for extravagant admiration any manifestation of talent simply because it comes from the ranks of the "humble." This very attitude of delight in the genius of the "humble" poisons the sincerity of democracy, for in the vocabulary of the true democrat there is no such word as "humble." Such a bias born of the democratic enthusiasm of the innately aristocratic will not serve to place either women or the "humble" upon any better plane than the formerly purely aristocratic bias which has ruled in the realm of the fine arts.[43]

Democratic breadth is fine: nevertheless, it does not solve but rather aggravates the problem of evaluation, just as full representation of a group's lived experience does not resolve but complicates its political relations with the rest of society. What is wanted is "the sincerity of democracy," unpoisoned.

Breadth of imagination is the antidote. An 1885 review of "Recent American Fiction" in the *Atlantic Monthly* by J. H. Morse suggested that Southern writers such as George Washington Cable and Charles Egbert Craddock were more successful than their Northern counterparts because "the North refines through a keen analysis. The South enriches through a generous imagination."[44] The author contrasts the "metaphysical temper" and "subtle distinctions" of Northern literature to "the breadth which characterizes the best Southern writing, the large, free handling, and confident imagination" (125). Meredith Nicholson's retrospective 1902 essay on Edward Eggleston uses similarly cosmopolitan criteria for both praise and censure. Eggleston understood that the United States "cannot be condensed into one or a dozen finished panoramas"; he had the requisite background reading since he "combined a personal experience at once varied and novel with a self-acquired education to which he gave the range and breadth of true cultivation, and, in special directions, the precision of scholarship"; his experience was also cosmopolitan, and though "he knew the use of books, . . . he vitalized them from a broad knowledge of life." But Eggleston was sometimes not cosmopolitan enough: "A fault of all of Eggleston's earlier stories is their too serious insistence on the moral they carried."[45] Morse had written something similar twenty years earlier: "We are delighted with the odd figures, with the strong human feeling, and we laugh and grow fat over the healthy sentiment" of Eggleston's *Hoosier Schoolmaster*, "but nearly all that a nice art and a balancing faculty would contribute is lacking."[46]

Charles W. Coleman Jr., writing about "The Recent Movement in Southern Literature," in an 1887 issue of *Harper's*, makes it clear he finds a relation between the profession of letters and writings that bear the "impress of clime." The "provincial flavor" of Southern writing was half responsible for its literary qualities (along with "delicate and exquisite workmanship") and half responsible for its viability as a product—the "freshness" of the Southern authors, the fact that their "many and various peoples and dialects have for the first time entered into literature" and that they depict people who may "otherwise be unknown to us," is what gives their stories value.[47] Coleman talks about the way these texts work for "us," and by this he means both Southern and Northern audiences. Coleman notes that Richard Malcolm Johnston, who wrote his "Dukesborough Tales" for *Southern Magazine,* was encouraged by fellow Georgian Sidney Lanier to "seek a wider audience; the subsequent stories of the series were published in Northern magazines. With this enlarged audience the publication of these admirable character studies continued" (842). The provincial flavor needs the "enlarged audience" if it is to do its cosmopolitan work.

When Howells reviewed Paul Laurence Dunbar for the first time, he introduced him as a writer with ties to Ohio, Indiana, Kentucky, and Illinois, and as the first man "of pure African blood" to "feel the negro life aesthetically and express it lyrically."[48] Dunbar's "unique achievement," Howells asserts, "was to have studied the American negro objectively," with both sympathy and unblinking truthfulness. It causes Howells to muse that perhaps "the arts . . . were to be the final proof that God had made of one blood all the nations of man" (280). He imagines "the hostilities and the prejudices" vanishing in the arts. At the same time, Howells does not want difference to vanish altogether. Dunbar's poems are "evidence of the essential unity of the human race, which does not think or feel black in one and white in another, but humanly in all. Yet it appeared to me then, and it appears to me now, that there is a precious difference of temperament between the races which it would be a great pity to ever lose" (280). He praises Dunbar for preserving these differences, and the two impulses together, the ability to preserve difference while making it vanish, produce what Howells calls "literary interpretation of a very artistic completeness" (281).

   This same understanding is at work in criticism today. Brodhead recognizes the revolt against subjugation in Chesnutt's text, but adds "conjure's resistance, if it is never impotent, is never omnipotent either; and Chesnutt's tales are at their most moving when charting the limits of such power" (200–201). Brodhead hovers between arguing for the ideological and cultural complexity of the conjure tales and dismissing them as local colorisms, by which he means texts whose cultural work is the normative abolishment of difference. Brodhead tells two tales: in the first, a tragic racist necessity determines Chesnutt's literary career, and he is obliged to stay with the dialect tales rather than write conventional novels, as he would have preferred; in the second, Chesnutt's stealthy artistry of resistance and exploration prevails in those same tales. Chesnutt "could win access to the ranks of authors on the condition that he . . . write the fiction of black life—local color life—that his audience was interested to hear" (209); he could continue to publish "to the extent that he helped maintain preferred fictions of racial life" (210). The suggestion in such statements is that the preferred fictions were racist, and it is worth noting that this argument gets its moral force from its invocation of inclusion—all authors should write all kinds of texts, nothing and nobody should be excluded. But it also wreaks havoc with Brodhead's own reading of the text, which suggests that the tales are precisely not the "preferred fiction of racial life" in the sense he means. They are, however, preferable for anyone interested in the full range of racial experience. Brodhead is right to suggest that Chesnutt had to write what "his audience wanted to hear," as is necessarily the case in all commercial publications, but the evidence is that literary readers wanted not the polemics of Chesnutt's other fictions but the sophisticated multiplicity of the conjure tales, exactly the stories that Brodhead and Sundquist and others describe. The way literary readers read in the nineteenth century, the way they evaluated literary texts, the way they understood the cultural work of literature, and thus the way they understood the literary itself, were all closer to the way we read now, in other words, than critics and scholars generally admit.

1900—1930

The Ends of Local Color

"The classical episode of 'local color' in American fiction may now be said to be ended," an anonymous critic wrote in the *Nation* in 1919.[1] The surface differences from region to region have no real importance or interest, this critic argued, because the nation has turned out to be "even more homogenous than it knew" (427). In fact, there are no deep cultural differences, the critic suggests; the people in the nation's geographical and cultural backwaters simply do not have the gumption to join modernity and thereby become truly interesting. People are tired of reading about "the village concerns of that part of the population which had been too conservative—often too dull or timid—to move about the country after the manner of the bolder spirits" (427). The critic thus dismisses regional difference by appealing to cosmopolitan ideals. Although local fiction is dead, poets such as Robert Frost, Edgar Lee Masters, and Vachel Lindsay with his "New Localism" are worth reading, the critic explains, but again not because they are interpreters of local folkways. They have literary value because they give us "real tragedy," and thus write about the fullness of human experience. Frost's poetry has "more of essential tragedy and idyl than in all the older stories of New England" (427). Masters "has made Spoon River an American village which belongs to the world" (427), and it is the world, not the village, that is of primary importance.

The *Nation* critic was a bit premature in announcing the demise of regionalism. The 1910s, 1920s, and 1930s would see a new burst of regional writing, including Willa Cather's work, that of the writers in the "revolt from the village" school (named by Carl Van Doren in an essay, also in the *Nation,* two years later), the Southern Renaissance, the Harlem Renaissance, the folklore movement, the "new regionalism" in social thought, and popular writing and film that explored (or exploited) regional cultures.[2] At the same time, a new regionalist movement swept through the country's university and college English departments, resulting in the creation of little magazines dedicated to regional literary production, including John T. Frederick's *Midland* (1915–1933) and the Agrarians' *Fugitive* (1922–1925). The latter's contributors included the core of the Twelve Southerners who would write *I'll Take My Stand* at the end of the 1920s. By the 1930s, the Federal Writers' Project would turn American regional writing into a small, government-subsidized industry. Robert L. Dorman, in *Revolt of the Provinces: The Regionalist Movement in America, 1920–1945* (1993), the most important survey of the period, claims that regionalism in these decades is "the signal of a critical juncture in the centuries-long transformation of this country from a rural, frontier, decentralized, producerist, farm and village society—the older America—into the modern, commercialized, consumerist, and mechanized mass society of the metropolis."[3] In this he follows the general historical consensus, at least since Robert Wiebe's *The Search for Order* (1967), that by the 1920s the "island communities" of the nineteenth century had disappeared, replaced by a national system "derived from the regulative, hierarchical needs of urban-industrial life."[4]

Both Wiebe and Dorman assume that these developments begin in the 1870s, but they are interested in characterizing the differences between pre– and post–World War I culture. Literary critics and historians, following Van Doren, also have stressed the distinctions between nineteenth-century local color and postwar regionalism, but in many ways literary regionalism before and after the war, at least in the broad sense I am using here, remains very much the same. Critical arguments pro and con, much like those that surrounded nineteenth-century local literature, accompanied the revived literary regionalism of these years. Describing those debates in 1936, B. A. Botkin wrote that "regionalism has given rise to a lively controversy, in which, in this case, not only literary critics but scientists have engaged. Because of its equivocal position between art and science, regional literature has drawn fire from both sides. Thus on the one hand, the sociological pretensions of literary regionalism have irked the social scientists" and, on the other, Botkin adds, regionalism's sociological bent has irked the belletristic types.[5] Botkin was one of a group of academic folklorists who worked for universities and government agencies and who made folk culture a respectable area of academic study—Botkin was professor at the University of Oklahoma, folklore editor of the Federal Writers' Project (1936–1939), and chief editor both of the Library of Congress's Writer's Unit (1939–1941) and the Archive of American Folk Song (1942–1945). Like Howells and other nineteenth-century commentators, Botkin argued that regional cultural production was an important force in the making and sustaining of a pluralistic society.

Also like Howells, many of the regionalists in the 1920s and 1930s saw regionalism as necessarily the essence of culture in a vast and diverse country. Mary Austin, whose *Land of Little Rain* (1903) and other fiction and nonfiction on the Southwest had made her one of the country's most widely known regional writers, argued that regionalism is the condition of literature in "any country which is large enough to cover more than one type of natural environment."[6] Assuming a Hippolyte Taine–like belief in the influence of a writer's environment, she claimed, in an oft-quoted 1932 essay, that "art, considered as the expression of any people as a whole, is the response they make in various mediums to the impact that the totality of their experience makes upon them, and there is no sort of experience that works so constantly and subtly upon man as his regional environment" (97). A corollary for Austin was that some environments are better for people than others.

Howard W. Odum, sociologist at the University of North Carolina, and his student Harry Estill Moore, later of the University of Texas, claimed that "the theme of American regionalism is, after all, essentially that of a great American Nation, the land and the people."[7] Odum and Moore and their colleagues, sometimes called the "Chapel Hill Regionalists," were unabashed proponents of American exceptionalism. In the diverse regional cultures of America, they claim, because of their "continuity and unity of development, through a fine equilibrium of geographic, cultural, and historical factors, must be found not only the testing ground of American democracy but, according to many observers, the hope of Western civilization" (3). They saw themselves as preservationists, collecting cultural artifacts on the brink of extinction. The Agrarians, to whom they are often contrasted since they were less interested in folk culture than in high culture, nonetheless argued something similar: that industrial civilization was homogenizing and destroying culture, and that the Enlightenment ideals upon which the country was founded can survive only in places (necessarily away from the large cities) that are as insulated as possible from the world of machines and their money.

The "region" in regionalism meant different things for each of the many schools and arguments; it was sometimes a large geographical entity like "the South" (variously bordered), sometimes smaller political areas (especially individual states), sometimes cultural groupings (based on race, ethnicity, religion, class, or combinations of these). Mary Austin even argued that the world of fairy adventure and fantasy—she mentions Lewis Carroll, Hans Christian Andersen, and Rudyard Kipling—constituted a form of regionalism. But despite differences of definition, twentieth-century regionalists of many stripes saw themselves as a countercultural force, offering not just a window on the past and the passing, but a vision of an alternative future. As Patrick Mazza sums it up:

In the period between the two world wars, as metropolitan, mass consumerist society was decisively wiping away the remnants of an earlier, ruralist United States,
a cultural and intellectual movement rose in challenge. To the centralizing, corporate system that was coming to dominate American life, this movement posed the
region as an alternative framework for reconstructing society. The regionalists of
the '20s, '30s and '40s sought in the cultural survivals of the older America the root-
stock for a revitalized, re-regionalized "symphonic nation," as regionalist Benton
MacKaye called it. In particular, the regionalists found resources for renewal in the
folk life of agrarian and immigrant communities, and the tribal cultures of Native
Americans. In these they saw the raw materials for a new "civic religion" powerful enough to break the spell of the emerging mass consumer culture.[8]

Odum, for instance, argued that "scientific" regionalism uses local materials to
give "both explanation and power to the whole social fabric as well as to the
separate regional units," and was, finally, in the service of "the study of the present and the future."[9]

The regionalists were far from alone in decrying industrial mass culture, of
course. The publication of Harold Stearns's *Civilization in the United States*
(1922), with contributions from many of the best-known Young Turk intellectuals and literati, was seen as a battle cry on the part of those who found American civilization at once both too much and too little. Stearns's contributors
damned American civilization for its deadening and leveling propensities, for its
overdevelopment as a system of social control, and for its lack of sophistication,
its underdeveloped accumulation of art and thought. In his contribution, Lewis
Mumford writes, "Since we have failed up to the present to develop regional
cultures, those who do not wish to remain barbarians must become metropol-
itans. That means they must come to New York or ape the ways that are fashionable in New York."[10] The standardization of American life demanded, in its
wake, increased standardization.

As Mumford himself came to realize, the development of regional cultures
was not as much of a failure as he had suggested, in part precisely because regionalism saw itself as an alternative to the aping of New York fashions. John
Dewey, writing at the end of the 1920s about the critique of civilization and the
regionalist boom, argued that the "national" news, "national" advertising, everything national, all appeared "thin," lacking substance. The only thing truly national, he suggested, besides Prohibition and the high cost of living, was the
"devotion to localisms," and he praised "the awakening of criticism and of sympathy" in regionalist writing.[11] One of the major responses to the Stearns collection was *These United States,* portraits of local cultures organized by state
published serially in the *Nation* in the early 1920s and later compiled by the editor, Ernest Gruening. The series was meant to counter the claim leveled by

Stearns et al. of a cultureless America.[12] The editors claim they are going to show the "riches of variety" that remain despite "that increase of similarity which in spiritual and intellectual affairs has standardized the land" and made it "one vast and almost uniform republic."[13] The "hope" of the editors is that

> there be the least possible surrender of the essential differences which soil and weather, social habit and ethnic stock, experience and ambition have raised up among the varying regions of the country. Though centralization and regimentation may be a great convenience to administrators, they are death to variety and experiment and, consequently, in the end to growth. Better have the States a little rowdy and bumptious, a little restless under the central yoke, than given over to the tameness of a universal similarity. (27–28)

The cultural critics gathered by Stearns had been influenced by Freud and others to see civilization as the curbing of instinct and therefore the limiting of human possibility, to see social proprieties as restraints, containments. They had been taught by a tradition culminating in Henry James and T. S. Eliot that American civilization was impossibly rudimentary and unformed compared to European civilization. They had learned from the Boazian anthropologists to consider a broader array of cultural possibilities and to understand their own culture as fundamentally artificial, or as we would say now, socially constructed. Like the nineteenth-century literary writers, literary writers in the 1920s, who made up the bulk of contributors to both series, could not pretend to know human sexuality in the precise way the physiologists or the psychologists did, or to understand economics the way an economist might. But they did suggest that they understood the significance of the full range of knowledge being produced better than the overspecialized professionals in other fields. And for a large group of these literary intellectuals, regional writing was still a prime arena for displaying this full range.

If what some of the Agrarians and folklorists offered in the face of standardization and cultural loss was preservation and revival, many regionalist writers offered something a little different. The Harlem Renaissance writers, for instance, who contributed to the *Messenger*'s series, "These 'Colored' United States" (which was itself an answer to the lack of racial diversity in Gruening's series), held a range of attitudes toward cultural difference that went well beyond the preservationist impulse to include satire, scolding, feigned incomprehension and feigned celebration, as well as reverence and respect.[14] And in their literary texts, the Harlem Renaissance writers worked toward a balance among these options. Jean Toomer's *Cane* (1923), especially in the first of its three sections, gives a hearty nod to the beauty and sensual pleasure of the more primitive rural Southern life, but also chronicles the degradation and loss involved.

James Weldon Johnson's *Autobiography of an Ex-Colored Man* (1912) suggests that the ex-colored man, in losing his relation to African American culture, has become deracinated and alienated from his own experience, but his cosmopolitan attainments are also at the center of whatever moments of full connectedness he has felt. Claude McKay's heroes, in *Home to Harlem* (1928) and *Banjo* (1929), offer advice on living in premodern happiness within the modern world by simultaneously embracing primitive vitality and modern intellectual consciousness. What McKay and others suggest is that, in assimilating to modern American cultural norms, African Americans lose the true value of their own culture, while lack of exposure to European and Euro-American high culture represents another deplorable loss, another kind of cultural deprivation. Not quite interested in preservation or revival, the Harlem Renaissance authors offered a cosmopolitan mixture of critique and celebration.[15]

The "revolt" literature, according to Van Doren—he is writing primarily about Masters's *Spoon River Anthology* (1915), Sherwood Anderson's *Winesburg, Ohio* (1919), and several novels from 1920, including Floyd Dell's *Moon-Calf* (1920) and Sinclair Lewis's *Main Street* (1920)—was equally concerned with deadening standardization, but instead of seeing traditional, rural culture as an antidote to urban alienation, these novelists saw it as the seedbed of conformity. They rejected both the promise of modernity and the "cult of the village" as redress, according to Van Doren, and worked to dispel the myth of the village as the protector of traditional healthy values. Van Doren sees Masters and Lindsay as the precursors of Anderson and Lewis, but mentions E. W. Howe's *Story of a Country Town* (1883), Twain's "The Man Who Corrupted Hadleyburg" (1899), and Clarence Darrow's *Farmington* (1904) as "mordant, neglected testimonies," and he writes that Howe "made it cynically clear—to the few who read him" that villages "might in fact be stagnant backwaters or dusty centers of futility" (407). He finds these to be exceptions, however.

> For nearly half a century native literature has been faithful to the cult of the village, celebrating its delicate merits with sentimental affection and with unwearied interest digging into odd corners of the country for persons and incidents illustrative of the essential goodness and heroism which, so the doctrine ran, lie beneath unexciting surfaces. . . . The village seemed too cosy to be disturbed. There it lay in the mind's eye, neat, compact, organized, traditional: the white church with tapering spire, the sober schoolhouse, the smithy of the ringing anvil, the corner grocery, the cluster of friendly houses, the venerable parson, the wise physician, the canny squire, the grasping landlord softened or outwitted in the end, the village belle, gossip, atheist, idiot, jovial fathers, gentle mothers, merry children, cool parlors, shining kitchens, spacious barns, lavish gardens, fragrant summer dawns, and comfortable winter evenings. (407)

Van Doren seems to be having some fun with this list of clichés, but as we have seen, these materials in literary regionalism have always been offset by drudgery, poverty, frailty, ignorance, and worse. The "revolt" novelists were in fact using the same basic techniques as the writers Van Doren believes they are leaving behind.

There are also quite wide areas of agreement between the "revolt" novelists and the Agrarians, who might appear to be on opposite ends of the cultural argument about modernity and the village, since the "revolt" fiction attempts to destroy the myth of small-town and rural life and the Agrarians insist on its continuing value as a model for the good life. Similarly, the "Old Crowd" Harlem Renaissance writers such as Jessie Redmon Fauset and the "New Crowd" writers such as McKay may seem to be antagonists on the question of civilization but in fact produce overlapping cosmopolitan arguments. At the subliterary edges of these movements one finds clear oppositions, but in their literary texts we find a much more balanced representation of cultural politics than partisan characterizations of their commitments would suggest.

Many other regionalist texts were published in the 1910s, including softer-edged fictions such as Sui Sin Far's *Mrs. Spring Fragrance* (1912), Harry Leon Wilson's *Ruggles of Red Gap* (1915), Zane Grey's *Riders of the Purple Sage* (1912), along with an outpouring of more novels and memoirs by Garland, Margaret Deland, Ellen Glasgow, Booth Tarkington, Grace King, Alice French ("Octave Thanet"), and Zona Gale. The way was paved for what would be received as the literary revolt against the provinces and the Agrarian revolt in their favor by these and a series of better texts: Jack London's *Valley of the Moon* (1913), Mary Austin's *The Ford* (1917), Robert Frost's *North of Boston* (1914) and *Mountain Interval* (1916), Willa Cather's *O Pioneers!* (1913) and *My Ántonia* (1918), and a few texts that, along with *O Pioneers!*, I will discuss in somewhat more detail: Edith Wharton's *Ethan Frome* (1911) and *Summer* (1917) and Edgar Lee Masters's *Spoon River Anthology* (1915).

These last texts show a new level of generic consciousness, demonstrating an attention to formal issues rarely seen in nineteenth-century local color literature. The murder of the adulterous Emil and Marie in a jealous rage in *O Pioneers!* and the incest, quasi-incest, and adultery in Wharton's texts are part of a revolution in regional fiction, but not because these were entirely new topics. E. W. Howe's *Story of a Country Town* (1885) had a jealous murder as a climactic event and Twain's *Pudd'nhead Wilson* (1894) features a son selling his mother into slavery and murdering the uncle who adopted him. Mary Wilkins Freeman's "Old Woman Magoun" (1909), in which a father tries to sell his daughter to another gambler and the girl's grandmother poisons her to save her from that fate, is as interested in the darkest human motives as anything from the 1910s and 1920s. But it is true that, already in the few years between the suppression of *Sis-*

ter Carrie in 1900 and its heralded republication in 1907 and 1908, the breadth of acceptable subjects for explicit representation in fiction had been radically extended, and in the next few years Masters, Wharton, and Cather helped bring a closer look at such transgression into regionalist literature. The more important change in these stories is the implication that such transgressive passions are not exceptional at all, but common, normal. And the formal devices they developed help these writers make exactly this point.

The best of these texts can be seen as congenial to all the regionalist movements—preservationist, reactionary, progressive—since they strip the village of its myths while decrying modern standardization and alienation, and celebrate the primitive while demonstrating the value of civilization. As I have been arguing, something like a revolt from the village had always been part of literary regionalism, and something like regional pride and commitment continued to infuse the best "revolt" literature. We will see this same combination in the premier regionalist magazine, *Midland,* as well, which despite its self-advertisement as an alternative to New York hegemony maintained a thorough commitment to the same literary world as the New York writers and editors.

The first section in what follows is a reading of Willa Cather's *O Pioneers!* If Hamlin Garland's *Main-Travelled Roads* was the prototypical regionalist text of the second half of the nineteenth century, *O Pioneers!* stands as an exemplary one for the first half of the twentieth. The most obvious difference is the move from story collection to novel, the preferred form for regionalist literature from the 1910s to the present. Other formal differences and thematic shifts are evident as well, but the basic mechanics of representation, like the basic literary values involved, remain the same. The second section examines the other texts and contexts in the 1910s, the third section looks at selected texts of the "revolt" in the 1920s, and the fourth and fifth the Southern and Harlem Renaissances of the 1920s.

Willa Cather's Parables
of Authorship

Willa Cather's *O Pioneers!* (1913) opens with a fairly dark, classic image of the plains: "One January day, thirty years ago, the little town of Hanover, anchored on a windy Nebraska tableland, was trying not to be blown away."[16] Larry McMurtry's *The Last Picture Show* (1966), to use a somewhat more recent example of a local color argument for the value of art, opens with the same wind-blown scene of cobbled-together buildings (the wind is even stronger in the 1971 film version), and it has the same effect: everything seems endangered. Cather's narrator says that none of the buildings in the town appear permanent and that the rest of the land is even less marked by human habitation:

> The houses on the divide were small and tucked away in low places; you did not see them until you came directly upon them. Most of them were built of the sod itself, and were only the unescapable ground in another form. The roads were but faint tracks in the grass, and the fields were scarcely noticeable. The record of the plow was insignificant, like the feeble scratches on stone left by prehistoric races, so indeterminate that they may, after all, be only the markings of glaciers, and not a record of human strivings. (15)

The prospect of the prairie here is to always be what it is, barren, inhospitable, with antlike humans washed out with every rain, their attempts to write themselves into the landscape indistinguishable from natural signs.

The opening suggests one of the framing dichotomies that will structure the novel's literary oscillations: the human and the nonhuman. The land, from what we might call a proto-ecological perspective, suggests a set of values distinct from the values of civilization and related to the prehistoric, animal existence of human beings rather than to their contemporary social existence. The land's constant threat is to reclaim its own from the "feeble scratchings" of humans; human desire and imagination are the counterforce. As Alexandra drives home from the little town at the very end of the first chapter, "the rattle of her wagon . . . lost in the howling of the wind," the human is nearly overwhelmed by the nonhuman, "but her lantern, held firmly between her feet, made a moving point of light along the highway, going deeper and deeper into the dark country" (14). This invocation of a civilizing mission, expressed in the language of the Enlightenment, ends the introduction, but it is far from the last word. The claims of nature will be balanced against the claims of the human throughout the text.

The first sentence also suggests that another time frame (besides the geologic-human one) will be important: "thirty years ago," the novel begins, a time interval that had already become a standard for local color writers. This sets up an immediate readerly understanding (one common to the genre) that the relation of the past to the present is up for discussion, as is the relation of tradition to the modern, since local populations were taken to be more traditional, less transformed by modernization. The historicized recent past, like the structuring distinction between the city and the country, sets up and frames various discourses for and against innovation and progress, stability and convention. The first character we meet is the five-year-old Emil, and the description of him offers us an artful take on this conventional aspect of the genre: "He was a little country boy, and this village was to him a very strange and perplexing place, where people wore fine clothes and had hard hearts" (5). He sees this tiny, wind-blown village, in other words, as villagers stereotypically see the city, and we are encouraged to notice this, to smile at the boy's lack of perspective. We also meet the young Marie, fresh from Omaha, who is clearly a "city child," dressed "in what was then called the 'Kate Greenaway' manner" (9), and with a little girl's version of city ways, including a flirtatious manner with men; because of her age, this also produces both an aura of danger around and a comic distance from the very distinctions of urbanity, style, and modernity she represents. Nonetheless, whatever the cute gloss, the gauntlet is raised on the competing claims of city, town, and country.

The third major axis of cultural debate is also introduced immediately: gender. When we meet the "tall, strong" Alexandra, she is walking "rapidly and resolutely," wearing "a man's long ulster (not as an affliction, but as if it were very comfortable and belonged to her; carried it like a soldier)" (5), while Carl, on the other hand, "was a thin, frail boy, with brooding dark eyes, . . . a delicate pallor in his thin face, and his mouth was too sensitive for a boy's" (8). The first descriptions of Carl and Alexandra, who will agree to marry at the novel's close, thus bring up a wide set of discourses about men and women, complicated by the suggestions of sex that follow. When Alexandra takes off her shawl, a sales-man sees her and exclaims, "My God, girl, what a head of hair!" (6). He does this "quite innocently and foolishly," but Alexandra gives him such a withering look that his hands are still shaking when he gets his drink in the saloon across the street. "His feeble flirtatious instincts had been crushed before, but never so mercilessly," the narrator comments. "Was he to be blamed if, when he chanced upon a fine human creature, he suddenly wished himself more of a man?" Mean-while, Marie, the lovely little girl from the city, is charming all the rough cronies of her uncle, her "lusty admirers" who smell of "spirits and tobacco" and who demand that she choose one of them as a sweetheart. She chooses her uncle, but in exchange for candy and toys she gives each of them a kiss. Her uncle hugs her until she cries, "Please don't, Uncle Joe! You hurt me." Every available res-olution is undercut: when the men seem threatening the uncle is a haven, but then the uncle is threatening. The salesman is too much of a man in his flirta-tiousness, not enough of one in his withered feebleness. Carl is not enough of a man, and a little bit too much of one. Alexandra is right to break the gender mold, but she goes too far and loses touch with her sexuality altogether.

The short first chapter also initiates a discourse on art, as Alexandra finds Carl "turning over a portfolio of chromo 'studies' which the druggist sold to the Hanover women who did China painting." Carl has also bought a magic lantern that "makes fine big pictures." It came with slides of "hunting pictures in Ger-many, and Robinson Crusoe and funny pictures about cannibals." This mixture of commercial art, folk art, and commercial folk art is our introduction to what will be a central thread of the text. "I'm going to paint some slides for it on glass, out of the Hans Andersen book" (13), Carl adds, and similar combinations of creativity and imitative commercial reproduction will continue to structure Carl as a representative of inadequate art. Carl has skill but not much imagination, and imagination is what art is all about.

Imagination is also the only thing that changes the prairie, in Cather's esti-mation. Alexandra differs from the other farmers in that she has vision; when we first meet her, we are told that "her blue eyes were fixed intently on the dis-tance" (5), and it is a distance few of the other characters can see, which is why few of the other farmers are as successful as she is. "A pioneer should have imag-ination" (37), the narrator later tells us, explaining the unfitness of Alexandra's dull-witted brothers for the life. A pioneer "should be able to enjoy the idea of things more than the things themselves" (37). The result is that Alexandra man-ages to wring her vision from the land and make a farm such that "a stranger, approaching it, could not help noticing the beauty and fruitfulness of the out-lying fields. There was something individual about the great farm" that Alexan-dra built over the next fifteen years, "a most unusual trimness and care for detail," and we are told that "it is in the soil that she expresses herself best" (62–63).

Alexandra is, in other words, not just a farmer but an artist. In her flower garden, "you feel again the order and fine arrangement manifest all over the great
farm; in the fencing and hedging, in the windbreaks and sheds, in the symmet-
rical pasture ponds" (63). Alexandra's imagination is a powerful force in her relation to the land, and the general lack of it, on others' part and sometimes on
hers, is at the root of all problems among family, friends, and neighbors. Imagination is necessary for adequate human relations and the lack of it is deadly.

Carl's relation to the world of art is as flawed as Alexandra's artistic relation
to the land is successful. He starts out as an artist who goes to learn engraving
as a trade. While he is away he sends some watercolor paintings to Alexandra
and she thinks of him as a painter. But when he returns he corrects her. "Paint?
. . . Oh! I'm not a painter, Alexandra, I'm an engraver. I have nothing to do with
painting." The watercolors he sent as remembrances, he explains, "not because
they were good" (80). He began his career as a wood engraver, which he feels
is a more artistic process than metal engraving, but "everything's cheap metal
work these days, touching up miserable photographs, forcing up bad drawings,
and spoiling good ones" (91). Engraving, done primarily for the newspaper and
magazine trades, is not just a degraded art, it destroys art. One of the enemies of
art is mass culture, in other words, and we get a sprinkling of other images expressing the paucity of representation and truth in newspapers and other mass
formats.[17] Alexandra is the real artist, Carl feels, and he makes the point explicitly: "I've been away engraving other men's pictures, and you've stayed home
and made your own," he says, gesturing to the gardens and fields (87). Alexandra is as close as we get to a representation of an artist.

The problem with Carl's art is not, however, simply its modernity, its implication in processes of mechanical reproduction. Cather turns the standard debate between rural tradition and modern innovation on its head by making
Alexandra's farmwork the site of modern, scientific innovation and Carl's modern commercial artwork a form of slavish repetition, like traditional ways a repli-
cation of what already exists. While still a young girl, Alexandra "read the papers
and followed the market" (18), and when she decides to run the farm she starts
by doing her own survey of farming methods, driving through a nearby valley
known for its innovations, interviewing farmers about their methods. She
spends a day with a farmer "who had been away at school, who was experi-
menting with a new kind of clover hay" (49), and her real success dates from
that visit. Her art is just as dependent on modern communication and tech-
nologies as Carl's engravings.

She is also equally dependent on modern capital. The mortgage has often
been used in regionalist texts as a symbol of modernity's destruction of traditional rural values, but Alexandra's decision to remortgage the family farm and
buy up neighboring farms by taking out further mortgages has made her busi-

ness possible; she is the landlord from "Under the Lion's Paw" rather than the farmer. She has to fight her dullard brothers, Oscar and Lou, to succeed. Oscar was the kind of man, we are told, "you could attach to a corn-sheller as you would a machine" (42). He was tireless and energetic. "But he was as indolent of mind as he was unsparing of body. His love of routine amounted to a vice" (42). Lou is flightier, but both are stuck in tradition and conformity. They "hated experiments," we are told, for the smallest of reasons: "Even Lou, who was more elastic than his older brother, disliked to do anything different from their neighbors. He felt that it made them conspicuous and gave people a chance to talk about them" (34). Every successful move Alexandra makes she does over the objections of these traditionalists. What she wants to create, and ends up creating, is an agribusiness, with more land than they can work alone and with employees drawn from their neighbors and the new immigrants. The end result is that Oscar and Lou become modern bourgeois with all the latest in consumer goods. As staunchly conservative and conventional as ever in their attitudes, they are by the end of the novel completely transformed into modern beings.

Alexandra's embrace of modern novelties is balanced in several ways. As she is returning home from her introduction to experimental agriculture, she hums an old Swedish hymn, and the narrator offers this burst of speculation:

> For the first time, perhaps, since the land emerged from the waters of the geologic ages, a human face was set toward it with love and yearning. It seemed beautiful to her, rich and strong and glorious. Her eyes drank in the breadth of it, until her tears blinded her. Then the Genius of the Divide, the great, free spirit which breathes across it, must have bent lower than it ever bent to a human will before. The history of every country begins in the heart of a man or a woman. (50)

Alexandra's modernity and her traditionalism, her agricultural science and her mystical passions, her knowledge and her imagination combine to make her the kind of artist she is. And just as the brothers' traditionalism leads them unwittingly into a modern relation to farming, Alexandra's modernizing does not seem to disturb her archaic, old-country, mystical streak. She just manages, while communing with "the quail and the plover and all the little wild things that crooned or buzzed in the sun," to feel "the future stirring" (54).

When Carl returns from his time in the city, Alexandra speaks of herself as if she were a typical premodern farmer. "You have lived where things move so fast," she says to him, "and everything is slow here; the people slowest of all. Our lives are like the years, all made up of weather and crops and cows" (99). When Carl complains of urban anomie and of slaving all day in anonymity to pay exorbitant rent, Alexandra responds: "We pay a high rent, too, though we may pay differently. We grow hard and heavy here. We don't move lightly and easily as you do, and our minds get stiff" (92). Like the prairie itself, oscillating between verdant paradise and barren desert, Alexandra shifts from scene to scene from the fast-moving, knowing, unstoppable modern to the thick, slow peasant.

Alexandra's relation to tradition is also represented by how she cares for Crazy Ivar, the old hermit who can talk to the animals and has lived in such ecological harmony that he spent three years living next to his pond "without defiling the face of nature any more than the coyote that had lived there before him had done" (28). He reads and quotes his Norwegian Bible and keeps track of the calendar only so he knows when it is the Sabbath. He does not believe in guns, the instruments of the most modern form of violence, and he has a mystical love of the land similar to Alexandra's. His home is, like Alexandra's, simple and simply furnished, like a monastery. Alexandra is his protector and takes him in when people want to have him committed. Just as she is the only one who embraces the experimentalist future, she is the only one (besides Ivar himself) who embraces the immigrant, animist past. Ivar gives Alexandra her first agricultural advice, on how to keep pigs from falling ill, based supposedly on his mystical closeness to the animals, but sounding remarkably like the latest directive from an agricultural station on the value of farm hygiene. In cases like this the argument seems to be that tradition and full modernity are already reconciled. But it is only for the visionaries, like Alexandra and the implied author and reader, that this is true; even Ivar, we are told, had lost his own farm due to "mismanagement" (65), due to insufficient modernity. Alexandra, quite pointedly, becomes more alone the more successful she is as a farmer, as if in payment for an excess of modernity. "Can you understand it?" (266) she asks Carl in the end, after her closest relative and her closest friend have betrayed her, and this time he understands better than she does herself. But readers are meant to understand it all in ways that not even Carl can, and thus readers, finally, are the only visionaries.

The novel is a fable about art, a parable of authorship and reading, then, not simply because Carl is an inadequate artist and Alexandra a better one. Alexandra's imagination fails her at other times as well. "Her mind was slow, truthful, steadfast," the narrator says. "She had not the least spark of cleverness" (46). Much as we are meant to like Alexandra, this is a strong criticism, especially since we have been enjoying Cather's cleverness on a regular basis. Her brother Emil has been in love with her married friend Marie for some time, and, we are told, "If Alexandra had had much imagination she might have guessed what was going on in Marie's mind, and she would have seen long before what was going on in Emil's. But that, as Emil himself had more than once reflected, was Alexandra's blind side" (151). We understand Emil and Marie, we understand that they are having an illicit love affair, but Alexandra is oblivious. "Her life had not been the

kind to sharpen her vision," the narrator goes on, in one of the many oscillations away from Alexandra's "clear deep" sight. Her training was all practical,
pragmatic, and "her personal life, her own realization of herself, was almost a
subconscious existence; like an underground river that came to the surface only
here and there, and then sank again under her own fields" (151). In a recurring
dream and daydream Alexandra is picked up and carried across the fields by a
big, strong, muscular man. Whenever she has had this dream, Alexandra takes a
cold bath, feels disgusted with herself, and refuses to think about it. She is the
text's best model of vision, but she cannot see what is in front of her eyes. She
is a paragon of imagination who has not enough of it, the spokesperson for understanding who does not understand her own desire.

Early in the story, as the young Carl is leaving, Alexandra says to him: "It's by
understanding me, and the boys, and mother, that you've helped me. I expect
that is the only way one person ever really can help another" (39). This would
be a very odd statement for a farm woman to make, since at this time people
not only could but necessarily did help one another out in more fundamental
and material ways. But it is in terms of exactly this kind of understanding that
readers meet the implied author in a silent agreement outside the discursive
movement of the text and agree with her about what really matters. The implied author of the text forges a bond with her readers, one that says Emil knows
something of Alexandra's lack of imagination, but that we literary readers know
even more.

At one point Alexandra has a quarrel with her brothers Lou and Oscar about
whether she should marry Carl. They find the idea vulgar (she's too old, Carl's
after her money) and she kicks them out of the house. She goes to her younger
brother and favorite, Emil, who is home from college, looking for a sympathetic
ear. As one reviewer pointed out in 1913, Alexandra had sent Emil to college
to "procure for him the advantages of education which shall give him a larger
horizon, more flexible interests, than her own."[18] But his horizons have not
widened, they have somehow narrowed—he is obsessed with his neighbor's
wife—and he is too self-involved to listen to Alexandra's problems. When he
does finally hear what she is saying, he finds the idea of her marrying far-fetched
and laughs at it. Hurt, feeling abandoned, Alexandra says, "I had hoped you
might understand, a little, why I do want to. But I suppose that's too much to
expect" (132). As we see Alexandra alone with her problem, we realize the limitations of Alexandra's family and culture, especially compared to the culture we
share with Cather. No one in the novel understands Alexandra at this juncture,
and yet we do. The characters' misunderstanding is interested—Lou and Oscar
worry about who will own what land and how they will appear in the community, Emil worries about his own problems—while we have a Kantian dis-

interested interestedness. Our aesthetic relation to these human problems is a form of broad understanding, our understanding both the means and the end of our aesthetic experience.

Emil and Marie head toward their adulterous affair necessarily shrouded in misunderstanding. They want others to misunderstand, to think they are just friends, and they sometimes join in the fiction themselves. Emil, frustrated at their predicament, turns on Marie, and says: "Sometimes you seem to understand perfectly and then sometimes you pretend you don't. You don't help things any by pretending. It's then that I want to pull the corners of the Divide together. If you *won't* understand, I can make you!" (117). But, as Marie explains, "If I understand, then all our good times are over, we can never do nice things any more. . . . And, anyhow, there's nothing to understand!" (117). We and the author are the only ones who really have the breadth of understanding necessary to the situation, and we bond over this mutual understanding by seeing its lack represented. Again in contrast to Alexandra's aloneness, the text offers us membership in such a literary community of understanding. We never establish the same imaginative bond with Alexandra, however much we like her, in part because the author keeps giving us cues not to, as when she points to Alexandra's lack of "imagination," her unconsciousness of her own unconscious. And we bond, finally in the realm of art, an art that is tied to both understanding and memory. Carl and Emil are almost artists, and they almost understand what they need to; Alexandra is a better artist, and she understands more, but not enough. We readers do because, unlike Alexandra, we are modern, cosmopolitan people, and we know about such things, we and Cather, the real artist.

Rather than having individuals represent poles of the cultural debates as in Garland's fiction, Cather collapses the distinctions into the characters, just as Alexandra's eyes "saw so far in some directions and were so blind in others" (131). Ivar is prototypically premodern in his shoeless love of nature, and prototypically modern in his radical individualism: it is Ivar who condemns Lou and Oscar for their conventionality, condemns America because "the way here is for all to do alike" (69). And at the same time he is the character so out of touch with modernity that the brothers want him institutionalized. Carl becomes the most modern character, with his "yellow shoes," but he also manages not to "become a trim, self-satisfied city man" (86). The brothers are self-satisfied bourgeois lumps, but they are also populist firebrands. The textual oscillations do not so much use the characters to represent poles as flip them from one side to the other of the cultural debates.

Thus, *O Pioneers!* is antimodern in its rejection of mass culture, promodern in its respect for agricultural science and psychology, antimodern in its respect for old Ivar, promodern in its rejection of social convention. We are asked to agree not so much with the antimodern or the promodern position as with a

very specific way of incorporating and in effect annihilating the differences between them, the very incorporations of difference I take to be central to the
cosmopolitan ethic of literary culture. Even the land itself is subject to such incorporative oscillation. As Ronald Weber has suggested, Midwestern writers'
complex response to the cultivated landscape is one of "passionate awareness
combined with indifference, affirmation with denial."[19] The landscape is, in
Cather's novel, the sum of the differences in apperceptions of it.

This openness to difference takes different forms and is variously motivated.
When we and Cather "understand" old Ivar, we see him not as a representative
of biblical authority, which he cites regularly, not as a representative of pre-
Christian Nordic animism and therefore immigrant culture (with which he is
also associated), and not as one of the new spiritualists or psychic researchers,
though we see hints of them as well. We, with our cosmopolitan ability to comprehend multiple perspectives, see all these possibilities, and we are absolved
from specifically endorsing any one; we are allowed, in effect, to have our faith
and deny it too. The rest of the text works to add to our perspectives, visiting
the "foreign" cultures of the French settlements, taking us down crazy Ivar's religious path, even, in the end, forcing us to understand the murderer, Marie's
jealous husband. And even Alexandra grasps that this breadth of understanding
is necessary to the fully realized life. "If the world were no wider than my corn-
fields, if there were not something beside this," she tells Carl, "I wouldn't feel
that it was much worth while to work" (92). She then tells him the story of Carrie Jensen, who "got despondent" about the monotony of farm life and tried to
kill herself "once or twice." Her parents sent her to visit relatives in Iowa, and
ever since "she's been perfectly cheerful, and she says she's contented to live and
work in a world that's so big and interesting. She said that anything as big as the
bridges over the Platte and the Missouri reconciled her. And it's what goes on
in the world that reconciles me" (93).

Cather's criticism, even in her earliest reviews from the 1890s, is sprinkled
with references to what I have been calling "literary cosmopolitanism." She
praises Frank Norris because "his horizon is wide" and he is "not limited by literary prejudices."[20] The fault of most writers, she says, is their lack of "magni-
tude; they are not large enough; they travel in small orbits, they play on muted
strings. . . . Flaubert said that a drop of water contained all the elements of the
sea, save one—immensity. Mr. Norris is concerned only with serious things, he
has only large ambitions. . . . His canvas is large enough to hold American life."[21]
Part of Henry James's perfection is that he does not "throw any light on his subject" but instead manages "to turn on so many side-lights."[22] Sarah Orne Jewett wrote so well about Maine because she "loved it by instinct, and in the light

of wide experience, from near and from afar." Cather takes the last sentence of Jewett's "Marsh Rosemary" to be an "unconscious piece of self-criticism," Jewett's own allegory of authorship. She quotes Jewett: "Who can laugh at my marsh Rosemary, or who can cry, for that matter? The gray primness of the plant is made up from a hundred colors if you look close enough to find them."[23]

And in her essay on Walt Whitman, Cather makes it clear that literature is not simply a random collection of colors, but a motivated one. Whitman was "a poet without an exclusive sense of the poetic" who was morally "neither good nor bad," and who found both the ocean and flyspecks beautiful. This is good, she feels, but not good enough. She criticizes Whitman for being too indiscriminate, for having "no conception of a difference in people," and claims that because of this, some of what he wrote was ridiculous. Literature is not the same as dictionary writing, she argues; its survey of difference is motivated by "conscience" and "responsibility," and this is where, despite his energy and spirit, Whitman is insufficiently poetic, insufficiently literary.[24]

Cather virtually disowned her first novel, *Alexander's Bridge* (1912), because she came to feel that it failed this basic literary test. In a preface written ten years and several Nebraska novels later (*Alexander's Bridge* is set in Boston and London), she remembers the advice that Jewett gave her: "One day you will write about your own country. In the meantime, get all you can. One must know the world *so well* before one can know the parish."[25] And in an essay written another ten years later, she belittles her efforts in *Alexander's Bridge* (and in *The Song of the Lark* [1915]) for their conventionality. *The Song of the Lark,* she felt, had "too much detail," so much so that it destroyed its formal balance, "what painters call 'composition.'"[26] The first novel is not literary enough because, although it knows the world, it does not know the parish. "I thought a book could be made out of 'interesting material,' and at that time I found the new more exciting than the familiar" (963). The overly detailed latter novel, like Whitman's encyclopedia, does not manage to keep its elements in equilibrium and loses sight of the motivation for arraying cultural options in the first place.

In *My Ántonia* (1918), Cather again represented a near-artist as her protagonist, and again oscillated between the available perspectives on country and city, men and women, progress and tradition. "She was one of the truest artists I ever knew," Cather told an interviewer about the model for Ántonia, "in her keenness and sensitiveness of her enjoyment, in her love of people and in her willingness to take pains."[27] She uses a double frame with two narrators: Jim Burden, who, as an interpolated author, is also a near artist; and the opening narrator, who has a wicked wit and functions, at least at first, almost like an implied author. Jim is not quite an artist, and in fact his text is not quite what we read; it is "substantially" Jim's text, but it has apparently been revised by the first narrator. We are also told that Jim's wife, among her other habits that disgust the

narrator, finds it "worth her while to play the patroness to a group of young poets and painters of advanced ideas and mediocre ability" and has had one of her
own plays produced.[28] Our narrator is herself a writer, and Jim becomes one in
his decision to write about Ántonia: after he makes the decision to do so, "his
eyes had the sudden clearness that comes from something the mind itself sees"
(713). Burden is a classic unreliable narrator, and the frame tale contrasts the
clearly superior perspective of the first narrator to Burden's blind spots and eva-
sions. The text uses many of the same dichotomies—foreigner/native, local/na-
tional, traditional/modern, nature/culture, young/old—and the same basic
technique of oscillation. It also is sprinkled with classical and literary allusions.
The critical debates—whether the text is in fact retrospective, suggesting that
the past is both "precious" and "incommunicable" as the famous last line has it,
or vehemently modern and forward-looking, for instance—are kept alive by
critics who make the mistake of seeing only half the argument the text makes.[29]

My Mortal Enemy (1926) is Cather's most rigorous example of the novel
démeublé, the unfurnished novel, which Cather argued in the 1920s was the
highest literary art.[30] In it a young girl from Nebraska learns about the city and,
over the course of the novel, comes to reassess several times the glamorous city
relatives she had idolized. Whether we agree with Sharon O'Brien that "the observer's acknowledged and unacknowledged investment in the subject is the
story itself," or with James Woodress when he finds in it both "the most bitter"
and the closest thing to "perfect" art Cather produced, or with any of the other
double readings, we do so in part because it follows the same patterns of oscillation leading us to transcend both the accomplished cosmopolitanism of the
city relatives and the developing cosmopolitanism of the protagonist, and leaves
us very well furnished with a sense of our own breadth of vision.[31] Cather's
other novels use the same techniques to the same effect: *One of Ours* (1922), *The
Professor's House* (1925), *Death Comes to the Archbishop* (1927), *Lucy Gayheart*
(1935), and many of the stories are structured by the same literary understanding.

Of course, this is a view not shared by many of Cather's current critics. Anne
E. Goldman, for instance, takes Cather to task for her anti-Semitism, her Ori-
entalism, her imperialism, her racism, and even her "brutal voyeurism."[32] Elizabeth Ammons worries about her "reactionary and racist" views and her "love
of empire."[33] And since the 1920s critics have found fault with Cather's views,
as Joan Acocella argues in her review of Cather scholarship: she has been attacked for her gentility, for her conventionality, for her lack of political passion,
for her lack of scope, and in recent decades, for her lack of gay pride, her phal-
locentrism, and for the various forms of imperialism just mentioned.[34] Acocella,
whose *New Yorker* article on Cather was one of the most significant pieces on
the function of criticism written in the 1990s, finds that the history of Cather

criticism, starting in the 1930s, became "less and less about literature, and more about 'whose side are you on,'" and she argues that this is an impoverishment of literary discussion.[35] These critics, it should be noted, all take as their moral ground the cosmopolitan ethos I am describing here, and fault Cather for not achieving it in her fiction. I do not deny that Cather is less cosmopolitan in some ways than these later critics. I am, like Acocella, simply finding Cather's own literary-cosmopolitan glass more than half full. Jewett wrote to Cather early in her career with literary-cosmopolitan advice, after having read the Nebraska stories in *The Troll Garden* (1905). Cather, Jewett felt, was not keeping enough distance from her Nebraskans. "You don't see them yet quite enough from the outside,—you stand right in the middle of each of them when you write, without having the standpoint of the looker-on who takes them each in their relations to letters, to the world."[36] At least by the time she wrote *O Pioneers!* however, Cather had learned exactly how to follow Jewett's advice, to write the local from the inside and to remain a looker-on, always conscious of the relation "to letters, to the world," and always conscious of the two in fruitful apposition.

The Critical Distance of Wharton, Johnson, Masters, and Frederick

Ethan Frome (1912) is a framed story of a particular kind, since the narrator, a man working for an engineering firm and temporarily staying in rural Starkfield, Massachusetts, announces that he is going to tell us a story that was told to him, but told in bits and pieces that did not add up. The very first line of the story sets us up for a narrative that is told from multiple perspectives but nominally controlled by one: "I had the story, bit by bit, from various people, and, as generally happens in such cases, each time it was a different story."[37] Unlike the classic local color frame tale, in which an urban perspective bounces off that of rural characters, this urban narrator admits he is making up large chunks of the narrative. "Although Harmon Gow developed the tale as far as his mental and moral reach permitted there were perceptible gaps between his facts, and I had the sense that the deeper meaning of the story was in the gaps" (6); and so he fills those gaps in as best he can. He imagines a story that he stitches together from morsels of conversation among people to whom he is a stranger, and we are warned, slyly but regularly, that the bits themselves are not to be trusted.

The last line, spoken by Mrs. Ned Hale, one of the narrator's main informants, is just such a bit: "I don't see's there's much difference between the Fromes up at the farm and the Fromes down at the graveyard; 'cept that down there they're all quiet, and the women have got to hold their tongues" (157). In a novel full of grotesquely pregnant silences, a novel in which blame is, in classic literary fashion, quite evenly distributed, this line undermines itself and the rest of Mrs. Hale's testimony. Ethan is again and again described as silent, inarticulate, and we meet him in relation to his "silent ache." Ethan's mother was famously silent before she died, and she hears voices in her head, a kind of communication that takes place in silence. Ethan's wife, Zenobia, has a harsh, accusing tongue as she complains about her illnesses, but the rest of her conversation takes place through gesture and insinuation. The conversations between Ethan and Mattie are largely inarticulate. In the end, Zenobia has returned to silence and Mattie has learned to complain, but even so, holding tongues has led to more problems than it has solved. Ethan has kept his desires—for a different life, for love—quiet, and this has, in effect, crippled him.

In an "Author's Introduction" Wharton added for a 1922 edition, she explains her technique in terms of the narrator's cosmopolitanism: "Each of my chron-iclers contributes to the narrative *just so much as he or she is capable of understanding* of what, to them, is a complicated and mysterious case; and only the narrator of the tale has scope enough to see it all, to resolve it back into simplicity, and to put it in its rightful place among his larger categories" (xvi). The narrator has a similar attitude toward his informants: he introduces Mrs. Hale to us in the same terms of social distinction that Wharton uses to describe him. "It was not that Mrs. Ned Hale felt, or affected, any social superiority to the people about her," the narrator assures us. "It was only that the accident of a finer sensibility and a little more education had put just enough distance between herself and her neighbors to enable her to judge them with detachment" (9). Mrs. Hale's mind was "a store-house" of anecdotes, volumes of which were brought forth by any question, but on the subject of Ethan she is "unexpectedly reticent" (9). Like Harmon Gow, who at one time is described as barely articulate and at oth-ers as the narrator's "village oracle" (10), Mrs. Hale never tells the narrator what he would like to know, and yet tells him most of what he does know. The "gaps" in the story, then, filled in by the narrator's imagination, must be reopened by readers. Wharton's introduction cautions us not to trust her narrator: the narra-tor is the "sympathizing intermediary between his rudimentary characters and the more complicated minds to whom he is trying to present them" (xv), but he is also a construction of her own designed to accomplish her artistic goals. He "is capable of seeing all around" the other characters, but we are urged to see "all around" the narrator as well. "This is all self-evident," she adds, congrat-ulating us for our cosmopolitan superiority, "and needs explaining only to those who have never thought of fiction as an art of composition" (xv). Wharton offers her readers membership in this very exclusive club of "complicated minds," more complicated, in fact, than the "few friends" to whom she "tentatively out-lined" her scheme and who met it with "immediate and unqualified disap-proval" (xv). We are meant to be smarter than those friends and recognize the artistry, the technique: this is not your grandmother's local color tale, she sug-gests, but something more "complicated."

Her art has a serious purpose, and that purpose is the same as that of the ear-lier local color writers; she just wants to do them one better. Even before Wharton moved to New England and it became familiar to her, she writes, before her "initiation" was complete, she recognized the life around her as inadequately represented in fiction:

> I had the uneasy sense that the New England of fiction bore little—except a vague botanical and dialectical—resemblance to the harsh and beautiful land as I had seen it. Even the abundant enumeration of sweet-fern, asters and mountain laurel, and the conscientious reproduction of the vernacular, left me with the feeling that the outcropping granite had in both cases been overlooked. (viii)

Wharton, like the other writers of regionalist texts in the 1910s and 1920s, defined herself against what they declared was the soft-pedaling local color of previous generations, claiming for herself a starker view. Wharton sets in play the relation between cultural centers and cultural peripheries, and the issues of class, tradition, and alienation that had long been central to the genre of the local color tale. Starkfield, Massachusetts, is a town from which "most of the smart ones get away," as Harmon Gow puts it, and as such is a classic backwater. Its dreariness is so pervasive that even the narrator succumbs to it: "I chafed at first, and then, under the hypnotising effect of the routine, gradually began to find a grim satisfaction in the life" (7). He recognizes that Starkfield was not quite as backward as it had been in the recent past, but he names the advances with a patronizing smirk: "I had come in the degenerate day of the trolley, bicycle and rural delivery, when communication was easy between scattered mountain villages, and the bigger towns in the valleys, such as Bettsbridge and Shadd's Falls, had libraries, theatres, and Y.M.C.A. halls" (7). The supposed advances make the picture starker, a fitting backdrop for the extremely stark story of the Fromes.

Wharton suggests that she has written with more realism than her predecessors, then, but she nonetheless, much more clearly than the previous generation of localists, foregrounds the issue of art and form. Judith Fryer has called Edith Wharton's New York novels "urban pastorals" because they prize the imagination and art over the other values—the values on either side of Lily Bart's dilemmas, for instance—available in the texts.[38] And we are reminded of questions of art frequently in *Ethan Frome* as well. Zenobia's name may suggest the powerful third-century queen of Palmyra and thereby issues of political power and gender, and it may aurally suggest xenophobia and thereby conflicts between populations, but the name also alludes to Zenobia in Hawthorne's *Blithedale Romance,* just as Ethan Frome is a reference to Hawthorne's Ethan Brand, the character whose Unpardonable Sin is his willed isolation from the brotherhood of humanity. This set of literary and cultural allusions serves to confirm both our difference from and our brotherhood with men like Ethan Frome and the narrator, and women like Zenobia and Mrs. Ned Hale. But more important, the explicit constructedness of the tale, the unnamed narrator functioning as a kind of quasi-artistic, untrustworthy author, himself a product of the implied author's imagination, keeps the question of art at the forefront. Because this narrator is some kind of professional involved in the construction of a power station, he stands as a modern vis-à-vis the locals, but his failure as a storyteller also suggests the superiority of the literary over the scientific purview.

Wharton's *Summer* (1917), without using a frame tale and without the help of an author's introduction, works in a similar way. At first glance Judge Royall represents upright town society while the folk on the Mountain are degenerate primitives. As R. W. B. Lewis noted some years ago, the Mountain "looms portentously over the little village: the home of illiterate outlaws, a scene of chilly squalor, violence of speech and gesture, and probably incestuous passions."[39] Charity Royall is "brought down" from the Mountain to live with the lawyer Royall, the "biggest man in North Dormer," and this is to be her salvation.[40] But Charity is bored by the small town and helplessly attracted to a young architect from the city, another classic local color urban interloper. The backwoods is contrasted to the town, and then the town to the city, doubling the usual dynamic, and then these three are equated to one another through their sexual crimes: incest on the Mountain, impregnation and abandonment on the part of the city professional, and quasi-incest on the part of the lawyer. *Summer*, however, has never been thought to have the literary merit of *Ethan Frome*, and for good reason. The villains are a bit too villainous, the spreading of blame too caustic, the appeals to the reader's superiority somewhat too blatant. The text nevertheless does manage to make strong claims for the literary, since the lawyer and the architect, having competing claims to cosmopolitan knowledge, both are shown to fall short of the literary in terms of their ability to deal with ethical complexity and to see the validity of all sides in human conflict.

As the overly brief description of these texts shows, the genteel teacups Sinclair Lewis would mock in his Nobel Prize acceptance speech a decade and a half later had already stopped tinkling. *Ethan Frome*, as I suggested, can be fruitfully considered the earliest text in what Carl Van Doren would call, by 1921, the "revolt from the village." Histories of regional fiction have tended to ignore Wharton's contribution to the genre while Wharton scholars have generally looked at these two texts as aberrations or genre exercises within her oeuvre. Alfred Kazin in his survey of literature and landscape, for instance, mentions Wharton only as a depicter of New York City.[41] Eric J. Sundquist mentions Wharton in "Realism and Regionalism," his essay in the *Columbia Literary History*, only as a practitioner of the "novel of business."[42] She is not mentioned in Thadious M. Davis's chapter on regional literature in the early twentieth century in *The Columbia History of the American Novel*.[43] Ronald Weber mentions her criticism of Sinclair Lewis but not her work in the genre.[44] Ammons, who

writes about her extensively elsewhere, does not mention her in the introduction to *American Local Color Writing, 1880–1920*. Anthony Channell Hilfer
begins his survey with Edgar Lee Masters in *The Revolt from the Village, 1915–
1930*.[45] Van Doren, in his 1921 article, places the revolt in 1919 and 1920, with
Spoon River Anthology as a forerunner, but Wharton's revolt, like Cather's, came
earlier.

Van Doren, as I have suggested, was wrong to see these authors as revolting
against a tradition of idyllic pastoral. They were simply revolting, as American
authors would continue to do, against the exclusions, the "gaps" in the story-
telling that had preceded them. They were determined to be more cosmopolitan than their predecessors, which is to say they were determined, like their
predecessors, to be literary artists. Wharton's foregrounding of her art in *Ethan
Frome*, like Cather's thematizing of art and imagination in *O Pioneers!* reminds
readers that they are in the realm not of reportage but of art, that they are being offered a view that only art can offer. Wharton is not, in fact, revolting against
the village; as she says in her introduction, she is simply revolting against subliterary representations of village life, just as the literary regionalist authors before
her had, and just as the writers who followed Wharton would revolt against what
they would come to see as her gentility, her timidity, her inability to represent
the full story. Literary cosmopolitanism is constantly in revolt against its own
past.

Other writers in the 1910s pushed representation into new populations and
arenas. Originally published in 1912, *Autobiography of an Ex-Colored Man* is as far
from Chesnutt's Uncle Julius stories as *Summer* is from *Deephaven* in its breadth
of subject matter and the explicitness with which contemporary issues are addressed. The publisher's preface to the first edition invokes the literary-cosmopolitan overview: "In this book the reader is given a glimpse behind the
scenes, . . . he is taken upon an elevation where he can catch a bird's-eye view
of the conflict being waged."[46] The novel, written as a first-person autobiography, follows the protagonist back and forth across the color line four times as he
decides to pass or not for various reasons. This constructs a large alternating
structure of values, compounded by movements in and out of Southern and
then European perspectives, high and low society, more and less racist white
groups, and bourgeois and bohemian society. The novel ends with the ex-colored man expressing a sense of remorse that he has given up the fullness of his
being in exchange for being white in the eyes of the world. When Carl Van
Vechten convinced Knopf to reissue the novel in 1927, he wrote an introduction to this second edition, claiming that in 1912 the book was alone in offering "an inclusive survey" of race (xxxiii). Although Ross Posnock feels that the

narrator represents a failure of cosmopolitanism, he notes that Johnson's "own life of interracial race work and mastery of multiple art forms, high and popular, resolved and redeemed contradictions that his novel would not."[47] Henry Louis Gates Jr., introducing the 1989 edition, praised Johnson for allowing "his political convictions to *inform* his theory and practice of art without succumbing to the temptation of becoming 'propagandistic' or overly didactic" (x) and for being "intent upon establishing a commonality of the human condition, shared at a most fundamental level by every human being" (xxiii); this last, Gates claims, is what makes the book "a classic of American literature" (xxiii).

The narrator discusses breadth of vision explicitly throughout the novel, and claims in fact, contra DuBois and his notion of double consciousness, that the "dual personality" (21) of African Americans is simply an effect of their self-censorship in the presence of whites. Rather than having a double consciousness, African Americans suffer from a diminished, limited consciousness. The "dwarfing, warping, distorting influence which operates upon each and every coloured man in the United States" is that "he is forced to take his outlook on all things, not from the view-point of a citizen, or a man, or even a human being, but from the viewpoint of a *coloured* man" (21). The opposite of cosmopolitan, literary vision, this diminished view means that everything is seen "through the narrow neck of this one funnel" (21). The white man in the South has a similar problem, the narrator later suggests, and for the same reason: because of the "Negro question," the white man's "mental efforts run through one narrow channel" (76). The narrator, because he has lived on both sides of the color line (and both sides of the class line), can see the world from the full variety of perspectives, and offers readers a model for cosmopolitan consciousness. Nevertheless, he often regrets the incompleteness of his own survey: "I regret that I cannot contrast my views of life among coloured people in New York," he says at one point. "But the truth is, during my entire stay in the city I did not become acquainted with a single respectable family" (114).

Throughout the novel the narrator digresses into sociological speculations. While discussing his work as a tobacco stripper in Jacksonville, he tells us that "the coloured people may be said to be divided into three classes, not so much in respect to themselves as in respect to their relations with the whites" (76). One class comprises tradesmen, independent workers, the educated, and well-to-do people, a second the servant class, and a third the "desperate class" (76–79). He describes in great detail the different kinds of people who frequent a club—again, not as individuals but as groups defined by psychosociological attributes. He discourses on the different emotional cultures of the French and the Germans, on the nature of African descendants raised in England, France, and America, and on other arrays of populations. He manages, in interpolations within his regionalist narrative, to give us his explicit opinions on the very stuff of regionalist narrative.

Over the course of the novel, since it starts when the narrator is still a boy and follows his adventures through adolescence and young adulthood, readers are encouraged, in classic *Bildungsroman* style, to assume that growth and maturity will expand the narrator's purview. The novel represents itself as a retrospective telling, but the narrator adheres closely to the consciousness he supposedly had at each point in his life. Besides this conventional blindness to his later knowledge, however, the narrator may seem to have few of the markers of unreliability that Wharton employs in *Ethan Frome,* and by the end of the novel, as he reflects on his life and where he has ended up, he seems possessed of an intelligent, reasonable, cosmopolitan consciousness. Still, by invoking his own nostalgia for the road not taken, the narrator suggests an even larger perspective, one in which his own bourgeois concerns for his children's future, which he claims, in the end not entirely convincingly, have directed his final choice to pass, are made to seem provincial and shortsighted. He has decided to be a white man, and this decision leaves him disconnected from large parts of his own past experience. When, as a young adult, he decides to embrace his African American cultural heritage and become a "Negro composer" (144), his white patron tries to dissuade him. "This idea you have of making a Negro out of yourself," the patron says, "is nothing more than a sentiment" (145), and the narrator has to agree with the analysis—he has not thought out all the ramifications of such a decision. But in the end, the decision to "make a white man out of himself" is more than a sentiment; it determines the entire shape of his life. The perspective of the individual ex-colored man is important, broad, and valuable, but we are asked to consider a wider perspective, one that allows us to understand, in a way that encompasses the understandings of the narrator and more, the social forces of his world.

There is a more subtle strand running through the text as well, with dozens of hints about the narrator's sexuality, encouraging readers to read beyond the narrator's revelations.[48] The hints begin early; as a boy, he tells us, he sometimes burst into tears at the beauty of his own playing, and threw himself into his mother's arms. "As big a boy as I was, . . . she, by her caresses and often her tears, only encouraged these fits of sentimental hysteria" (27). This is an obvious auto-feminization. His relations with men often resemble cruising. He is picked up by a Pullman porter who brings him to his boardinghouse; in the morning, "bored and embarrassed" by him, he tries to go off on his own; after losing all his money, however, he accepts the porter's offer to sleep in his closet (53–58, 64–65). On the ship on his way home from Europe he is particularly struck by "a tall, broad-shouldered, almost gigantic, coloured man":

In fact, if he was not handsome, he at least compelled admiration for his fine physical proportions. He attracted general attention as he strode the deck in a sort of
majestic loneliness. I became curious to know who he was and determined to
strike up an acquaintance with him at the first opportune moment. (149)

He approaches the man one day and offers him a cigar.

There are other examples as well, but the most central is his relationship with
the patron, who begins by hiring him to play piano at parties and ends up taking him along on his European travels. He meets the patron at the club where
the narrator sometimes plays a few songs on the piano, and his description hints
at his homosexuality:

> Among the white "slummers" there came into the club one night a clean-cut, slen-
> der, but athletic-looking man, who would have been taken for a youth had it not
> been for the tinge of grey about his temples. He was clean-shaven and had regu-
> lar features, and all of his movements bore the indefinable but unmistakable stamp
> of culture. He spoke to no one, but sat languidly puffing cigarettes and sipping a
> glass of beer.

The patron sends the narrator a five-dollar tip through a waiter every time he
plays, and eventually sends for him and hires him to play an "engagement," a
dinner party attended by "blasé" women and "girlish-looking" youths (118). The
narrator plays not just for parties but for the patron's private pleasure, and an air
of expectancy hangs over the scene. The patron sometimes seems to the narrator
"to be some grim, mute, but relentless tyrant, possessing over me a supernatural power," but eventually there "grew between us a familiar and warm relationship, and I am sure he had a decided personal liking for me. On my part, I looked
upon him at that time as about all a man could wish to be" (121). The narrator
regularly makes excuses for not telling the entire story of his relationship: "My
affection for him was so strong, my recollections of him are so distinct, he was
such a peculiar and striking character, that I could easily fill several chapters with
reminiscences of him; but for fear of tiring the reader I shall go on with my narration" (148). By this he means, of course, that he will go on narrating something other than his relation to his bachelor benefactor.

The last chapter, in which the ex-colored man, now a successful "white" businessman, is about to ask a white woman to marry him, thus has a double tension, "for I had more than the usual doubts and fears of a young man in love to
contend with" (199). He had until that time been playing the role of a white
man "with a certain degree of nonchalance," but he worries that he cannot perform the role of a married white man: "My acting had called for mere external effects. Now I began to doubt my ability to play the part. I watched her to

see if she was scrutinizing me, to see if she was looking for anything in me which made me differ from the other men she knew" (199–200). Again, the explicit issue is race, but the secondary one of sexuality looms as well. He tells of having a crush on his female music teacher as a young boy, but the closest he comes to a woman in the rest of the narrative is when he has drinks with a rich widow whose thrown-over sweetman shoots her moments later. Even that, like his patron "renting" him to others, has a flavor of prospective prostitution more than anything else.

The talk about sexuality never gets any more explicit, however, and the muted innuendo of these scenes and passages are simply that: they work not so much to develop a major theme or subplot as to push us to think of the intelligence behind the narration, and therefore about Johnson's motives as well. I understand that in making this claim I am reading this text differently from Eve Kosofsky Sedgwick's model; it may be that this "love that dare not be too explicit" gains force by being underground, as she suggests, but my argument here is that it also announces the text's sense of its multiple audiences, and thereby the text's own cosmopolitanism.[49] And as it does so, readers share a perspective the narrator is represented as not fully willing or able to share with us. The possibilities for reading this textual thread open the world of the text further than even our very cosmopolitan narrator can, despite his position as a "privileged spectator" of black and white, Northern and Southern, American and European, high and low cultures.

Spoon River Anthology was first published serially in Reedy's Mirror, edited by William Marion Reedy, a magazine that at the time had a larger circulation than Dial, Atlantic Monthly, and the Nation combined and a reputation for literary excellence.[50] In "The Writer of Spoon River," Reedy claims that "Masters moves from particulars to universals," and that this is what makes his work great art.[51] "He saw and knew his Spoon River so well that when he came to write it out of himself, with his personality added to what he saw and knew, he wrote the life of man everywhere, or at least everywhere in America" (3). Masters clearly attempted to represent all sides of what John E. Hallwas calls the "Illinois cultural divide" between North and South, East and West, as well as both sides of the other important literary and cultural debates of his day.[52]

The bulk of Spoon River is made up of 240 epitaphs, almost all first-person reveries, supposedly spoken from the same graveyard, since the graveyard, Masters explained to a newspaper reporter, is the "only democracy."[53] These reveries argue for the necessity of atheism in the modern world and for the consolations of religion. They represent the value of the Jeffersonian past and of social progress. They dissect the psychology of blinkered provincialism and the alienation of open-eyed modernity. Masters's other work never manages to keep these forces in balance and has never been considered particularly successful, and critics have long been divided as to how well he accomplishes this in the *Anthology*. His early admirers were sure he had succeeded: Amy Lowell called it "Dostoevsky in *vers libre*," and William Stanley Braithwaite also compared the volume to a Russian novel, claiming that Masters "was superior to the novelist . . . in his strict impartiality; he never bestows his sympathy as a novelist does; standing wholly aloof he merely exhibits the actors, and leaves us to our own opinions."[54]

Many of the epitaphs, as epitaphs sometimes do, directly address the reader: "Oh, you young radicals and dreamers . . . who pass by my headstone" (324); "Do you remember, passer-by" (319), "Listen to me, ye who live in the senses" (314); and (with an almost comic baldness) "You are alive, I am dead" (204). These addresses create an implied reader of the fictional tombstone, the addressee imagined by the speaker of each epitaph, as well as providing a space for readers to imagine the author of the *Anthology*. Several of these direct addresses obviously cover all readers, alive in the world of the senses, while others suggest a more specifically literary community: "Very well, you liberals, / And navigators into realms intellectual, / You sailors through heights imaginative," (191) begins the epitaph for Thomas Rhodes, for instance. Or this, from Jeremy Carlisle: "Passer-by, sin beyond any sin / Is the sin of blindness of souls to other souls" (325). This last, a call to universal understanding, tempered a few lines later by the speaker's admitted "acrid skepticism" (325), is also a call to literary community, to what one epitaph calls "the vision, vision, vision of the poets / Democratized!" (320).

Even those epitaph-poems that do not directly address the reader participate in the construction of a cosmopolitan literary community, quite distinct from the community represented in Spoon River. Masters himself explained this years later, in reference to "Anne Rutledge":

> Finally, "Anne Rutledge" does not say that the Republic will bloom forever; it simply expresses an imploration on the part of this obscure voice speaking from beneath the weeds of that lonely graveyard, that the Republic will bloom forever from the dust of her bosom—something that Anne Rutledge never thought of, and never could have thought of in her simple heart; but which I, as the creator of the Anthology, did think of, and with the fervent hope that the Republic will bloom forever, nourished by every life that can give it sustenance out of poetry or prose, fact or fiction.[55]

The creator of the *Anthology*, in other words, not the "obscure voices" themselves, offers the poem to readers, the implied author that constructs, along with the reader, the cosmopolitan compact.[56]

Following the 240 free verse epitaphs is the "Spooniad," a satirical rhymed mock epic on the model of Pope's "Dunciad," and an epilogue in the form of a verse play. Many critics have complained about these, feeling that they destroy the unity of the piece and break its mood.[57] They have the effect, however, of broadening the purview of the *Anthology* by opening the materials in the epitaphs to satire and to the kind of mythic treatment the epilogue offers. The "characters" in the epilogue are not Spoon Riverites but Beelzebub, Loki, Yogarinda, God, and, finally, the Milky Way, an almost ludicrously cosmopolitan cast. In a letter to Mencken, Masters claimed that the "Spooniad" is "the epic binding together of the more than two hundred dramatic expressions of the microcosm," bound together precisely by their own "conflicts."[58] The imaginative transcendence of conflict is what makes life whole. "And so you appeared to me, neglected ones," says Jeremy Carlisle, "and enemies too, as I went along / With my face growing clearer to you as yours / Grew clearer to me. / We were ready then to walk together / And sing the chorus and chant the dawn / Of life that is wholly life" (325).

In moving from rural Illinois to Chicago, Masters learned, he said later, "that the city banker was no other than the country banker, the city lawyer the same as the country lawyer, the city preacher the same as the country preacher, and the theology, finance, jurisprudence, society and the antithesis of good and evil the same in the city and the country town."[59] The village virus, Masters might just as well have said, is the same as the urban virus. The "revolt from the village," in this sense, might more accurately be considered the incorporation of the village, the renunciation of its special status. In "Isaiah Beethoven" and "Elijah Browning," the penultimate and antepenultimate poems in *Spoon River Anthology*, the two characters are each named after a biblical prophet and a famous artist, suggesting this same sense of the village as all the world and history, the world as the village. Elijah, "amid multitudes who were wrangling," ends by touching a star, delivered to "Infinite Truth." Isaiah looks at Spoon River and thinks, "O world, that's you!": the cosmopolis the small town, the small town the cosmopolis.

The first two regional "little magazines" were started the same year *Spoon River Anthology* was published as a book—the *Midland* (1915–1933) and *Texas Review* (1915–1924; from 1924 on *Southwest Review*). They would be followed in the 1920s by others, including the *Frontier* (1920–1939), *Fugitive* (1922–1925), *Prairie Schooner* (1927–), *New Mexico Quarterly Review* (1931–1969), and *Southern Review* (1935–). The *Midland*, the most important of these regional little magazines, was founded by the then twenty-one-year-old University of Iowa undergraduate John T. Frederick, and on the first page of the new journal he articulated his editorial position and the justification for his magazine.[60] His rationale reads like an apologetic, tentative recapitulation of Garland's call to arms:

> Possibly the region between the mountains would gain in variety at least if it re-
> tained more of its makers of literature, music, pictures, and other expressions of civ-
> ilization. And possibly civilization might be with us a somewhat swifter process if
> expression of its spirit were more frequent. Scotland is none the worse for Burns
> and Scott, none the worse that they did not move to London and interpret Lon-
> don themes for London publishers.[61]

All qualified: possibly a gain, possibly somewhat swifter progress, or at least none
the worse. In later issues he would become slightly firmer, claiming that Midwestern writers, forced to deal with Eastern editors and publishers, tended to
misrepresent their region: "A result has seemed to be a tendency to false emphasis, distortion, in literary interpretations" (6 [1920]: 3). Even here, however,
instead of Garland's fiery rhetoric, Frederick still hedges—the result "has seemed
to be" rather than is, and has seemed so not in entirety, but as "a tendency," and
not a tendency to falsification entirely, but simply a tendency to "false emphasis."

Garland argued that the West was the place of a revitalized life and real literature, but Frederick was always more circumspect, suggesting that some day, soon
perhaps but not yet, the Midwest would produce its great literature:

> The traveler in the middle west today is likely to think that we have forgotten how
> to dream. He is likely to see from his train window, in the hundreds of farms so
> much alike and the scores of little towns with their huddled laundries, garages,
> bake-shops, and pool-rooms, no evidence of that vision without which people per-
> ish. Even some who have lived among us have made books which deny we have
> souls. But those who love the middle west know that its people have their dreams,
> sometimes distorted to be sure by ignorance and untoward circumstance, but of-
> ten as intelligent and noble as could be desired. Perhaps nowhere else in this crazed
> and saddened world is the spirit so eager, so wistful, so unafraid. In the end we shall
> have beauty. We shall have splendor. Give us time. (8 [1922]: 40)

According to Frederick, Eastern editors distort, but then so do the untoward
circumstances of Midwestern life, even if sometimes things are as good as "could
be desired." In the end, he asks not for equality but for patience. Even his most
brazen statements are oddly careful: "The challenge of the diverse literary materials in America is not likely to be heard by those closest to the tinkling teacups
of literary New York. It will be answered, if at all, by others" (16 [1930]: 375).
The tinkling teacups were already a stock image of gentility (Frederick is practically quoting Lewis's Nobel Prize speech here), and since no one identified
with the teacups, the charge could offend no one. The suggestion in the last sentence ("if at all") is one of doubt rather than insurgency. The obvious question
is this: why was Frederick so tentative, so seemingly unsure?

The *Midland*'s place in literary history would suggest he had no reason to be. The magazine burst on the literary scene due primarily to the laudations of two Eastern tastemakers: H. L. Mencken and Edward J. O'Brien. O'Brien, the editor of the "Best Short Stories" series from 1914 to 1940, classified every one of the ten stories the *Midland* published in its first year as "distinctive," and singled out the journal as the "one new periodical" that "claims unique attention this year. . . . It has been my pleasure and wonder to find in these ten stories the most vital interpretation in fiction of our national life that many years have been able to show. Since the most brilliant days of the New England men of letters, no such white hope has proclaimed itself with such assurance and modesty."[62] H. L. Mencken wrote to Frederick in 1920 that he thought the journal "full of excellent stuff," and invited Frederick to use the quotation in promotional materials; in 1923 he wrote in the *Smart Set* that the *Midland* "is probably the most influential literary periodical ever set up in America."[63] By the mid-1920s, O'Brien was ranking the journal as one of the three best in the country, giving it his "100 percent" rating alongside only the *Dial* and *Arena*. Frederick J. Hoffman, Charles Allen, and Carolyn Ulrich, in their history of the little magazine movement in 1946, argued that Pound, Williams, and other little magazine editors in this period were driven by "discontent," and that Frederick's discontent, like Garland's, was with Eastern literary dominance. They give the journal pride of place in the regionalist movement: "Literary regionalism was given its first conscious statement in *The Midland* and the little magazines that followed it."[64] And John Tebbel claimed in the *American Magazine* in 1969 that the *Midland* did in fact help the Midwest "break away from eastern dominance."[65] Already in 1930, O'Brien was arguing that it used to be Boston, but "the geographical center today is Iowa City."[66]

Taken as a whole, Frederick's writings show that he believed strongly in various aspects of regionalist thought, especially the agrarian strains that become more prominent in his writing after his back-to-the-land experiments in the early 1920s. "Earth has healing for bodies and souls of those who love her," he wrote in the magazine during his return to the farm, and he eventually wrote two farm novels. But his undergraduate years were also suffused with ideas gleaned from the ongoing (and national) debate that pitted the Germanic philological tradition of scholarship against an anti-academicism shared by the general culture, the literary avant-garde, and a sprinkling of professors around the country. Lewis's Nobel Prize speech, in which he claimed that "our American professors like their literature clear and cold and pure and very dead," was the temporary culmination of a volley of such statements in the 1910s and 1920s. The professors who agreed with such sentiments managed by the 1920s to start small literary magazines at many universities (all eight of the journals listed above were university-based) and to include the study of more contemporary literatures (such as American literature) in their curricula. The leader of this contingent on the Iowa campus in the 1910s was Frederick's mentor, C. F. Ansley, who in 1911 founded the Athelney Club, where like-minded students and teachers met to discuss literature and literary values, and where the idea for a journal like the *Midland* incubated.[67] Ansley was a vocal proponent of the "Higher Provincialism" of Josiah Royce, who had first presented his ideas on the value of local affiliation and culture in a 1902 Phi Beta Kappa speech at Iowa, which Ansley is assumed to have attended.[68]

According to Royce, the country was in danger of losing its cultural base, which was always local, and varied because it was local, to the standardizing and leveling effects of industrial culture. It was the job of writers and intellectuals to know and nurture their own local cultures and save society from the despotism of machines: regional affiliation gives people "the power to counteract the leveling tendencies of modern civilization" (79). For Ansley, this meant teaching students Iowan as well as Anglo-Saxon culture, and trying to convince university administrators that the English faculty's own creative efforts in fiction, poetry, and the essay were as significant as any scholarship they might produce on classic literary texts. Ansley left the university in 1917 (to move onto a farm on the northern Michigan "frontier") during a battle over whether the English department could consider, in hiring and promotion, contemporary literary production as equal to historical monographs. Thirteen years later, Frederick would resign his own professorship (for the last time) over the same issue.

Frederick was more devoted to literature than to scholarship, and, it is fair to say, more devoted to literature than he was to the Midwest. As Ruth Suckow, the *Midland*'s most illustrious fiction writer, wrote in a letter to Frederick, "country, after all, is background in human life—I don't believe it should be made to bear too much burden."[69] The history of the magazine under his direction is one of a movement away from stricter definitions of region and toward national contributors, subscribers, and significance. The magazine began its life in Iowa, but moved several times as Frederick attempted to improve the magazine's funding by negotiating with various Midwestern universities. This was always with an eye to his own salary rather than to an actual endowment for the journal, since Frederick was determined to have it remain free of "academic" influence and therefore direct funding; he makes a point of the fact that he made up the annual shortfall from his own pocket (and later the pocket of his coeditor, Frank Luther Mott).[70] But the distinction was somewhat tenuous. In 1917 he took a job at State Normal College in Moorhead, Minnesota, and the following year was back at Iowa; in 1919 he moved to a farm in Glennie, Michigan, at the northern end of the Lower Peninsula, and moved the editorial office of the journal there as well; in 1921 he was once again at Iowa; the

1922–1923 year saw a move to Pittsburgh, and then back again to Iowa. Each of these moves was prefaced by negotiations for a higher salary, and a salary for his wife. The universities made clear that they were interested in Frederick primarily because he was bringing the journal with him. When the pot was sweetened enough he moved to his new academic post and paid the journal's expenses out of his increased salary. The journal's vaunted freedom from academic support was primarily an imaginative act on Frederick's part.

In 1930, after resigning for the last time in protest, Frederick moved from Iowa to Chicago, where the magazine would be published for its last three years. (He split his time between Northwestern and Notre Dame until 1945 and from then until retiring in 1962 he taught full-time at Notre Dame.) The move to urban Chicago was still, Frederick insisted, part of a regionalist project of resisting New York's hegemony: "Chicago seems among American cities most likely to make a challenge to New York's domination immediately effective" (16 [1930]:370). Nonetheless, he did change the name from *Midland: A Magazine of the Middle West* to *Midland: A National Literary Magazine*. This change, he wrote, was due to "the somewhat belated recognition of the fact that almost from the beginning the material printed in the magazine has come from all parts of the country" (16:[1930]:60). Subscriptions too came from across the country. Already in 1922, when Frederick began a campaign to sign up "sustaining subscribers" who would contribute twenty-five dollars to defray the accumulated red ink, he received a total of fourteen checks, eight from Iowa and the others from Pennsylvania, New York, and California. Regular subscribers were scattered around the country as well, with an increasing number from New York and California over the years. It is very clear that the success the journal enjoyed, even locally, was due to its national reputation: it was important to the magazine's success nationally that Mencken and O'Brien reviewed it the way they did, and important to its local audience and contributors that it got that kind of prestigious attention. The magazine could "open doors," as one Iowa contributor wrote, because of its national standing.[71]

More significantly, Frederick himself never stopped courting New York publishers for his own work. He sent his fiction to New York magazines (and Mencken's Baltimore ones) rather than the other regional magazines, and his novels were published by Knopf rather than by his own Midland Press (which he began as an adjunct to the magazine). Even his textbook on the short story and his two anthologies of Midwestern writing were published by Knopf instead of his own regional press. He also regularly attempted to land an east coast editing position. His most sought-after job was with the *Nation,* to which he sent several letters over the years offering his services as an editor. While arguing for the necessity of regional outlets, against the "barrier of commercial standardization" (18 [1932]:1) and against the Eastern cultural monopoly, in other words, Frederick was busily scheming to join forces with the bad guys in New York.

What I earlier called the hegemonic reading of regionalism would explain this as simply the bubbling up of Frederick's own bad faith; he is in league with the enemy, packaging up his region's culture and selling it off to the highest bidder. But such a symptomatic reading is a bit too easy, it seems to me, or at least too quick to deny the conscious authenticity of the last 150 years of regionalist writers' and readers' commitments and understandings. The fact that Frederick wanted a job in New York does not mean that he was always really writing about New York and New Yorkers' self-estrangement when he thought he was writing about Iowa.

Frederick's hesitancy, his seeming timidity, is his acknowledgment of the fact that regionalist writing, if it is to be literary, needs to attend to both local and more global concerns. When Frederick taught Cather's *My Ántonia* in his classes, he praised it because its characters were "representative of socially important groups of the time and place," but Frederick was always interested in what regionalism as a literary form said beyond the particular.[72] Reviewing Masters's *Spoon River Anthology*, Frederick praised not just the representation, but the fact that Masters had "produced a *Comédie Humaine* in miniature, an inclusive, detailed picture of humanity" (1 [July 1915]: 243.) Midwestern authors have something important to say about the Midwest, Frederick suggested, but they have something to say about the rest of the world as well. Frederick sometimes argued a preservationist line, but he was never willing to forget the second half of this literary equation. Frederick believed, in Phillip Joseph's phrase, in the "region as redeemer of the nation," just as Royce had and just as the Southern Agrarians would.[73] But he also understood literary art to encompass both region and nation. Mott, Frederick's coeditor after 1925, reviewing Iowa author Roger L. Sergel's new novel, *Arlie Gelson,* writes that Sergel uses Iowa as a background because he knows it, and this is meant to be high praise. But the title of Mott's review is "On the Importance of Belonging to the Human Race." In an early editorial, Frederick argued that when we teach literature, it should not be "aesthetic appeal" that is important; "the world today is laying the emphasis upon other values and points of view" (1 [March 1915]: 7). To read Keats, he writes, it is better to have a background in economics than in metrical forms. When Frederick reviewed Edgar Lee Masters's *New Spoon River* in 1925, he was disappointed: "The world has changed since 1915," he wrote. "And Masters has changed less than the world." He did not write that Masters had changed less than Spoon River, Illinois, but less than the world. The world, not the local, is the frame.

This doubleness can be found across the regional little magazine movement. Harold G. Merriam, editor of the *Frontier,* for instance, wrote in 1934:

> I should like to have writers understand regionalism not as an ultimate in litera-
> ture, but as a first step. . . . The "universal" when healthy, alive, pregnant with val-
> ues, springs inevitably from the specific fact. This conception of the interpretation
> of life I would oppose to the idea of cosmic-minded people that understanding
> springs from abstract ideas and images in the mind—in the soul. To such an ex-
> tent regionalism, in my judgment, is earth-minded.[74]

Hoffman, Allen, and Ulrich use this passage to condemn the "grave fault" of "pedantic and self-conscious preoccupation with the region" (134) in some re-gional writing, and to praise those magazines, like *Frontier* and *Midland,* that did not fall into the trap but instead showed "a broad streak of cosmopolitan, eclec-tic interest" (139).

Little magazine regionalism was thus in the mainstream of cosmopolitan American literary culture. "The besetting weakness of regionalism," wrote Lewis Mumford, another iconoclast at the center of literary culture in the 1920s, "lies in the fact that it is an attempt to find refuge in an old shell against the turbu-lent invasions of the outside world, armed with its new engines: in short, an aver-sion to what is, rather than an impulse toward what may be."[75] Mumford goes on about the "sentimental regionalist" and his "neurotic retreat" from the pre-sent for several more pages, but his simple point is one that Frederick, Merriam, Mott, and the others working in regional literary production, including the Twelve Southerners, were well aware of—that literary regionalism is necessar-ily cosmopolitan. Mott, in fact, quotes much of this passage by Mumford in his own history of the magazine in 1968 (139).

And this is why, even at the end of the magazine's run, Frederick could say, "I believe that New York's literary despotism is bad: bad for criticism . . . bad for writing," and yet still send his next manuscript there. What is bad about the despotism is that it is a kind of provincialism, the Lower Provincialism—New Yorkers do not know enough about the world, as Frederick makes clear in his review of Fannie Hurst's attempt to describe a Midwestern farm, which led him to "immoderate, irreverent, vulgar mirth" (14 [1928]: 157) at its string of inac-curacies. In reviewing McKinlay Kantor's novel *Jaybird,* by contrast, what he praises is not its fidelity but the fact that it is providing another perspective on Midwestern life, highlighting the "bright threads": "Some of us have been un-just to our material. We have seen only dull threads in a pattern which is really of exuberant variety and intensity of contrasts" (19 [1933]: 55). A commitment to exuberant variety made for Frederick's qualified embrace of the local, just as the intensity of contrasts in regional fiction is what makes it literary, what makes it available to such radically opposed critical readings, what makes it, for better and for worse, cosmopolitan.

The streak of anti-academicism represented by reluctant academics such as Frederick continues to be very strong in literary culture. To the extent that scholarship is interested in definition, in pinning down the facts, in making summary judgments, Ansley and Frederick suggested in the 1910s, it is at war with the literary spirit, and one can find this idea recapitulated at the slightest prompting in any present-day creative writing program and in the annual MLA-bashing pieces that show up in the *New York Times* and elsewhere. Despite this, literary studies has been, throughout the last hundred years, the academic discipline most hostile to discipline, most ready to attack its own institutions, most gleeful in tearing down its crumbling idols. And, of course, despite all the quarrels, it is still the most congenial place for literary ventures like the little magazines. Frederick qualifies his editorial comments because, more than anything, he was concerned that they be literary, that he be part not just of a faculty or a regional movement, but of the literary world. The highly entertaining anti-academic rants of H. L. Mencken in these same years offered a similar literary argument against literary study, which helps explain his recognition of Frederick and company as fellow travelers. Criticism works against itself, necessarily.[76] Nowhere is this clearer than in the *Midland*'s combination of critical provincialism and literary cosmopolitanism. Like the Southern Agrarians, Frederick offered the provinces as an antidote to the standardization and stultification of modern life, and at the same time he published fiction very much like that of the "revolt from the village" writers, who were picking apart the myth at the very foundation of that claim.

The Revolt from the Village: Anderson, Lewis, Suckow

S herwood Anderson's contribution to "These United States," the *Nation's* series on the states in 1922, does not appear to have helped the editors accomplish their goal.

> Have you a city that smells worse than Akron, that is a worse junk-heap of ugliness than Youngstown, that is more smugly self-satisfied than Cleveland, or that has missed as unbelievably great an opportunity to be one of the lovely cities of the world as has the city of Cleveland? I'll warrant you have not. In this modern pushing American civilization of ours you other states have nothing on our Ohio.[77]

The editors had wanted to celebrate the diversity of regional cultures and to combat the critique that "centralization and regimentation" had resulted in a homogenized, dead-end society, but Anderson does not think they can do it: "This business of writing up the states in the pages of *The Nation* is, I'll bet anything, going to turn out just as I expected. There'll be a lot of knocking, that's what I'll bet."[78] Anderson was half right. Had the editors truly wanted it to be otherwise, they would not have asked Anderson or H. L. Mencken for essays. Mencken's "Maryland: Apex of Normalcy," is as caustic as one might expect: what is life like in Maryland? "I answer frankly and firstly, it is dull. I answer secondly: it is depressing. I answer thirdly: it steadily grows worse" (165). Maryland represents "a massive triumph of regimentation" (167). Other writers in the series were more positive, as when Cather finds Nebraska somewhat under the sway of materialism but assumes it is just a phase, since the people "are as clean and full of vigor as the soil."[79] Dorothy Canfield Fisher finds that because of faith in the principles of liberty and self-determination, "we Vermonters can cock our feet up on the railing of the porch and with a tranquil heart read the news of the modern world and the frightened guessing of other folks at what is coming next!"[80] But in choosing the likes of Mencken, Sinclair Lewis, and Anderson, the editors knew they were in for at least as much critique as celebration.

Anderson and Lewis, who wrote the piece on Minnesota, had by this time already been identified in the pages of the same magazine as in revolt against the provinces. Anderson's *Winesburg, Ohio* (1919) and Lewis's *Main Street* (1920) were Van Doren's prime exhibits of the new, demythologizing approach to the American village. *Winesburg, Ohio* is a collection of short stories, most of which have young George Willard as a central or peripheral character, and he provides one level of cosmopolitan consciousness to the text. A frame tale offers another. The introductory "Book of the Grotesque" tells the story of an old writer who wants to have his bed raised so that he can see out the high windows of the house, a little allegory of the writer's need for a commanding vista. The writer, we are told, thought that he had "known many people, and known them in a peculiarly intimate way that was different than the way you and I know people." Hubris, the narrator suggests, but then asks, "Why quarrel with an old man concerning his thoughts?"[81] (24). The writer has a theory that people become grotesque by believing in truths, and this may seem to suggest that an openness to multiple truths is the preferable option, but again the narrator keeps some distance. As in the case of Wharton's *Ethan Frome,* we have an untrustworthy frame tale: Irving Howe noted some years ago that if in the introduction the grotesques are represented as victims of their own fanatic willfulness, "in the stories themselves grotesqueness is the result of an essentially valid resistance to forces external to its victims."[82] The frame tale appears to offer us a larger, contextualizing, literary panorama, but readers are meant to understand that the "old writer's" outlook, albeit wider, is insufficient.

George Willard, a reporter for the local paper (another standard representation of a poor competitor to the literary writer), has cosmopolitan desires. He wants to see the world, "to meet the adventure of life" (246), to escape the limited purview of Winesburg. "I've been reading books and I've been thinking," he tells Helen White in "Sophistication": "I'm going to try to amount to something in life." He wants, in fact, to be better than the rest of the people in the town, to be "a big man" (236), and this is related to his growing sophistication. In this story, the last before "Departure" (in which George leaves for the big city and the novel ends), sophistication is a concept akin to cosmopolitanism. Sophistication comes when one takes "the backward view of life" and thinks about the future simultaneously, when one's sense of life is saturated by a realization of death. "A door is torn open and for the first time he looks out upon the world, seeing, as though they marched in procession before him, the countless figures of men who before his time have come out of nothingness into the world" (234). This brings, the narrator claims, not a sense of mastery but a sadness. This "sadness of sophistication" (234) infuses the book, suggesting a melancholy version of literary cosmopolitanism, driven by the impulse to understanding. It is explicitly contrasted to false cosmopolitanism. Helen White dated an instructor from a local college, who, though he was also from a small town in Ohio, had begun "to put on the airs of the city. He wanted to appear cosmopolitan" (238). He is a classic failed cosmopolitan outsider, who adopts a patronizing attitude toward the people of Winesburg, glad to have the chance to "study" them (238). His talk wearies Helen, however, who is more interested in the newly (and we assume more truly) sophisticated George.

George, when he becomes sophisticated, wants human contact, wants to "touch someone with his hands, be touched by the hands of another," but his desire is not exactly for sex: "He wants, most of all, understanding" (235). Sophistication is both the gift of someone with "imagination" and the curse. There are no happy idiots, the book shows, and no happy wise men, and readers, sharing the larger view with our implied author, are meant to understand that the best we can do is be sad and wise, sophisticated. As Van Doren wrote, the grotesques "see visions which in some wider world might be dispelled by the light but which in Winesburg must lurk about till they master and madden with the strength which the darkness gives them" (409). It is the light of that "wider world" that Anderson trains on his town, writes Van Doren, and although reviewers who did not like the book saw it as a complete condemnation of the small town and its inhabitants, Van Doren notes the breadth of Anderson's sympathies: "He broods over his creatures with affection, though he makes no luxury of illusions. Much as he has detached himself from the cult of the village, he still cherishes the memories of some specific Winesburg" (409). Maxwell Anderson wrote in the *New Republic* that the book "will shatter forever what remains of the assumption that life seethes most treacherously in cities and that there are sylvan retreats where days pass from harvest to harvest like an idyll of Theocritus."[83] Rebecca West wrote that the novel is in some ways similar to Jewett's and Freeman's provincial tales, but that it is "not fiction. It is poetry. . . . It delights in places where those who are not poets could never find delight; . . . it seems persuaded that there is beauty in everything, in absolutely anything."[84] And H. L. Mencken congratulated Anderson on his ability not to take sides, an advance over his earlier novels: "The national vice of ethical purpose corrupted [Anderson's earlier novels]; they were burdened with *Tendenz*. Now, in *Winesburg, Ohio*, he throws off that handicap."[85]

The critics who more simply applauded or denounced Anderson's negative take on the small town were not all wrong. The stories do show the intolerance of village life destroying characters' lives. Wing Biddlebaum in "Hands" is the most obvious case, a man falsely accused of pedophilia who barely escapes lynching and lives in terror with hysterically fluttering hands for the rest of his life. Alice Hindman's sexual repression in "Adventure" sends her running naked through the streets, Elmer Crowley's oversensitivity to the "public opinion of Winesburg" in "Queer" makes him unpredictably violent (194). The deadening, stultifying force of small-town public opinion is a clear theme, producing what there is of a larger arc to the stories: George's gathering desire to leave the confines of Winesburg for the wider world.

But this "revolt from the village" is only half of a more cosmopolitan story. These characters all are complicit in their own oppression, and the argument against the anti-individualistic nature of village life is necessarily cosmopolitan: it is made by alluding to the various possibilities excluded by the standardizing small-mindedness of provincialism.[86] Simply to take a stand against such small-mindedness, against the debilitating, vitiating, crippling force of village surveillance and standardization is, as Van Doren argued, to be in revolt against the local. But the alternative is the urban and national scene, where other, larger, perhaps even more sinister forces of standardization are afoot. If Winesburg, Ohio, is a mess, then so are Akron, Youngstown, and Cleveland; and if, as Anderson suggested, the other states and their cities "have nothing on Ohio," we can assume that this applies to Chicago, New York, and Philadelphia as well. *Winesburg, Ohio* is indeed an indictment, but not a simple indictment, of the small town. As George and Helen sit in the grandstand of the fairgrounds late at night, after the fair is over and everyone has left, and feel the "ghosts, not of the dead, but of living people" in the "terrifying" silence, the narrator reflects on what it means to apprehend the life of a small town in its actual absence, thus providing one of the metaphors for regionalist literary art: "One shudders at the thought of the meaninglessness of life while at the same instant, and if the people of the town are his people, one loves life so intensely that tears come into the eyes" (240–41).

※

Sinclair Lewis, at our remove from his time and issues, can seem a bit sophomoric. For instance, even he described his *Man Who Knew Coolidge: Being the Soul of Lowell Schmaltz, Constructive and Nordic Citizen* (1928) as a series of "drools," and reviewers were almost entirely united (and in retrospect entirely correct) in finding it boring.[87] Lowell Schmaltz is a blowhard Babbitt figure, but unlike Babbitt, whom Lewis manages to represent from "within and without," Schmaltz never exists on the page as anything but schmaltzy. When Mary Austin described Babbitt as a representative of "the generalized, 'footless' type which has arisen out of a rather widespread resistance to regional interests and influences, out of a determined fixation on the most widely shared, instead of the deepest rooted, types of American activity,"[88] she described Schmaltz more than Babbitt. Schmaltz expresses many of the same attitudes as Babbitt, but without Babbitt's various saving graces and without the dense context and ideological oscillations of the earlier novel. Thanks in part to Mencken, who coined the term, "Babbittry" became synonymous with small-minded, unimaginative, commerce-constructed vacuity. But Lewis was in fact much more evenhanded in the novel than that.

When Babbitt says that "in other countries, art and literature are left to a lot of shabby bums living in attics and feeding on booze and spaghetti, but in America the successful writer or picture-painter is indistinguishable from any other decent businessman," it is in the context of the picture of the "decent businessman" Lewis has already drawn (including Babbitt), and in that of Babbitt's own infatuation with the bohemian enclave in Zenith.[89] The omni-directional insult is one of Lewis's gifts: his satire leaves no target unhit, in this case neither the stereotypical bohemian nor the stereotypical antibohemian. Babbitt's affair with Mrs. Judique represents a reversal of his distaste for her countercultural ways, but by the time the affair is over, he has begun to see the tawdriness of his own actions and hers. When Babbitt convinces his friend Paul to go for a vacation to Maine, in part to cure Paul's depression, they have comically opposite responses; Paul, who had been extremely depressed, becomes more and more chipper despite disbelieving in the "camp cure," while Babbitt, who had been mindlessly extolling its virtues, becomes wearier and more irritable. As the text zigzags through these perspective changes, the ironic distance of the narrator maintains the duality. Which is better or worse, the text asks, the standardization of culture or the paltry revolts against that standardization? And the answer never quite comes.

The discourse of standardization that runs through the novel addresses a central cultural issue. Fordism and Taylorism, assembly lines and mass culture and advertising, the return to normalcy—all these *Babbitt* represents as problems undermining individuation, but in ways that keep alive the benefits involved in economic progress. In *Arrowsmith* (1925), the protagonist rages: "Damn the great executives, the men of measured merriment, damn the men with careful smiles, damn the men that run the shops, oh, damn their measured merriment."[90] But in *Babbitt* the critique, satirically rendered, is, if no less harsh, more complex. When the histologist Dr. Kurt Yavitch complains that in Zenith people have "standardized all the beauty out of life," Seneca Doane, the "radical lawyer," replies: "When I buy an Ingersoll watch or a Ford, I get a better tool for less money, and I know precisely what I'm getting and that leaves me more time and energy to be an individual in" (85). They argue about whether the café life of Paris is as standardized as the cocktail parties of Zenith, and Yavitch tells Doane, "You're a broad-minded liberal, and you haven't the slightest idea what you want. I being a revolutionist, know exactly what I want—and what I want now is a drink" (86). The passages on either side of this interchange show that the standardization being attacked and defended is itself an inaccurate representation of the state of affairs: there are not only malcontents, bootleggers, and bohemians in Zenith, but cocaine runners murdering prostitutes, young men committing suicide, fifteen thousand people in an evangelical tent meeting, GAR veterans who still think the world is flat, Marxist union organizers, poets writing rondeaux, and research scientists staying up for days trying to synthesize rubber.

Babbitt's opinions are all standardized, adopted without thinking, and he just blabs out the contradictions: "We got no business interfering with the Irish or any other foreign government. Keep our hands strictly off. And there's another well-authenticated rumor that Lenin is dead. That's fine. It's beyond me why we don't just step in there and kick those Bolshevik cusses out" (24). Edith Wharton, to whom Lewis dedicated *Babbitt,* wrote Lewis that she found *Main Street* (1920) to be a better novel, "because in [*Main Street*] you produce a sense of unity & of depth by reflecting Main Street in the consciousness of a woman who suffered from it because she had points of comparison, & was detached enough to situate it in the universe—whereas Babbitt is in and of Zenith up to his chin & over, & Sinclair Lewis is obliged to do his seeing and comparing for him."[91] Readers who, like Wharton, find Lewis's implied author too judgmental and opinionated do not rate the novel highly, but, far more than *The Man Who Knew Coolidge* and many of Lewis's later novels, *Babbitt* does accomplish the literary work of open-ended comparison. Readers can laugh at the way Babbitt's received notions contradict one another, at his lack of understanding, but his intermittent yearnings for something more, his near-accidental decencies, his final investment in his son's future unconventionality—all these complicate the portrait of Babbitt in exactly the way Wharton suggested it should be complicated.

Main Street, according to Lewis's biographer Mark Schorer, was "the most sensational event in twentieth-century American publishing history."[92] It was an immediate best-seller and the other revolt novels of 1920 surged in sales when they were mentioned in reviews alongside it. H. L. Mencken, who had found Lewis to be an idiot ("Of all the idiots I've ever laid eyes on, that fellow is the worst"), wrote to George Jean Nathan in obvious surprise: "That *Lump* . . . has done the job! It's a genuinely excellent piece of work."[93] Carl Van Doren was not so sure. In "The Revolt from the Village," he suggests that Lewis is too partisan to be fully literary:

> Mr. Lewis hates such dullness—the village virus—as the saints hate sin. . . . The question, of course, arises whether the ancient war upon stupidity is a better literary cause to fight in than the equally ancient war upon sin. Both narrow them-

selves to doctrinal contentions, forgetting for the moment that either being virtuous or being intelligent is but half—or thereabouts—of existence, and that the two qualities are hopelessly intertwined. The greatest novelists, as they do not condemn lapses of virtue too harshly, so also do not too harshly condemn deficiencies of intelligence. (410)

Van Doren feels the same about Mary Borden's *The Romantic Woman* (1920): "She hails, in a way, from the village and has hints of mystical fervor; she has, however, the hard outward manner of the worldling who has passed beyond village bounds. . . . She looks at Chicago from the post of a secure outsider, sometimes vexed, sometimes smiling, sometimes ready with approbation, but always critical" (411). Conversely, Floyd Dell, Van Doren thinks, gets it right: "Mr. Dell writes . . . as if he regarded their war upon the village as an ancient brawl which may now be assumed to have been as much settled as it ever will be" (411), so that the two sides are not to be cheered for but understood. Van Doren praises Dell, using the same classic cosmopolitan understanding that drives his criticism of Lewis, through the use of paired antinomies: "He can be at once downright and graceful, at once sincere and impersonal, at once revolutionary and restrained, at once impassioned and reflective, at once enamored of truth and scrupulous for beauty" (412).

Other demurrers also found *Main Street* too unrelievedly critical of the small town, and they were much less restrained than Van Doren. According to Schorer, "no reader was indifferent to *Main Street:* if it was not the most important revelation of American life, it was the most infamous libel upon it" (269). The controversy over the book was heightened when the Pulitzer Prize jury voted for it, only to be overturned by the trustees of Columbia University, who gave the prize to Edith Wharton's *Age of Innocence* (1920). The novel could cause this kind of stir precisely because it was not just about the "village virus" (Lewis's working title), but about civilization itself. "This is America," the narrator tells us in an epigraph. "Main Street is the continuation of Main Streets everywhere. . . . Main Street is the climax of civilization." The novel uses Carol Kennicott as the semicosmopolitan intruder who marries into Gopher Prairie life and feels spiritually and culturally starved and stultified. The critics who found the text too one-sided have tended to identify the text's argument with Carol Kennicott's dissatisfaction, as have the critics who gleefully agree with her assessment. But we are encouraged by the novel over and over again to see Carol's problems in terms of broader debates. She protests, for instance, that she wants "the primitive forest with hooded furs and a rifle, or a barnyard warm and steamy, noisy with hens and cattle" (113). But what she finds are the gray, desolate farmhouses of Hamlin Garland, the "yards choked with winter ash-piles, . . . roads of dirty snow and clotted frozen mud" (113). Carol's perceptions are constantly being reversed throughout the text, suggesting that these two views, the romantically picturesque and the pessimistically realist, are simply ways of seeing the same objects. A kind of double double take gets applied to everything, first from the perspective of Catherine and then in the narrative's perspective on her.

Lewis makes it clear on the first page that although he is staging his drama in a specific region, Minnesota, "the story would be the same in Ohio or Montana, in Kansas or Kentucky or Illinois, and not very differently would it be told Up New York State or in the Carolina hills" (3). And early on he makes his claim for literary representation, its superiority to the one-sided views in subliterary genres:

> In reading popular stories and seeing plays, asserted Carol, she had found only two traditions of the American small town. The first tradition, repeated in scores of magazines every month, is that the American village remains the one sure abode of friendship, honesty, and clean sweet marriageable girls. . . . The other tradition is that the significant features of all villages are whiskers, iron dogs upon lawns, gold bricks, checkers, jars of gilded cat-tails, and shrewd comic old men who are known as "hicks" and who ejaculate "Wall I swan." This altogether admirable tradition rules the vaudeville stage, facetious illustrators, and syndicated newspaper humor, but out of actual life it passed forty years ago. (3)

Lewis, of course, sees his own work as avoiding both traps, and to the extent readers have agreed that he succeeded in doing so, they have found his work literary.

⤳

What Mencken praised in *Main Street* he also praised in the work of Ruth Suckow, whose stories he read in the *Midland* and immediately solicited for his own publications. In a letter to Frederick, he said Suckow "writes like the devil" and asked to be put in touch with her.[94] In a letter to Lewis, Mencken wrote, "I lately unearthed a girl in Iowa who seems to me to be superb. She follows after Dreiser and Anderson, but she is also a genuine original."[95] He said that Suckow was "unquestionably the most remarkable woman . . . writing stories in the republic."[96]

Suckow's "Uprooted," originally published in the *Midland,* depicts a family discussion about the fate of their aging parents; the children persuade the parents to leave the old, run-down farm and move in with a daughter in town. Suckow's "A Start in Life," published in Mencken's *American Mercury* in 1924, is the story of a young girl leaving home to become a servant in a nearby farmhouse: the end of one rural life of hardship, the start of another. Both stories, collected in her first collection, *Iowa Interiors* (1926), contain deromanticized visions of rural poverty. And in both, the question of staying home, which means staying poor, or going away and perhaps doing better, is paramount. In "Uprooted," it is Sam, the businessman-son who has moved to the big city (Omaha), who sees the dilapidated state of the farm he grew up on and where his poor parents still live: the gnarled trees, the dank, musty rooms of the farmhouse, the weather-beaten buildings, the weeds and peeling paint. "It was strange how people seemed to take root in a place. He should think anyone would be glad to leave this run-down, miserable spot. See how the steps were coming apart!"[97] In "A Start in Life" it is Daisy, the young daughter, who, as she is being driven away to her new job for the first time, sees the home she is leaving with new eyes:

> In that moment, Daisy had a startled view of home—the small house standing on a rough rise of land, weathered to a dim color that showed dark streaks from the rain; the narrow sloping front porch whose edges had a soaked gnawed look; the chickens, grayish black, pecking at the wet ground; their playthings, stones, a wagon, some old pail covers littered about; a soaked, discolored piece of underwear hanging on the line in the back yard . . . the old swing that hung from one of the trees, the ropes sodden, the seat in crooked. (17)

As this suggests, it is leaving home that allows one to see it, to have a perspective on it, or at least to have this kind of dreary perspective on it.

Both the young Daisy and Sam's elderly parents want to stay where they are; even considering options makes them feel alienated, rootless, put upon. Sam himself wants nothing more than to be through with the family discussion about what to do with his parents and to go home himself: "The vision of a large leather chair at home, in which the hollows were his own, filled him with homesickness" (107). As Sam's leather chair suggests, this yearning for home is not about one's roots: he cannot wait to get away from the house he grew up in. Daisy begins to realize that the main difference between her old life of poverty and her new life as a servant in a clean, linoleumed, freshly painted household with its modern car, hot water heater, gasoline-powered water pump, and so on, is that she does not "belong" (17). She is simply the help and no one cares about her homesickness, her confusion. She wants to go home not because she is rooted there but because she quite understandably does not like where she is, does not want to be a servant or to be treated like one. She is on the same patch of land, basically, only twenty miles away. Her social position, not her regional roots, creates her desire for home.

In "A Home-coming," another story in the same collection, the protagonist comes back to her childhood home after being away for more than fifteen years. "She was at home. She looked about the room—familiar, unfamiliar. More real than any other place, and yet not real at all. Part present, part past" (31). After vacillating, in the end she decides that it is all she needs, and that traveling from place to place would be no better. The decision, of course, does not make her happy. As she wanders about the house looking for solace, she tries to read a modern novel, but it is too hard, too shrill. "Where were the books tender enough for her weariness?" she asks herself, and thinks of *Cranford*. "But there was something deeper than 'Cranford.' Where were the books," she asks, in the story's advertisement for itself, "tender, and yet deep?" (32). The protagonist cannot answer the question, but the text does. In a world in which homes are sinks of poverty and habit, and everywhere else is a new form of alienation, literary antinomies offer the closest thing to resolution. The story we are reading, presumably, answers its protagonist's call for a literature adequate to representing the relation of the traditional to the modern, of the present to the past, both tender enough and deep enough.

"The Top of the Ladder," like other stories of success in the 1920s, contrasts the admiration of the poor for the rich to rich people's own sense of alienation. As in another story, "Renters," the rich and poor are not symmetrically, but rather comparably, miserable and neither understands the nature of the other's misery. And in all Suckow's stories, if the grass is greener, it is not so for long. "Retired" follows an old man around his muddy small town. He has moved off his farm and into town, as he had dreamed of being able to do, but now he just finds himself bored. He goes to the store where the other old men gather, and one tells him to make himself "to home" (135), which he tries to do. But as the men talk and the old man listens "glumly" (136), he realizes that the stoveside is as boring as his lonely walk, and more aggravating. Although he does not miss the farm exactly, he feels useless, alienated from both his own past and his present. As Sam, the wealthy businessman-son in "Uprooted" thinks, "It was too bad that the way of life was as it was" (109), but that does not change it. The retired man does not want to go home to the farm, and does not even want to go home to his new town house. Suckow's texts often work by spreading the gloom evenly.

Young Daisy wants to go home again, but we know that is not going to happen. The elderly parents want to stay in their home, but that cannot happen either. Sam, the story's representative of the modern world, does have the means and the desire to go home. "Lord!" he thinks, in the last line: "He would be glad to get out of that hotel and back to his home again" (109). But for most readers, especially those in, say, New York, Sam's sense of rooted comfort in Omaha is as absurd as his parents' befuddled inertia. And the same is true of Daisy's alternative: Daisy's "wealthy" employers live at a similar distance from Suckow's readers: their house is on a mud road, the new shiny linoleum is, after all, linoleum. Daisy's sense of their extreme modernity and wealth is a sign of ignorance; as Suckow's readers know, they do not represent the epitome of modern luxury.

Suckow herself was no Daisy and had a cosmopolitan Midwestern upbringing. As a second-generation German American she was surrounded by immigrant relatives, and as an itinerant preacher's child she moved constantly as a child. Later, at Grinnell College, she encountered the cosmopolitanism of institutionalized higher education, and finally, like Garland, she too moved to Boston in her early twenties, and then to Denver. At twenty-seven she returned to Iowa and submitted stories to the *Midland,* later working with John T. Frederick and his miscellaneous group of immigrants to Iowa City. In the course of her life Suckow lived in the college town of Cedar Falls, in Greenwich Village, in Vermont (in Robert Frost's home), in Chicago, Tucson, and Claremont, California. Although she wrote a little about Greenwich Village and California, she wrote continually about Iowa, up through her last novel, *The John Wood Case* (1959), in which rural characters still dream of "intellectual and metropolitan sophistication" and city characters still come looking for "the wholesome air and restful quiet of this solid, homespun part of our country" that the imaginative young people cannot wait to get away from.[98]

In Suckow's novel *The Odyssey of a Nice Girl* (1925), the protagonist, coming home for the first time to the Midwest after attending school in Boston, brings with her a poetry magazine as talisman and emblem of her new cosmopolitanism. "There was a difference that she felt in books, although she did not know how to name it," and it is this difference that had led her to want to go to Boston to study.[99] But she never becomes quite cosmopolitan enough, and her "studies" are not finally able to counter "the bleak emotionless grind of all these days" (285). Here again, Suckow's is an equal opportunity despondency, in which the rich man with thirty-six servants commits suicide and tenant farmers face their bleak futures. But, at the same time, things are not entirely hopeless in Suckow's fiction. In a piece about Suckow in 1931, Frederick wrote that Suckow avoids the problems of prettifiers such as Zona Gale and pessimists such as Masters and Lewis. "She is not hostile to the Middle West—not a resentful critic. This does not mean that there is nothing of the ugliness of middle western life in her books. There is plenty. But it is always balanced by something else."[100] In a few of her stories, this balance is achieved by the characters; in "A Rural Community," for instance, the returning son comes home and finds both his own alienation and a sense of the "deep stabilities of country life."[101] But in most of the stories, that balance is achieved by the implied author and readers rather than

by the characters themselves. Daisy never finds that "something else," but readers are supposed to, just as readers are meant to feel Sam's dilemma more pro-
foundly than Sam himself is able to do. The distance the texts establish between
characters and implied reader and author provides, in these stories of quiet des-
peration, the only real "tender, yet deep" insight, the only real available sense of
belonging.

The Southern Renaissance
and the World's Body

In 1917, H. L. Mencken, supporter of Suckow and cheerleader of the revolt from the village, published "The Sahara of the Bozart," which was exactly the kind of opprobrium that the Southern Agrarians—the theorizers, participants, and promoters of the Southern Renaissance—were shortly to fight against. In the South, Mencken wrote,

> A poet is as rare as an oboe-player, a dry-point etcher or a metaphysician. It is, indeed, amazing to contemplate so vast a vacuity. One thinks of interstellar spaces, of the colossal reaches of the now mystical ether. Nearly the whole of Europe could be lost in its stupendous region of fat farms, shoddy cities and paralyzed cerebrums . . . and yet, for all its size and all its wealth and all the "progress" it babbles of, it is almost as sterile, artistically, intellectually, culturally, as the Sahara Desert. There are single acres in Europe that house more first-rate men than all the states south of the Potomac. . . . Elegance, esprit, culture? Virginia has no art, no literature, no mind or aspiration of her own. Her education has sunk to the Baptist seminary level; not a single contribution to human knowledge has come out of her colleges in 25 years; she spends less than half upon her common schools, per capita, than any northern state spends. In brief, an intellectual Gobi or Lapland.[102]

A decade later, the Agrarians argued the opposite, that the cultural desert was the rest of the country. "The arts," they claimed in *I'll Take My Stand* (1930), do not "have a proper life under industrialism, with the general decay of sensibility which attends it."[103] In order to create art, an artist needs "a right attitude to nature; and in particular . . . a free and disinterested observation of nature that occurs only in leisure" (xliii). Since industrial civilization demands that people work harder and longer and spend whatever free time they have consuming, "neither the creation nor the understanding of works of art is possible in an industrial age except by some local or unlikely suspension of the industrial drive" (xliii). They admit that there is not enough art being produced in the South either, but argue that since it is the region least desertified by industrialism, it is the most likely place for new art to be born.

The Southern Agrarians would seem to be a limit case for my argument, since they came together to make a sustained argument for local affiliation, against modernity, and at least occasionally, quite loudly and explicitly against relativism in values. The literary writers among them, however, nonetheless maintain primary allegiance to the values of literary cosmopolitanism as I have sketched them here. It is true that their manifesto, *I'll Take My Stand,* contains many arguments that are starkly anticosmopolitan, but many are the opposite. The most partisan of the comments come from the contributors to that volume who were social scientists, and even many of these have an overlay of cosmopolitanism. The historian Frank Lawrence Owsley is responsible for what is undoubtedly the single stupidest sentence in the book—the South after the Civil War, he writes, "was turned over to the three millions of former slaves, some of whom could still remember the taste of human flesh and the bulk of them hardly three generations removed from cannibalism"—and he also provided the most stark appraisal of the relation between Northern industrialism and Southern agrarianism. But after pages of withering criticism of the soulless, merciless North, he concludes:

> The struggle between an agrarian and an industrial civilization, then, was the irrepressible conflict, the house divided against itself, which must become according to the doctrine of the industrial section all the one or all the other. It was a doctrine of intolerance, crusading, standardizing alike in industry and in life. The South had to be crushed out; it was in the way; it impeded the progress of the machine. So Juggernaut drove his car across the South.[104]

Just like Lewis and the other Revolt writers, he argues against intolerance, and therefore appeals for tolerance, against "crusading, standardizing" culture and therefore for open, diverse culture. Although noticeably intolerant in obvious ways, even Owsley and the other nonliterary Agrarians consistently invoked cosmopolitan arguments to make their stand.

The literary writers among the Agrarians were even more clearly invested in the values of literary cosmopolitanism, and the few who have been remembered—John Crowe Ransom, Allen Tate, Robert Penn Warren, and Donald Davidson—in *I'll Take My Stand* and elsewhere, all claim for literary art the same

power and value as the mainstream of literary cosmopolitans. Davidson echoes
Howells, for instance, when he claims that

> we cannot define regionalism unless at the same time we define nationalism. The
> two are supplementary aspects of the same thing. Regionalism is a name for the
> condition under which the national American literature exists as a literature: that
> is, its constant tendency to decentralize rather than to centralize; or to correct over-
> centralization by conscious decentralization, or it describes the conditions under
> which it is possible for literature to be a normal artistic outgrowth of the life of a
> region.[105]

He commends the "broad sense of the world which comes, paradoxically, from
a comparative retirement from the world," suggesting that his and his fellow
Agrarians' separatist arguments are all, finally, in the service of a more cosmopolitan breadth of perspective. The regionalist must, from his region, "confront the total and moving world" (277), Davidson writes. In his contribution
to I'll Take My Stand he repeats Garland's claim to the literary fecundity of the
provinces and criticizes the false cosmopolitanism of the cities:

> Our megalopolitan agglomerations, which make great ado about art, are actually
> sterile on the creative side; they patronize art, they merchandise it, but they do not
> produce it. The despised hinterland, which is rather carefree about the matter,
> somehow manages to beget the great majority of American artists. True, they of-
> ten migrate to New York, at considerable risk to their growth; they as often move
> away again, to Europe or some treasured local retreat. Our large cities affect a cos-
> mopolitan air but have little of the artistic cosmopolitanism that once made Paris
> a Mecca.[106]

To be fair, this is just one argument among a vast array, many of which are out-
right contradictory, that Davidson tosses out in his essay, and it is not the main
thrust of the piece, which is simply that industrial society is ruining everything.
But to make that argument, Davidson often suggests that industrialism narrows
the scope of experience and that to nurture provincial cultures is to broaden the
cultural repertoire, or at least keep it from shrinking any further.

Allen Tate begins his essay in I'll Take My Stand with a footnote that makes
the same point. He feels "constrained to point out," he writes, that the title of
the book is not really true to what he takes to be its aims: "It emphasizes the
fact of exclusiveness rather than its benefits; it points to a particular house but
omits to say that it was the home of a spirit that may have also lived elsewhere."[107] His argument is about cultural belief, and he chides Southerners for

not having enough. The American religion is pragmatic, and so is interested not in "the whole horse," but "only half the horse," the horsepower. Tate is arguing for a culture that has "respect for the full-dimensioned, grass-eating horse" (157). Again the arguments all push toward a broader perspective. The partial view adopted by the North, all abstraction and instrumentalism, is what the South resists and should continue to resist. In "The Profession of Letters in the South" (1935), Tate suggests that both Northern and Southern arguments about the South tend to overgeneralize, because "the South is an immensely complicated region."[108] In a later essay on regionalism, Tate argues for regionalism but against provincialism, claiming that regionalism always assumes a relation both to history and to the rest of the world, but that provincialism does not.[109]

John Crowe Ransom, like the rest of the Agrarians, identifies industrialism as the enemy. "Industrialism is a program under which men, using the latest scientific paraphernalia, sacrifice comfort, leisure, and the enjoyment of life to win Pyrrhic victories from nature at points of no strategic importance."[110] He, like Davidson, argues that only in semileisure, away from the city, can true, harmonious art be created, unconfused by the "gospel of Progress" (7). Industrialism, along with its ideological handmaidens, progressivism and individualism, wrote Ransom, was destroying local cultures in favor of a standardizing ethic, and though Ransom understood that "the further survival of the South as a detached local remnant is now unlikely" (21), he argued nonetheless that local traditions were worth saving and could be marshaled to shape or direct the inevitable progress of commercial and industrial culture. Like the earlier regionalists, he found that the "important benefit" of the regional way of life is that it "feels right, it has aesthetic quality," and he adopts, in "The Aesthetic of Regionalism," the very cosmopolitan pose of the "philosophic regionalist."[111] Reinventing Schiller's distinction between the naïve and the sentimental, in that piece Ransom writes that truly regional people like the Southwestern Indians "do not have to formulate the philosophy of regionalism" because they are completely integrated in their own lives and culture (48). But, he adds, we in the modern world do, because we are necessarily aware of multiple philosophies of life and therefore cannot have a naïve relation to our own experience.[112] The philosophic regionalist is born of an already existing cosmopolitanism, the burden and privilege of being able to see one's own culture from within and from without.

In I'll Take My Stand's introductory "Statement of Principles," the Twelve Southerners argue that the New Humanists (Irving Babbitt, Paul Elmer More, Stuart Pratt Sherman, Norman Foerster) are too abstract—they are guilty of an abstract form of thinking the Agrarians associate with the scientific, instrumentalist mind. A true humanism, they write, "is not an abstract system, but a culture, the whole way in which we live, act, think and feel" (xliv). They suggest that "we cannot recover our native humanism by adopting some standard of taste that is critical enough to question the contemporary arts but not critical enough to question the social and economic life which is their ground" (xlv). The New Criticism, with which Ransom, Tate, and Warren would remain associated, famously erected boundaries between literature and its social and historical context, but the Agrarians' support for the New Criticism always came with riders. Ransom, for instance, in the aptly titled (for my purposes) *The World's Body* (1938), wrote the following, in which a classic New Critical denial of the relation of literature to life is followed by an equally classic statement of literary cosmopolitanism. It also shows the continued necessity felt by literary culture to make its claims in relation to scientific knowledge:

> True poetry has no great interest in improving or idealizing the world, which does well enough. It only wants to realize the world, to see it better. Poetry is the kind of knowledge by which we must know what we have arranged that we shall not know otherwise. We have elected to know the world through our science, and we know a great deal, but science is only the cognitive department of our animal life, and by it we know the world only as a scheme of abstract conveniences. What we cannot know constitutionally as scientists is the world which is made of whole and indefeasible objects, and this is the world which poetry recovers for us.[113]

What Ransom, Tate, and Warren embraced in the New Criticism was the conviction that literature was a particular form of knowledge that could not be adequately paraphrased by any other science's or discipline's discourse. This bars certain kinds of critical statements that the New Critics considered "extrinsic," but, like Tate, Ransom always assumes regionalism's relation both to history and to the rest of the world.

And Ransom adds that literature reveals the world while other forms of knowledge conceal it. "As science more and more completely reduces the world to its types and forms, art, replying, must invest it again with body."[114] Over and over in Ransom's writings, the plea is to consider the full complexity of poetry ("Poetry is more complicated than . . . a scientific sort of act")[115] rather than reducing it to the psychology of the author or its political efficacy. The New Criticism, which, when it became the whipping boy of later movements, was represented as a simplification of the complexity of literary action, was itself a form of literary cosmopolitanism that saw its job as rescuing literary art from scientific reduction. As René Wellek and Austin Warren and Ransom and others set up their exclusionary boundaries for criticism—they all attempted to outlaw various forms of extrinsic criticism, dismissing what they saw as fallacious approaches—they nonetheless continued to evaluate texts on grounds quite similar to those of previous and future generations of literary cosmopolitans. "The history of aesthetics," Wellek and Warren write in *Theory of Literature* (1948), is "a dialectic in which the thesis and counter-thesis are Horace's *dulce* and *utile:* poetry is sweet and useful." Each has had proponents, they explain, art for art's sake and pure propaganda being the opposite poles, but "neither view, in isolation, can possibly seem acceptable. . . . We must describe the function of art in such a way as to do justice at once to *dulce* and *utile.*"[116] I. A. Richards, whose work laid much of the theoretical foundation for New Criticism, saw irony as the driving force of the literary work, and he defined irony as "the bringing in of the opposite, the complementary impulses."[117] Cleanth Brooks, "the model New Critic" according to Murray Krieger, took Richards's formula further, suggesting that the literary text was like a set of mirrors, infinitely bouncing opposing images back and forth.[118] The New Critics valued complexity and ambiguity in literary texts above all else, which is in effect another way of describing what I have been calling literary cosmopolitanism. As Ransom puts it, "What these works intend is, simply, the widest and most unprejudiced knowledge . . . that is possible."[119]

Ellen Glasgow, whom many of the Agrarians saw as a foremother, had an incorporative attitude toward scientific knowledge much like Cather's. *Barren Ground* (1925) retells the story of *O Pioneers!* in which a woman on her own pulls her farm out of the traditional past and into the modern age. Dorinda Oakley, like Alexandra Bergson, owes her success in part to the advances in scientific agriculture, advances both women assimilate and put into production before their neighbors and despite those neighbors' resistance and derision. Both end up so successful that they can buy up hundreds of acres around them made available by their neighbors' failures. Both get their man in the end, and not until the end. As Douglas Anderson has pointed out, the spate of farm novels in these decades with farm-owning female protagonists is one indication that the novels were more interested in addressing the concerns of their literary readers (the majority of them female) than in producing a sociologically accurate rendering of rural life.[120] And Glasgow herself was clear that even as she represented "the Virginia background" in her many novels, she was after a wider view. "I was faithful to my resolve that I would write of the universal, not of the provincial," she wrote in her autobiography, published posthumously.[121] "I knew my part of the South, and I had looked deep enough within and far enough without to learn something of human beings and their substance" (129). Her relation to this "universal" was itself the result of reading literature. She describes devouring every book she could find as a girl, fiction and nonfiction. She read Henry George's *Progress and Poverty* in her late teens; she also read *The*

Origin of Species so thoroughly that she "could have passed successfully an examination on every page" (88–89). After an aunt gave her a subscription to a mercantile library in New York, she breathlessly awaited the weekly parcels of books. With the subscription, she writes, "the doors of a new world were flung back" (90). This widening of her perspective was not just an accumulation of fact and erudition, but the adoption of a cosmopolitan culture of reading: when asked later in life by an interviewer what the South needed most, she said, "blood and irony" (104).

Barren Ground's protagonist, Dorinda Oakley, grows up with a severely depressive father and a mother with a religious mania, and these facts mark the text's modernity; they demonstrate the author's cognizance of the new psychology and her willingness to analyze the springs of sexual repression.[122] When Dorinda becomes pregnant, the father is not, as in Wharton's *Summer*, the urban interloper, at least not exactly. The man, Jason Greylock, is from a neighboring farm, albeit a larger and older one, who has been away in the city studying medicine. So while he represents the city, he also represents the New South. Jason's father is the novel's main representative of the old regime, living in the dilapidated big house with a bevy of black servants and having illicit relations with at least some of them. Hence, he represents the past, the worst of the Old South, just as his professionalized and citified son is supposed to represent the future.

After setting up that opposition, Glasgow complicates it by having Jason abandon the pregnant Dorinda and marry someone else. Dorinda then goes to the city to have the baby. While there she has a fortunate (plotwise) accident, losing the baby and coming under the care of a physician, Dr. Faraday, who finds her an interesting case. The doctor too brings an up-to-date psychological perspective to the mix. After Dorinda recovers from the accident and miscarriage, she goes to a concert with a certain Dr. Burch and is overwhelmed by the music. Burch watches her and soaks up her enthusiasm afterward. He admits that he was afraid the music would be too "difficult. . . . It wasn't an easy programme," but her response had been "pure sensation" (240, 239). Synesthetic and intense, her response included floods of memories, images, and colors. "Ecstasy quivered over her, while sound and color were transformed into rhythms of pure feeling" so strong as to be almost painful (239). But Burch remains distanced. "I never get that response to music," he tells her. "To me it is little more than an intellectual exercise." He tells her of a musician friend who claimed that his knowledge of theory had made pure enjoyment impossible. Again, the naïve and the sentimental, the alienated city dweller and the happy primitive.

But this is just a moment in the system of oscillations: we have already seen how alienated Dorinda was in the country and how barren lives there can be:

For twenty years [Dorinda and her mother] had lived in the same house together, yet they were still strangers. For twenty years they had not spent a year apart, and all the time her mother had dreamed of coral strands and palm trees, while she herself had grown into a thing as strange and far away as Africa. Were people like this everywhere, all over the world, each one a universe in one's self, separate like the stars in a vast emptiness? (184–85)

At the height of her love for Jason, the first time we have seen her overwhelmed by emotion and sensation, she can still ask, "Was this all there was in her feeling for Jason; the struggle to escape the endless captivity of things as they are?" (105). And we have also seen, between these moments of despair, moments of country-bred elation: "Had not the land entered into their [hers, her parents', Jason's] souls and shaped their moods into permanent or impermanent forms? Less a thought than a feeling; but she went on more rapidly toward the complete joy of the moment in which she lived" (128). The oscillations are underscored by a refrain of depressive rhetorical questions. Two weeks into her stay in New York City, she looks around and asks herself again, "After all the fuss that has been made over it . . . is this Life?" (203) At the end of the novel, when she has conquered the land and become an enormous success, she reflects again: "More than thirty years of effort and self-sacrifice—for what?" (518)

After the concert Dorinda and Dr. Burch talk about her farm life, and she asks him about scientific farming; a friend of his from the University of Wisconsin is coming to town to give a series of lectures about the latest developments in agriculture, and Burch will get her a reading list so she can prepare. As she reads and listens she gets an "idea of the land," and plots her return to the country (249). One of the ways the city broadens her perspective, in other words, is by providing her with a new image of the country, one that is divorced from her own experience of it, an urban-based, urban-derived image of the rural. With the help of this "idea of the land" and an infusion of capital from Dr. Faraday, she returns to her farm and transforms it into a modern factory, complete with machines for milking and for making butter into trademarked pats for a luxury hotel. The modernity of this successful farm ensures not only her own livelihood but a triumph over tradition, represented as a tradition of decay: her capitalist reinvigoration of her parents' farm reverses a process of deterioration and her further capitalist expansion allows her eventually to buy the Greylock farm, where Jason's father had been living out his degraded Gothic caricature of plantation life.

This description might suggest integration, a melding of city and country concerns in which modernity and tradition find resolution, but the text continues to shift from pastoral beauty to rural idiocy, from urban knowledge and possibility to urban angst and futility. When Dorinda first returns to the farm,

armed with her urban-inculcated ideas and ideals of rural life, she finds not integration but an incredible emptiness. "How small the station looked, and how
desolate, stranded like a wrecked ship in the broomsedge. What isolation! What
barrenness!" (255) Like the first impressions of Garland's returning characters as
they step off the train, Dorinda finds her idealizations immediately challenged:
"In her memory the horizon had been so much wider, the road so much longer,
the band of woods so much deeper. It seemed to her that the landscape must
have diminished in an incredible way since she left it" (255). The land will appear diminished many more times as the novel progresses, and it will also act as
a source of strength and beauty: "The storm and the hag-ridden dreams of the
night were over, and the land which she had forgotten was waiting to take her
back to its heart. Endurance. Fortitude. The spirit of the land was flowing out
again toward life" (524).

The other themes in the text are also structured by oscillations, ironies, and
unresolved antinomies: the decadent, decrepit, immoral, sexually promiscuous
(primitive) past versus sterile, dissociated, repressed modernity; repressed, Puritan, barren tradition versus the fullness of modern knowledge and possibility;
the dullness of the city and the vibrancy of the country; and vice versa. When
at the end John Abner suggests she might marry again, and she answers in an
"infinitely wise" way that she is "finished with all that" (459), we remember that
she has been saying this for years, and it was never quite true. The irony that, in
escaping her mother's form of religious mania and sexual repression, she ends
up in some ways the same, does not escape even Dorinda at times. But Dorinda's
and the other characters' moments of insight are always at best partial. The relation of things as they are, "the dull grey of existence" (117), to racial, agricultural, intellectual, and personal progress and to ecstasy, the correct relation
between repression and freedom, the relation between fate and volition, empathy and self-possession: the characters get glimpses, but only readers get the full
array. In the last line of the novel, Dorinda repeats her catchphrase, "I'm thankful to have finished with all that" (459), and only readers, along with the implied
author, know she is wrong, that nothing is ever finished.

Other Southern novels of the 1920s and 1930s follow the same pattern. Edith
Summers Kelley's *Weeds* (1923), a novel of impoverished tobacco farmers in
Kentucky, pauses midway to make explicit the point it has been making im-
plicitly all along:

> There is an idea existing in many minds that country folk are mostly simple, nat-
> ural and spontaneous, living in the light of day and carrying their hearts on their
> sleeves. There is no more misleading fallacy. No decadent court riddled with lust

of power, greed, vice, and intrigue, and falling to pieces of its own rottenness, ever moved under a thicker atmosphere than that which brooded over the little shanty where these four fresh-cheeked young country people stood stripping tobacco.[123]

This paragraph, along with any number of other moments of authorial direct address ("The only break in what would seem to an outsider an interminable stretch of tedium . . ." [10]; "In backwoods corners of America, where the people have been poor and benighted for generations . . ." [13]), is at the heart of what Kelley is trying to accomplish. In the interests of what Ransom called "the widest and most unprejudiced knowledge," she is showing the poor rural folk from the inside and the outside. This is a good book, however, not a great one. Like many regional texts, it sets up its protagonist as a quasi-artist (she sketches and keeps the drawings in a drawer), and it attempts to keep in equilibrium the specificity and universalism of its arguments. But in comparison to Glasgow's text, this one activates fewer cultural debates and does not balance its own partisanship in some of them. Matthew J. Bruccoli has made a pitch for the novel's literary status by claiming (conditionally) the opposite. "If *Weeds* has a chance for a permanent life, that chance stems from the fact that it is not a 'problem novel'—that is, it does not study a contemporary problem and call for reform."[124] But in fact it is more "Upton Sinclairesque" (his phrase) than Bruccoli admits—Kelley did spend some years as Sinclair's secretary, after all, and lived at Helicon Hall—and the capitalist enemy is clear.

It is considerably more successful, however, than Erskine Caldwell's *God's Little Acre* (1933), a despicable text that, because it exposed the poverty and vice of the rural South, and because it reveled in its characters' illicit sex lives, became a best-seller. The obscenity charges brought against it helped sales—the judge's decision appears as an appendix to the fifth and later printings. The novel was received well in the North, where reviewers applauded its portrayal of the real life of the rural South, and quite poorly in the South, where it was seen to be pandering to the worst stereotypes of Southern life. A sample from the text: one black man tells another of peeping in a white woman's window: "'What did you see, nigger? The moon rising?' 'What I saw made me just want to get right straightaway down on my hands and knees and lick something.'"[125] Or this description in the voice of the narrator, from whom we are to construct an implied author: "In the mill streets of the Valley town the breasts of girls were firm and erect. The cloth they wore under the blue lights clothed their bodies, but beneath the covering the motions of erect breasts were like the quick movements of hands in unrest. In the Valley towns beauty was begging, and the hunger of strong men was like the whimpering of beaten women" (100). This eroticization of the beaten woman has no balancing representation; in fact, the women themselves agree. Griselda's husband, Buck, likes to kiss "and things like that" (260) but her lover is different and better, as she explains to her father-in-law, because he really understands women. "'Will took my clothes off and tore them to pieces. . . . I didn't know I wanted him to do it before, but after that I was certain. After a woman has that done to her once, Pa, she's never the same again. It opens her up, or something. I could never really love another man unless he did that to me.'" For that kind of man, she would be "'like a dog that loves you and follows you around no matter how mean you are to him'" (261).

This is the text's standard approach to sexual and racial politics: it parades stereotypes from one side of the cultural debate as if they were exposés of forbidden knowledge. The regional politics are almost nil. The poor rural folk are just plain stupid. Here is the protagonist, Ty Ty, who is about to spend the rest of the book digging enormous holes on his farm, ruining it for cultivation, looking for gold that of course he never finds. He says to his son: "I wish you had the sense not to listen to what the darkies say. That ain't a thing in the world but superstition. Now, take me, here. I'm scientific. . . . All they know is that talk about diviners and conjurers" (5). Ty Ty's science consists of getting an albino to tell him where to dig; the "symbolism" of the "all-white man" is hard to miss, as is the pure patronizing distance between implied author and character. The problem is not the characters, since similar characters with similar attitudes, predilections, and faults can be found in much literature. The problem is the entire lack of balance. Ty Ty and company have nothing to offer readers except a sense of the readers' own superiority. Some readers mistakenly saw Caldwell as a literary writer in the 1930s because he seemed to be expanding the range of represented reality. As the novelty of his sex scenes wore off, however, his literary reputation suffered. He was not included in any American literature anthologies, not even in the latest Norton Anthology of Southern Literature, much to his die-hard fans' chagrin, and he is seldom taught.[126]

Faulkner's Sound and the Fury (1929) is everything that God's Little Acre is not. Like Toomer's Cane, the structure of the text suggests its cosmopolitan intentions. Four sections, three narrated by characters (Benjy, Quentin, Jason), the fourth by a narrator, each telling and retelling stories of the Compson family, multiply the perspectives, adding and revising and complicating the narrative that readers are required to construct. The reader-writer compact is particularly strong, as it is in much modernist literature, since the text frustrates easy reading, requiring an attention to the text as text. The last image of the novel, in which Benjy is howling because his carriage is circling the square in the wrong direction, is one of the many places the implied author chucks the chin of the knowing reader. When the horses are brought under control and the carriage circles in the right direction, the last sentence reads: "The broken flower drooped over Ben's fist and his eyes were empty and blue and serene again as cornice and facade flowed smoothly once more from left to right, post and tree, window and doorway and signboard each in its ordered place."[127] Only an idiot, in other words, would require a narrative to move in the orderly way of conventional prose fiction, readers scanning across the words from left to right, with everything in its regular place.

The high modernist prose style of *The Sound and the Fury* heightens the novel's heteromorphic effects. As the first (Benjy) section begins, we move from scenes in 1928 to those in 1909 and 1910 and back again, to 1898 and 1899 to 1913 and 1914 and back, and we are given very little explicit information marking these times; the readerly confusion makes them all prismatic refractions of one another, just as the retelling of the stories later in the novel will do again. The dream fugue of Quentin's section (the second), in which reality and fantasy become indistinguishable, in which again episodes decades apart melt into one another, makes for a densely layered sense of intertwined worlds that constantly forces the reader to apprehend the specificity of individual understandings and their inevitable lack of full overlap. And, in the tradition of American literary cosmopolitanism, these innovations are not just in the service of form but also work to make Faulkner's political points: "I love [the South] enough to want to cure its faults," he said. "And the only way that I can cure its faults within my capacity, within my own vocation, is to shame it, to criticize, to try to show the difference between its evils, its goods."[128] The South's "baseness" and what makes it "glorious" need to be pointed out in order that it might improve. The fact that baseness and glory coincide in characters such as Quentin and his father, who are both sublime and ridiculous, is part of Faulkner's argument, and the nontraditional narrative style helps him keep both in tension.

Faulkner said that he wrote the first section and was unsatisfied, and so wrote the second, and still was not happy. Even after the four-section novel was published, he felt that the story needed more telling, and added an appendix with more information about the characters, not to mention *Absalom, Absalom* (1936) and the rest of the Yoknapatawpha County novels, all of which bear on this story in one way or another. Faulkner's literary impulse was always additive. He kept adding the perspectives of different family members, of the older generation, of those who travel beyond the local, of those whose race or occupation or gender or family life or some combination of these make them see their local world in different ways.

In Faulkner's novels the characters themselves represent discrepant cosmopolitanisms. When Jason IV complains about his lot in life, he does so while recognizing the difference going to college meant to his father and brother: "I never had time to go to Harvard like Quentin or drink myself into the ground like Father. I had to work," he says, bristling with intrafamily class resentment. "I says no I never had university advantages because at Harvard they teach you how to go for a swim at night without knowing how to swim and at Sewanee they don't even teach you what water is. I says you might send me to the state University; maybe I'll learn how to stop my clock with a nose spray" (109). Jason's deprecatory sarcasm toward himself and others provides a kind of multidimensional commentary on the social distinctions in the text. When Jason says, succinctly, "I have nothing against Jews as an individual," the joke is both his and on him, and his misogynist ravings are both accurate representations of ways of seeing the world and critiques of those ways of seeing. Faulkner's cynical belief in human universality—"Man stinks the same stink no matter where"— was accompanied by a keen sense of the gaps in perspective between different populations and even between siblings.[129]

Of course it is difficult to say with any confidence what exactly Faulkner thought about these issues, because he was fully capable of stating, with the same folksy-oracular insouciance, several completely incommensurable opinions on any given topic. "Art is no part of Southern life," Faulkner says at one point, and at another: "The South . . . was the only part of the country that currently seemed interested in art."[130] The South, he said, echoing the Twelve Southerners, was the "only really authentic region in the United States," in which "a deep indestructible bond still exists between man and his environment" and where there still exists "a common conception of the world, a common view of life, and a common morality."[131] But his fiction asserts the opposite: Dilsey and Jason Compson IV, whose consciousnesses guide the third and fourth sections of the novel, respectively, share very little in the way of conceptions of the world, relations to a natural or cultural environment, or morality. In his fiction, Faulkner's ability to invest in contradictory axioms serves him well, and he succeeds at representing the South in classic cosmopolitan terms, as novel after novel continued to depict more and more groups of contemporary and historical people and their ways of apprehending the world. As fellow Southerner and New Critic Robert Penn Warren put it, "No land in all fiction is more painstakingly analyzed from the sociological standpoint."[132]

I quoted in the introduction Faulkner's statement on universality and the local, how he felt "that the verities these people suffer are universal verities," how people, whatever their race, suffer, aspire, act foolishly, and triumph in the same way. "That is, his struggle is against his own heart, against—with the hearts of his fellows, and with his background." In this sense, Faulkner said, there is no such thing as a regional novel. But again, his fiction, while it makes manifest this sense of universal verity, shows that the opposite is equally true. The characters all feel anguish, for instance, but Jason's anguish is almost always an occasion for high comedy, while Dilsey's is meant to be fully dignified. The anguish of Caroline, the hypochondriac mother, is not to be taken very seriously, while Quentin's finally suicidal anguish, or Caddy's anguished desire to see her daughter, are quite serious indeed. The meaning of these characters' distress arises from their particular, embedded social lives, from their specific relation to local facts.

Irving Howe has written that Faulkner's fiction, like that of Caldwell, Ransom, Tate, and Warren, "was conceived in an explosive mixture of provincialism and cosmopolitanism, tradition and modernity," that it was in dialogue with the European literary tradition and Northern literary ideas.[133] "Left to itself, a regional consciousness is not likely to result in anything but a tiresome romanticizing of the past and thereby a failure to understand the present," he continues, so that Faulkner's work, like the best Southern literature, could only come into being in a region "already cracking under alien influences" (26). Faulkner's "explosive mixture" in *The Sound and the Fury* is one of the finest enactments of literary cosmopolitanism we have, a novel that, from its ability to insert half a dozen sociolects in a single sentence to its restless inability to announce the end of its quest for completeness, asks readers to add, incorporate, multiply, contextualize, recontextualize, supplement, juxtapose, augment, and complicate, a novel that is driven by and incites an unquenchable desire for a fully cosmopolitan understanding. "Can a person really avoid judgments or value systems?" Faulkner was asked by a psychiatrist at the University of Virginia, and he answered: "He can as long as he is a writer. I think the writer is a perfect case of split personality."[134] To a graduate student in the same year he offered a more explicit explanation, in words that are as central to the American literary tradition as any: "I doubt if the writer's asking anyone to sympathize, to choose sides. That is the reader's right. What the writer's asking is compassion, understanding. . . . It's not to choose sides at all" (276–77).

The Passport to This World:
Harlem, Hester Street, and Beyond

The fictions written by members of racial and ethnic minorities in the 1920s tended to be vehemently cosmopolitan and were often as closely tied to a specific geographic locale as classic local color. Mourning Dove (Hum-Ishu-Ma)'s *Cogewea: The Half-Blood* (1927), though it fails in many ways as a literary text, works hard at a cosmopolitan balance of the competing interests of whites and Indians, of men and women, of settlers and natives, and stays close to the Pend d'Oreille River in eastern Washington. It is, finally, however, a "meller-dramy," in which the good-hearted but humble suitor and the rich nasty suitor fill their respective roles, both receiving their just reward.[135] The book resolves itself when the "half-blood" protagonist and her "half-blood" fiancé, unfairly ostracized by both whites and Indians, get together in a "zone of [their] own," inherit a pile of money, and face an exceedingly bright future.

Hum-Ishu-Ma was attempting a literary novel, with regular, if heavy-handed, oscillations of perspective and value, and references to Longfellow and other literary lights (the heroine also wonders, when the not-yet-exposed evil Easterner proposes marriage, whether she has found what she always wanted, "a husband who loved books" [137]). The protagonist Cogewea has the blood of both races and the ability to see the merits and problems in both cultures. She has a sentimental relation to books, but she maintains a naïve one toward nature, as she explains to the Easterner Densmore: "Birds and squirrels are good company. The wild creatures are primitive and are closer to the creative spirit than we imagine. I love them!" (83). The Eastern whites are blind to the values of the West, the Indians to the whites, both Indians and white to the special perspective of the half-bloods, and the novel regularly seesaws among these various claims.

Cogewea explains that "the whites cannot authentically chronicle our habits and customs. They can hardly get at the truth" (94). But Jim chides her, saying, "You sure hand it to the pale faces steamin' hot. . . . You've got to have your speil" (94). Speaking of the ravages of alcohol, the narrator tells us: "This is the heritage of the white man's civilization, forced—like the opium traffic of China—upon a weaker people by the bayonets of commercial conquest. It over-shadows all of the good resultant from the 'higher' life" (40). Moments later it is not simply the whites that are the problem but both civilizations: "Thus the primitive and the modern are ever at variance; neither comprehending or understanding the other" (40). So far, so good. But then the novel ends with a much more exclusive view—Cogewea and her new husband decide that their own zone, that of the half-breed, is inaccessible to anyone else, primitive, modern, Indian, white. Because of their special perspective between two worlds, they are left with not the whole world but simply their own special, isolated province. The novel fails, finally, with this argument that provides its resolution. The problem is not so much that the attempt at balance is figured by the special perspective of the "half-bloods," but that the author suggests we cannot share it, that it is available only to those in the "zone." It finally reneges on its literary promise to broaden the cosmopolitanism of its readers. And it is not, finally, a particularly compelling novel for this reason.[136]

Mike Gold's *Jews without Money* (1930) fails in another way. The majority of the memoir/novel represents the tenement life of immigrant Jews in New York's Hester Street ghetto with a wealth of detail and interpolated stories. Alfred Kazin likens Gold's lists of people and types ("pimps, gangsters, and red-nosed bums; peanut politicians, pugilists in sweaters; tinhorn sports and tall longshoremen in overalls") to Whitman's "inventories of the American scene," and the great strength of the book is its inclusiveness.[137] More than Abraham Cahan or his contemporary Anzia Yezierska, Gold tried to represent the full variety of the life in this specific locale. While *Cogewea* makes an argument for half-bloods as the only true cosmopolitans, Gold in the end argues that Communists are the only ones that see the whole world. The majority of the text oscillates between a love for the culture of the ghetto and disgust at the degradations of its poverty. The penultimate chapter ends with the protagonist's father telling him: "It's better to be dead in this country than not to have money," and making him promise to become rich. "This is my one hope now!" the father says. "I am a greenhorn, but you are an American! You will have it easier than I; you will have luck in America!" (302). His son is less sanguine. "'Yes, poppa,' I said, trying to smile at him. But I felt older than he; I could not share his naïve optimism; my heart sank as I remembered the past and thought of the future" (302). This interchange keeps the tension between the generational views alive. On the last page, however, after a quick description of years of degrading jobs, the protagonist hears a soapbox Communist speak, and this is the end of the novel:

O workers' Revolution, you brought hope to me, a lonely suicidal boy. You are
the true Messiah. You will destroy the East Side when you come, and build there
a garden for the human spirit.
O Revolution, that forced me to think, to struggle and to live.
O great beginning!

There is no ambiguity here, no irony, no further oscillations are expected or allowed. The truth has appeared and destroyed the literary. It would be possible,
of course, to end a novel with a protagonist finding a new Messiah in ways that
keep the tensions in the text alive, but it does not happen here; the novel turns
out to be simply a long preface to this little piece of didacticism, and Gold's career from then on, as a columnist for the *Daily Worker* and the *People's World,*
would consist of equally uncomplicated rehearsals of Party ideology. The ending is absolutely unsatisfying in literary terms because of its failed cosmopolitanism, even as it invokes the world.

Yezierska's *Bread Givers* (1925), a coming-of-age novel also set in the Hester
Street Jewish ghetto, is somewhat more successful. The novel is a hodgepodge
of styles—Ammons lists realism, fairy tale, melodrama, exposé, and rags-to-
riches myth; we can add local color—in which the protagonist comes to acquire
a cosmopolitan relation to her own assimilation and heritage.[138] Yezierska's
characters in this novel and elsewhere are swept up in the processes of modernization, including the forces of Americanization. Sarah Smolensky grows up
in a household dominated by a tyrannical rabbinical father, much like Al Jol-
son's father in *The Jazz Singer* (1927), except less intelligent, more selfish, and ir-
redeemable. "Since men were the only people who counted with God, Father
not only had the best room for himself, for his study and prayers, but also the
best eating of the house. The fat from the soup and the top of the milk went
always to him."[139] The father refuses to work, being a rabbinical scholar, and refuses to let his daughters marry because he does not want to lose their income.
The landlady screams "*Schnorrer!*" at him and his daughters live in fear and open
resentment. His traditionalism is shown to be more self-justification than belief
when he is snookered into a bad business deal—he has been sold a grocery store
in New Jersey, complete with stock, in what looks like a cushy deal until the
stock turns out to be displays of empty boxes. Sarah, called *Blut-und-Eisen,*
"blood and iron," is an entrepreneur from a young age who manages, unlike her
father, to be successful at it, and then to get an education and assimilate. She is
modern where her father is traditional, and open where he is closed; thus we
have a structure that veers, as Ammons notes, toward the melodramatic.

The novel is not a simple advertisement for modernity, however. Sarah, like
her father, is a lover of books, and thus from the start has her own ties to tradition. Although she wanted nothing more than to leave her traditional home,

while she is at college she constantly bemoans the fact that it leaves her "alone, alone" (208). She also finds that the moment of triumphant personhood she at first felt as a college student does not last long, so that shortly she is asking again, "Will I never lift myself to be a person among people?" (220). She graduates from college and moves into her own apartment and has another momentary sense of triumph. She has become a teacher and thereby fulfilled her desire to "be a person" in American terms, and she has acquired the apartment with its clean, white walls that she has been dreaming about for years. "This was the honeymoon of my career! I celebrated it alone with myself. I celebrated in my room, my first clean, empty room. In the evening, when I sat down to meals, I enjoyed myself as with the grandest company" (241). She should be happy, but instead is rife with doubt, in part because she has, in fact, no company. Her father's house was too crowded, but her own is too empty. And as Sarah oscillates between a romantic idealization of men and proud self-sufficiency several times during the novel, so the larger structure of her life moves from a rejection of her father's teachings to modified acceptance. Her father had always preached that "a woman without a man is less than nothing," and indeed it is only when she becomes involved with Hugh Seelig, the principal of her school, that she begins to be truly happy, implicitly proving him right.

She also vacillates between pride in and derision for her new profession, sometimes feeling that she and her colleagues are just "peddling their little bit of education for a living, the same as any pushcart peddler" (270). These oscillations about the value of her profession and her need for a man are related to her changing relation to her own Jewishness. On her first "date" with Hugh he asks her what she remembers of Poland, where they were both born, and she says nothing. As they part, he says, "Next time when we are together we must . . . try to remember more about Poland" (279). Hugh decides that he wants to take Hebrew lessons from Sarah's father, not because he is religious, but because he is interested in his own ethnicity. He wants to "remember Poland" and learn Hebrew as a way of acquiring a conscious heritage, a thing of value not as a blueprint for living, but because it is a kind of belonging, in two senses of the word: it is a possession for the individual and provides the basis of an imagined community.

Walter Benn Michaels has argued that in marrying Seelig, Sarah would effect "the restoration of the child to the father," and in the process, he claims, "Jewishness is made Jewishness again."[140] But it is Jewishness of a very different sort. In the final scene in the book, Sarah has decided to take in her now-homeless father, and immediately begins to resent him. He starts chanting his misogynist verses from the Torah and she feels she is losing her sense of self and her home. Hugo reassures her, "with easy enthusiasm . . . like a Tolstoyan," and gives her another way to understand her own relation to the tradition her father represents so vigorously. They walk down the hallway, away from the father's chanting, which "lowered and grew fainter till we could not hear the words anymore" (296–97). This, Hugo suggests by tightening his grip on Sarah's arm, is what it is all about. "We lingered for the mere music of the fading chant" (297), Sarah tells us. What is valuable about tradition is not its ethical or regulative function in one's life, in other words, but its aesthetic value. In rejecting the words and appreciating the music of her father's chant, in learning Hebrew as a secular rather than a sacred project, they reappropriate tradition and ethnicity as a set of aesthetic objects. The daughter is not restored to the father, but the father is, in a form he would not appreciate, restored to the daughter.

This resolution is one that readers had been prepared for by their own activity, appropriating Jewish culture as a series of aesthetic objects in the very act of reading Yezierska's text. And in a final coda, even this seeming resolution is left open. Hugo is happy with his modern, assimilated, secular aestheticization of his ethnic heritage, but Sarah is less sanguine. She wonders if this or any other rapprochement is possible: "I felt the shadow still there, over me," she says in the last lines. "It wasn't just my father, but the generations who made my father whose weight was still upon me" (297). The literary conclusion is not resolution but an openness to the fullness of history, an acceptance of the impossibility of resolution.

The aesthetic reappropriation of cultural difference (which is at the heart of our own multiculturalism as well) became common in the 1920s. *The Jazz Singer* works the same way, with the assimilated Jack Robin learning to appreciate his father's work as a cantor only after seeing a certain Rabbi Rosenblatt in Chicago sing a selection of sacred songs in concert, in a theater, with an applauding audience rather than a worshiping congregation. He goes home afterward, ready to approach his father for the first time in years. His mother is open to his jazzy ways, but his father is still closed, and when he yells at his father that his songs mean as much to his audience as his father's do to his congregation, the father kicks him out of the house again. The father will not consider his culture simply part of the aesthetic array of American possibility; he understands the depth of the rejection of tradition required by cultural pluralism. The father dies, however, and the son, as Michael Rogin has noted, is given the ability "to have it all, Jewish past and American future, Jewish mother and gentile wife."[141] Yezierska's heroine does not get quite the fantasy resolution of the Hollywood hero; her literary version of this story keeps past and future, Jew and gentile, in tension, acknowledging the weight of generations and their ongoing cultural transformation, and the continuing costs as well as the benefits they incur.

⇌

A very similar literary cosmopolitanism is at work in the major texts of the Harlem Renaissance. Jean Toomer's *Cane* (1923) is structured along these lines. The first section is a collection of poems and poetic narratives that are local color representations of rural Southern black life, the second section a collection of representations of Northern (or near-Northern) urban black life, and the third section a longer story of the return of a Northern, urbanized African American as a missionary educator to his ancestral South. But rather than offering a solution to the problems of rural violence and poverty and urban alienation, this third section, as Lucinda H. MacKethan has noted, "leaves only the ambiguities clear."[142] This structure follows Toomer's own experience, for it was in moving to Georgia to teach that he came upon his literary vocation. Moving to the South transformed him, but, he wrote, "My point of view has not changed; it has deepened, it has widened."[143] Seeing the rural South encouraged him to enter "the world of writers and literature. I saw it as my passport to this world."[144]

Toomer, like the Southern Agrarians, the folklorists, and the "revolt" novelists, wrote in protest against the standardization of culture. He saw the decline of interest in spirituals as one of many indications that folk culture was dying.

> I learned that the Negroes of the town objected to the spirituals. They called them "shouting." They had victrolas and player-pianos. So, I realized with deep regret that the spirituals, meeting ridicule, die out. With Negroes also the trend was towards a small town and towards the city—and industry and commerce and the machines. The folk-spirit was walking in to die on the modern desert. That spirit was so beautiful. Its death was so tragic.[145]

The first section of *Cane* was thus an act of recuperation. Even so, this section oscillates between the celebration of spiritual and pastoral moments and the recognition of brutality and oppression. Poems such as "Georgia Dusk," "Reapers," "November Cotton Flower," and "Face" erupt with moments of violence and dread amidst invocations of mythic African pasts and paeans to the folk spirit and folk sensuality.

Reviews of *Cane* recognized Toomer's attempt as literary rather than documentary, as did Waldo Frank's introduction. "This book is the South," Frank claimed. "I do not mean that *Cane* covers the South or is the South's full voice. Merely this: A poet has arisen among our American youth who has known how to turn essences and materials of his Southland into the essences and materials of literature."[146] Alfred Kreymborg gave him the cosmopolitan blessing, writing that Toomer is "fascinated by the larger, rather than the parochial interests of the human race."[147] And other reviewers agreed, even while displaying their own provincialisms, as in this case from the *New York Herald Tribune*:

> It can perhaps be safely said that the Southern Negro, at least, has found an authentic lyric voice in Jean Toomer, a voice and a heart, likewise, that is synchronized with the aspirations, the hopes and fears of the genuine darky. There is

nothing of the theatrical coon-strutting high-brown, none of the conventional dice-throwing, chicken stealing nigger of musical comedy and burlesque in the pages of Cane.[148]

This was meant as a compliment to Toomer's wider purview. W. E. B. DuBois found Toomer cosmopolitan almost to a fault: "Toomer does not impress me as one who knows his Georgia," DuBois wrote in his review of Cane, "but he does know human beings."[149] William Stanley Braithwaite claimed that in Cane Toomer demonstrated "an artist's passion and sympathy for life, its hurts, its sympathies, its desires, its joys, its defeats and strange yearnings," suggesting the text's oscillations. "Cane is a book of gold and bronze, of dusk and flame, of ecstasy and pain."[150]

Toomer famously refused to be marketed as a "Negro author," because he had, he claimed, "Scotch, Welsh, German, English, French, Dutch, Spanish," and either "Negro" or "Negro and Indian" blood (at another time he added Jewish and subtracted Scotch and Spanish), and claimed that he had "strived," in his writing, "for a spiritual fusion analogous to the fact of racial intermingling."[151] That oft-quoted line has much to do with the literary success of Cane and Toomer's failure to achieve literary success again. Shortly after completing Cane, the author came under the sway of G. I. Gurdjieff's philosophy of wholeness, in which the fragmented parts of one's being are fused. The philosophy is one that takes differences between East and West, of the various religious traditions, of conflicting cultural values, to be so much illusion, masking a deeper reality, one that Gurdjieffian techniques can help adherents achieve. It thus has a very different aim than literary cosmopolitanism; instead of holding cultural conflict in dynamic balance, Gurdjieffian thought would have us transcend those conflicts altogether. Everything Toomer wrote after his Gurdjieffian conversion was subliterary and virtually unpublishable. The challenge Lewis offers to Kabnis— "Can't hold them, can you? Master; slave. Soil; and the overarching heavens. Dusk; dawn. They fight and bastardize you"[152]—may be a challenge to fuse antinomies into unity, as Gurdjieff suggested, but in the story itself, these forces maintain their conflictual balance: this was the literary challenge Toomer achieved in Cane and then never again.

Toomer's text helped inaugurate the Harlem Renaissance, along with Claude McKay's book of poems, Harlem Shadows (1922), followed the next year by Jessie Redmon Fauset's first novel, There is Confusion (1924). Known as one of the midwives of the Renaissance for her work as literary editor of the Crisis, the official magazine of the NAACP edited by DuBois, Fauset encouraged and published Toomer, McKay, Countee Cullen, George Schuyler, Nella Larsen, and Langston Hughes.[153] From the 1920s on, Fauset has been seen to be clearly situated on one side of the ideological fractures of the New Negro movement, on the opposite side of the fence from Claude McKay, for instance. But if Fauset and McKay disagreed on the most politically appropriate shape for African American fiction and poetry, they agreed at a more fundamental level about the nature of the literary.

Zona Gale, known as a Wisconsin local color writer, provided an introduction to Fauset's *The Chinaberry Tree* (1931), in which she offered a classic regionalist defense of Fauset's subject: Midwesterners, Southerners, New Englanders, and "the uneducated Negro" have all been represented in fiction, Gale writes, but not until Fauset's novels did what would come to be called the black bourgeoisie appear. Gale of course is not entirely correct here; nevertheless she praises Fauset for her "wide interests and her American and European experiences" and her class for its "progress of art and music, science and social life."[154] In her own foreword to the novel, Fauset assures readers that "nothing,—and the Muses themselves would bear witness to this,—has ever been farther from my thought than writing to establish a thesis."[155] This was the third of four novels Fauset published, and the second, *Plum Bun: A Novel without a Moral* (1928), makes the same argument with its subtitle. Fauset's first novel, *There is Confusion,* like *O Pioneers!* is a parable of cosmopolitan authorship, in which the culmination of the protagonist Joanna's artistic career is a play entitled "The Dance of the Nations." The play has dances representing France, England, and America, and when Joanna comes on the scene, a white woman is dancing three parts to represent America, "one for the white element, one for the black, and one for the red."[156] Joanna replaces her as the dancer representing black America, at first dancing in a mask, later without. She is a big success, but she—and we as readers—are unsatisfied: "In spite of her vogue, her unbelievably decided success, Johanna frequently tasted the depths of ennui. She saw life as a ghastly skeleton and herself feverishly trying to cover up its bare bones with the garish trappings of her art, her lessons, her practice, her press-clippings" (233). The problem is that she is more interested in fame (it is a desire for fame that has driven her throughout the text) than in artistic achievement, more interested in "sensation" (230) than art. And we are meant to think about what such a celebratory dance leaves out of the equation, why dance is not the kind of complex art form literature is.

Fauset argued against the sensational in Negro art by arguing for the representation of a wider cross section of African American society than was available in what she saw as the sensationalist art of writers such as Claude McKay or the white primitivists T. S. Stribling, Waldo Frank, and Carl Van Vechten. Like McKay, in other words, she was determined to broaden the scope of black fiction in her novels. She counseled Toomer to "read voraciously, not only the moderns but the ancients. Get some translations of the Greek poets. Get together enough French to be able to read the imagist poetry of France."[157] She understood, as Deborah McDowell has noted, that "provincialism could be a dragrope around a writer's neck."[158] Like Toomer's refusal to be a Negro author, Fauset's refusal of sensationalism was based on a cosmopolitan understanding of literary art. Dismissed as an Old Crowd reactionary by many in the Renaissance itself and many critics since, interested in the "smiling side" of African American life, Fauset was in fact offering a corrective, as Gale suggested in her introduction, to what she saw as a provincial overemphasis on lower-class life.[159]

One of her antagonists, as I have suggested, was Claude McKay, who attempted his own corrective, his own broadening of the African American literary palette. McKay's texts cover the globe, representing the many cultures of the African Diaspora from Marseilles to the Caribbean to Harlem. Like W. E. B. DuBois's invitation to his reader to ride with him in the Jim Crow car, McKay's texts create a readerly space from which to survey not simply the specificities of black life, but the wider view afforded by traveling through that life.[160] DuBois himself was not a fan. In reviewing *Home to Harlem* (1928), he said that it "for the most part nauseates me, and after the dirtier parts of its filth I feel distinctly like taking a bath."[161] McKay, he felt, had "set out to cater for the prurient demand on the part of white folk for a portrayal in Negroes of that utter licentiousness which conventional civilization holds white folk back from enjoying." The *Pittsburgh Courier,* then the nation's leading black newspaper, agreed: "No book could descend lower and bear the slightest resemblance to literature; and no reputable publisher would dare to print anything more vulgar." And Marcus Garvey attacked him for portraying "looseness, laxity, and immorality."[162] But licentiousness is one of many different relations to sexuality represented in his fictions, and the sense of freedom from civilized restraint enjoyed by some characters is contrasted to a number of other options, good, bad, and ugly. McKay's critique of civilization is, in other words, itself more complex than DuBois and his other detractors suggest.

The vernacular culture represented in *Home to Harlem, Banjo* (1929), and *Banana Bottom* (1933) is contrasted not only to the culture of DuBois and Fauset's black bourgeoisie, but also to the deadening crush of Euro-American civilization, "the ever tightening mechanical organization of modern life."[163] Here is a typical passage on the eponymous Banjo:

That this primitive child, this kinky-headed, big-laughing black boy of the world, did not go down and disappear under the serried crush of trampling white feet; that he managed to remain on the scene, not worldly-wise, not "getting there," yet not machine-made, nor poor-in-spirit like the regimented creatures of civilization, was baffling to civilized understanding. Before the grim, pale rider-down of souls he went his careless way with a primitive hoofing and a grin. (314)

Although Banjo hits on the idea of starting an orchestra to make money in the first few pages of the novel, he does not just play for the money like white musicians: "They played in a hard unsmiling way, and only for sous. Which was doubtless why their playing in general was so execrable. When Banjo turned himself loose and wild playing, he never remembered sous" (40). The careless, big-laughing, grinning primitive is his own antidote to, or at least analgesic for, overcivilization and wage slavery.

And his music is similarly antitoxic to those around him. Ray, the character who represents, among other things, the overcivilized Negro (even to himself), is a "book fellah" who provides the other half of McKay's argument in *Banjo* and in *Home to Harlem*. Banjo has his banjo, and Ray has his pen, and while Ray's educated alienation is contrasted to Banjo's natural integrity, Ray also provides a road map to Banjo's sensibility for McKay's educated readers. Ray finds that music is the quickest and surest route to understanding Banjo's primitive sensibility. "But you're interested in race—I mean race advancement, aren't you?" an activist character asks Ray midway through the novel. "Sure," answers Ray, "but right now there's nothing in the world so interesting to me as Banjo and his orchestra" (92). Ray is interested in the problems of civilization, which he has thought about quite seriously, but more interested in the rewards of primitivism, which he knows less well and to which he finds an introduction in Banjo's world and music.

Influenced by D. H. Lawrence, whom he considered "a spiritual brother," McKay believed, along with Sherwood Anderson, H. L. Mencken, and a host of others in the 1910s and 1920s, that the deadening weight of civilization was choking people's primitive, vital life force.[164] McKay argued, in his fiction and criticism, that African American performative culture escaped this particular dilemma. In his fictional arguments the more "primitive" option tends to win, whether it is all-night dancing versus civilized bedtimes, the "colorful" speech of the uneducated versus the anglicized speech of the overcivilized Negroes, or the banjo and the fiddle versus the player piano and the symphony. McKay does not deny the value of European forms, musical, linguistic, or social, but he tips the balance toward the "earthy people," whose continued existence and continued expression he represents as heroic and salutary.

The argument is not to respect difference, as our own multicultural pieties would have it, but to evaluate. Diasporic African art is not just different from much Western art, McKay argued, it is in some ways better, which is why it is the wave of the future. Joyce Hope Scott has written that with his trickster characters McKay shows that the African American artist must embrace "his cultural heritage," but McKay is making an argument not just about African American artists but about art itself.[165] "Our age is the age of Negro art," McKay wrote in *The Negroes in America* (1923). "The slogan of the aesthetic world is 'Return

to the Primitive.' The Futurists and Impressionists are agreed in turning everything upside-down in an attempt to achieve the wisdom of the primitive Negro."[166] McKay represents the primitive as a progressive future, not as a past to
which we might return. In this he is taking a position contrary to the critique
of African American folk forms made by such "Old School" critics as Fauset
and DuBois, those who saw all primitivist culture as a rejection and refutation
of race progress. In McKay's review of the first all-black Broadway musical
Shuffle Along (1921), he rails against conservative critics who declare that "Negro art . . . must be dignified and respectable like the Anglo-Saxon's before it
can be good. The Negro must get the warmth, color, and laughter out of his
blood, else the white man will sneer at him and treat him with contumely. Happily the Negro retains his joy of living in the teeth of such criticism; and in
Harlem, along Fifth and Lenox avenues, in Marcus Garvey's hall with its ex-
travagant paraphernalia, in his churches and cabarets, he expresses himself with
a zest that is yet to be depicted by a true artist."[167] The argument finally is *against*
an exclusivity that would limit artistic and cultural palettes. McKay tips the balance toward the primitive because it is the primitive that is being excluded by
machine civilization.

In 1972, Sherley Anne Williams discussed the way McKay used black music
as "a symbol of liberation from a stifling respectability and materialistic conventionality which have an odor of decay about them," but found—wrongly, in
my opinion—that McKay "is content with implying this conflict through the
use of the jazz life as a framework."[168] Kathy J. Ogren has discussed, more aptly
albeit briefly, how McKay uses jazz clubs in *Home to Harlem* to "establish an open,
emotional, and participatory ambiance" and to create "an Afro-American aesthetic based on folk and working-class culture."[169] But while it is true that
McKay argues for the progressive force of primitivism, he also argues for the
continued value of Tolstoy and any number of other European artists, expressive and intellectual forms, and cultural values (the novels have lists of European
and American literary authors sprinkled throughout). McKay's argument is not
Afrocentric, in other words, or even, finally Afro-Americocentric; it is, I want
to show, cosmopolitan. That is, he exercises a kind of connoisseurship of cultural
value, picking through the best that the world has thought, written, composed,
and improvised, and he champions African Diaspora culture from the standpoint
of such cosmopolitan connoisseurship. Ross Posnock finds in these novels a "stasis," a representation of McKay's "knotted psyche" in the "malaise of [his] self-
divided hero."[170] I argue instead that McKay divides these novels between two
protagonists in order to represent not stasis, but dynamic, cosmopolitan balance.
McKay's aesthetic is fully in line with the cosmopolitan mainstream of American literature. He demonstrates that he knows both the great Russian novelists
and the blues, both white and black culture, both American and European, both

upper and lower classes. He shows that he knows what the race scientists, the anthropologists, the sociologists, and so on are saying, and thus offers a synthetic overview of African Americans' relation to civilization, and at the same time, of course, an advertisement for literary art.

In the opening chapter of *Banjo*, Banjo both declares his intention to start an orchestra as a way to make a living and announces his aesthetics: "I *is* an artist," (8) he says, and McKay agrees. Banjo has arrived in Marseilles and is one among the "great vagabond host of jungle-like Negroes trying to scrape a temporary existence from the macadamized surface of this great Provençal port" (68). Banjo assumes (as does McKay) that "the American darky is the performing fool of the world today," and this is true at least in part because of a lack of true economic opportunity, because whatever work is available is hard, unremunerative, and deadening. "We kain't afford to choose," Banjo tells his educated friend Ray, "because we ain't born and growed up like the choosing people" (319). But unlike most of those who cannot afford to choose, Banjo has an avocation he recognizes can earn him a living, which is more than just coincidence. McKay argues that African American performance is in demand the world over because it expresses the "irrepressible exuberance and legendary vitality of the black race," and that exuberance and vitality are at least in part due to the fact that the black race has not been fully deadened by civilized living.[171]

Several of McKay's poems that were published in Alain Locke's *The New Negro* (1925)—without McKay's permission—express his aesthetic at the time he was writing his first novels. "Like a Strong Tree," for instance, contains the lines:

> Like a strong tree that reaches down, deep, deep,
> For sunken water, fluid underground,
> Where the great-ringed unsightly blind worms creep,
> And queer things of the nether world abound:
> So I would live in imperial growth,
> Touching the surface and the depth of things,
> Instinctively responsive unto both. (134)

As Melvin Dixon has pointed out, this poem states McKay's artistic credo and expresses Ray's struggle, in *Home to Harlem* and *Banjo*, to negotiate the high and the low, cultivation and spontaneity, intellect and instinct.[172] Ray finally learns, haltingly and partially, to embrace both aspects of culture, to create stories out of "the fertile reality around him."[173] Dixon is right in seeing in this McKay's "critique of the cultural misdirection of the Harlem Renaissance, which favors portrayals of bourgeois respectability and assimilation" (49), and right that the music in these texts functions as both proof and harbinger of a common base for black art. But the poem goes further than this as well, as does another poem in the Locke collection, "Baptism," to which I will return in a moment. These poems embrace both "the queer things of the nether world" and the surface, both the conventional and unconventional.

In his first two novels, McKay examines the high and the low, the cultivated and the instinctual not just in music, but in speech patterns, eating practices, sexual mores, and ways of understanding black experience, through a somewhat schematic set of personifications. In *Home to Harlem* and *Banjo* he seems more interested in providing a Whitmanian catalog of types, positions, and roles than he is in plot or even character development. In both cases we are given the educated versus the uneducated, the happy primitive versus the anxious bourgeois, but also a series of minor characters representing other possibilities. Some of these (and they never fare very well) are shown to be completely unconscious, unthinkingly coming up against racism, economic hardship, and crime, unable or unwilling to think about the nature of the social world into which they have been born and through which they move. Bugsy in *Banjo* and Zeddy in *Home to Harlem,* for instance, are shown to be primitive and instinctual enough, but tainted, corrupted by civilized values, by the desire for money, prestige, luxury, leisure. "Primitive peoples could be crude and coarse, but never vulgar," McKay writes in *Banjo,* and Bugsy and Zeddy are vulgar. "Vulgarity was altogether a scab of civilization."[174] Other characters stand in for forms of black radicalism and black conservatism, as representatives of the parties of race pride, race uplift, radical individualism, and the like.

Readers are encouraged, in the first instance, to read in sympathy with the seeming protagonist, and so Jake and Banjo, with whom the novels open, are our first frames of reference. Readers are asked to enter into their enjoyment of the low life. They are, after all, "handsome, happy brutes" (*Banjo,* 48), and the narrator imperatively enjoins us to shake our things to the music they make and to which they dance:

> Shake to the loud music of life playing to the primeval round of life. Rough rhythm of darkly-carnal life. Strong surging flux of profound currents forced into narrow channels. Play that thing! . . . Sweet dancing thing of primitive joy, perverse pleasure, prostitute ways, many-colored variations of the rhythm, savage, barbaric, refined—eternal rhythm of the mysterious, magical, magnificent. . . . Oh, Shake That Thing! (*Banjo,* 57–58)

The language here mimics not just the tempo and syncopation of the music but its disregard for civilized conventions. It revels in its primitivisms—"savage, barbaric"—and yet stylistically it is strenuously modern. Such passages of primitivist absorption announce their own modernism in their abandonment of syntax, in their neologizing freedom, and in the combination of vernacular and literary diction. McKay rejected the most modern innovations in poetic form in his own poetry, believing that, as Wayne Cooper puts it, "'real' poetry adhered to Victorian poetic conventions, and . . . the modernists substituted novelty for discipline and incomprehensibility for beauty."[175] But in these passages he grants himself the modernists' freedom from formal convention and offers readers a verbal representation of the freedom from "civilized" constraints: "Oh, 'blues,' 'blues,' 'blues.' Red moods, black moods, golden moods. Curious syncopated, slipping-over into one mood, back-sliding back to the first mood. Humming in harmony, barbaric harmony, joy-drunk, chasing out the shadow of the moment before" (*Home to Harlem,* 54). Such passages are supposed to give readers some taste of the "joy-drunk" response to music the characters feel, and the more primitive those characters are the less trammeled the appreciation.

With the entrance of Ray, we are asked to rethink our sympathies, since Ray seems so clearly to be an authorial stand-in. He has the education that most of McKay's readers would have had, and he has the diction, seriousness of purpose, and relation to meaning making associated with literary communities. Here, just a few pages later, is a sample of Ray's thought: "But it was not by Tolstoy's doctrines that he was touched. It was depressing to him that the energy of so many great intellects of the modern world had been, like Tolstoy's, vitiated in the futile endeavor to make the mysticism of Jesus serve the spiritual needs of a world-conquering and leveling machine civilization" (66). At first this remarkable difference in mood makes us confront the difference in value that the vagabonds and primitives represent, making them appear frivolous and, in fact, somewhat unsatisfied with the vicissitudes of their lives. This is a regular oscillation in the novels, and is followed by others when Ray, enamored of the freedom and vitality of Banjo or Jake, sings their praises and abandons his own beliefs, and we are asked to reevaluate them once more. Whatever our first relation to the primitivist characters might have been—slumming, escapism, vicarious experience—after we approach these characters anew through Ray's emulative desire, we realize that the debate is being staged not so that we might take sides, but so that we might comprehend the debate. Ray, as our guide, moves back and forth and among the various possibilities: respect for an "African" mode of existence, envy of its carefree vitality, exultation at his own brief experiences of it, distress at its impossibility in the context of corrupt civilization, distaste for the ignorance that seems to be a prerequisite for it, irritation at its headlong refusal to contemplate tomorrow. These perspectives on the "joy-drunk" mode of existence are all represented as valid, and their orchestration for our benefit is not meant to resolve into a vote for or against a particular cultural style. "Dance down the Death of these days, the Death of these ways in shaking that thing," the "shake that thing!" passage in *Banjo* continues, "jungle jazzing, Orient wriggling, civilized stepping. Shake that thing!" Jungle jazzing and civilized stepping, with a little Oriental wriggling thrown in for good measure—a cosmopolitan inclusiveness is at the heart of the novel's ethos.

But this does not mean that anything goes. Banjo's music, Ray's angst, and Malty's shiftlessness at one level may amount to the same thing, after all—they all serve to condemn "leveling machine civilization." But we are not asked to approve of Banjo's lackadaisical energy over and above Ray's literary desires, any more than we are asked to condemn the various pimps or Marxists who make their appearances. We are asked to acquire, and the novel provides precisely this for us, a cosmopolitan overview of the positions offered by the text. And that cosmopolitan overview is sanctioned by the novel's literary genealogy. As critics have long noted, McKay's primary affiliation was with the literary life rather than with a specific racial program.

Toward the end of *Banjo*, Banjo pronounces a version of the cosmopolitan perspective in a speech about the war. The world went crazy, he says

> and one half of it done murdered the other half to death. But the wul' ain't gone a-mourning forevah because a that. Nosah. The wul' is jazzing to fohgit. . . . The wul' is just keeping right on with that nacheral sweet jazzing of life. And Ise jest gwine on right along jazzing with the wul'. The wul' goes round and round and I keeps right on gwine around with it.

Banjo sees the great whirl of life transcending the lines of national difference, and the job of individuals is to comprehend and live the fullness of life. Banjo's diction and predilections are primitive, but his sentiment is cosmopolitan.

In fact, McKay's interest in the question of the primitive is itself literary and cosmopolitan. The argument about primitivism and civilization is at the heart of the cosmopolitan novel of the 1920s, as we can see in a short roster of the writers who took it as an important subject in their fiction: the other Harlem Renaissance authors, Hemingway, Fitzgerald, Faulkner, Cather, Eliot, Wharton, Van Vechten, Dell, Lewis, Anderson. Take this well-known passage from Lawrence's *Women in Love* (1920), in which Birkin contemplates a statue of an African woman:

> She knew what he himself did not know. She had thousands of years of purely sensual, purely unspiritual knowledge behind her. . . . Thousands of years ago, that which was imminent in himself must have taken place in these Africans; the goodness, the holiness, the desire for creation must have lapsed. . . . Is our day of creative life finished? Does there remain to us only the strange awful afterwards of the knowledge in dissolution, the African knowledge, but different in us, who are blond and blue-eyed from the North?[176]

In Sherwood Anderson's *Poor White* (1920), black dockworkers throw parcels and words around, feeling their bodies and work and words all in harmony and "unconscious love of inanimate things lost to whites."[177] In *Dark Laughter* (1925) Anderson, himself influenced by Lawrence, uses the free laughter of the unciv- ilized Negro soul to provide ethical commentary on the ridiculousness of civ- ilized morality. For Lawrence and Anderson, primitive vitality and primitive wisdom had been lost, and theirs was a primitivism drenched in nostalgia. For McKay the cultural worlds of the primitive and the civilized coexisted, min- gled, created hybrids, and would continue to do so. McKay loved Lawrence, he wrote in his autobiography, because he represented "all of the ferment and tor- ment and turmoil, the hesitation and hate and alarm, the sexual inquietude and the incertitude of this age, and the psychic and romantic groping for a way out."[178]

McKay works in his fiction to the same effect, multiplying the ambiguities and uncertainties of contemporary civilization. At one point in *Banjo,* Ray grins to himself "at the civilized world of nations, all keeping their tiger's claws sharp and strong under the thin cloak of international amity and awaiting the first fa- vorable opportunity to spring" (135), thus showing civilization itself to be sav- age. The average white man, he muses, can be violently seized at any moment by his "guarded, ancient treasure of national hates" (135), and can revert to sav- agery. Ray "hated civilization," McKay tells us later in the novel. "Once in a mo- ment of bitterness he had said in Harlem, 'Civilization is rotten.' And the more he traveled and knew of it, the more he felt the truth of that bitter outburst" (163). And yet, at the same time, the carefree, laughing primitives live in a "slimy garbage-strewn little space of hopeless hags, hussies, touts, and cats and dogs for- ever chasing one another about in nasty imitation of the residents," their vaunted sensuality simply "low-down proletarian love, stinking, hard, cruel" (87). Even the music that so liberates Ray's senses and sense of human possibility can, as in the parties at Gin-head Suzy's apartment in Brooklyn, make for brawls and ug- liness (*Home to Harlem,* 53–74). Civilization is rotten, but so is primitive life. And just as the primitive life is full of benefits, so is the civilized: "The whites have done the blacks some great wrongs," McKay wrote elsewhere, "but they also have done some good. They have brought to them the benefits of modern civ- ilization" (*Long Way from Home,* 349).

These multiple valuations point to the real moral of the story, which is that the truly educated person is one with an aesthetic cosmopolitan openness to difference, someone with a broad enough purview to comprehend the myriad cultural forms that make up the world in which Ray and Banjo, McKay and his readers all live. Sometimes the arguments between characters are resolved quite explicitly in favor of a broader overview. In *Banjo,* for instance, a French bar- tender and a Senegalese student argue about the fate of Negroes in America, the bartender saying the African Americans are the most privileged and pro- gressive in the world, the student saying that they are lynched and Jim-Crowed into submission. Ray takes the overview: "You are both right," he says, and goes on to explain that both the facts of oppression as the student understands them and the facts of progress as the bartender understands them are true. This scene is followed by one in which Ray argues with his friend Goosey about the meaning of interracial marriage, and there Goosey is given the chance to up the cosmopolitan ante. Ray gives Goosey the cosmopolitan Marxist argument about class, to which Goosey replies:

> To me the most precious thing about human life is difference. Like flowers in a garden, different kinds for different people to love. I am not against miscegenation. It produces splendid and interesting types. But I should not crusade for it because I should hate to think of a future in which the identity of the black race in the Western World should be lost in miscegenation. (*Banjo*, 208)

The point is not to acquire some kind of predetermined cosmopolitan correctness, but to develop a habit of cosmopolitanism perspectivalism.

McKay announces, in a poem from the mid-1920s, "Baptism," that he will go to hell and back for his poetry:

> In the furnace let me go alone;
> Stay you without in terror of the heat.
> I will go naked in—for thus 'tis sweet—
> Into the weird depths of the hottest zone.
> I will not quiver in the frailest bone,
> You will not note a flicker of defeat;
> My heart shall not tremble its fate to meet,
> Nor mouth give utterance to any moan.
> The yawning oven spits forth fiery spears;
> Red aspish tongues shout wordlessly my name.
> Desire destroys, consumes my mortal fears,
> Transforming me into a shape of flame.
> I will come out, back to your world of tears,
> A stronger soul within a finer frame. (*New Negro*, 134)

That these verses equate hell and desire, sex and removal from the world, is not surprising, given McKay's regular if somewhat muted defenses of homosexuality. McKay, like many other writers of fiction at the time, adopted the necessary role of one who comprehends the social proprieties and the advance of civilization but who understands them as contingent rather than natural and who can survey all the realms, including the hells, that propriety tries to keep at bay. This ideal is much closer to someone Ray is in the process of becoming than to someone like Banjo, of course. The model is someone like the readers of these texts after reading them, someone, indeed, like McKay, who knows, appreciates, and can experience the primitive and the civilized, the hetero and the homo, the licit and the illicit, someone who has the cosmopolitan chops to hang with the band and to assess novelistic representations of hanging with the band. "Ray had found that to be educated, black, and his instinctive self was something of a job to put over," McKay writes, and that is the chore he sets for his readers as well.

Ray, Jake, and Banjo represent what James Clifford has called "discrepant cosmopolitanisms," in that they all have a cosmopolitan view of the world, made up in each case of a variety of perspectives, positions, and experiences.[179] McKay's *Banana Bottom* is full of discrepant cosmopolitanisms: Crazy Bow plays classical European music, American Negro spirituals, New World dance music, and West Indian folk music. Squire Gensir is a British aristocrat who collects Anancy stories, puts together dictionaries of slang, attends native religious observances, and collects the "songs, jammas, shey-sheys, and breakdowns," and any other peasant music he can find: the "songs of the fields, the draymen's songs, love songs, satiric ditties of rustic victims of elemental passions" (71). Gensir is not the ultimate cosmopolitan, however. "Being an enthusiast of the simple life, he was like many enthusiasts, apt to underestimate the underlying contradictions that may inhere in his more preferable way of life" (176). Gensir mentors the protagonist Bita as she comes to terms with the relation of her British musical training to her life in the Jamaican countryside and as she deals with sex and sexual transgression. In the end she decides, however, that "love and music were divine things, but none so rare as the pure flight of the mind into the upper realms of thought" (314).

McKay suggests that, in our pure flights of mind, we as the literary community can be the true cosmopolitans, the ones who empathize with all these characters and understand their hell and their glory. For those who would complain that such Enlightenment-inflected cosmopolitanism is itself ideologically saturated, indeed imperialistic, McKay might have responded, in the words of his poem "Like a Strong Tree," "So I would live in imperial growth, / Touching the surface and the depth of things, / Instinctively responsive unto both" (*New Negro*, 134). Addison Gayle Jr. is right to say that McKay's "wandering from one city to another" brought to his work "a cosmopolitan perspective that few of his contemporaries possessed," and we can say that McKay, who cites not just the instinctive primitivist Lawrence but also Whitman, the great encompasser of multitudes, as a formative influence, sees vagabonding through "the weird depths of the hottest zone" and back into the "world of tears" as the basis of literary representation.[180] He understands literature as the great song of himself that can introduce his readers to the fullness of the world and the self made possible through such imperial, cosmopolitan, literary vagabondage.

The Rest

I have selected these few writers to discuss not necessarily because they are representative but because they otherwise had very different careers and very different relations to regionalism, and thus represent a range of regionalist options. Hundreds of other texts and authors could have been used to make similar points, and indeed it is my contention that this kind of reading can be applied to any literary text and can help explain why others are not considered literary. Sui Sin Far's stories about Mrs. Spring Fragrance, for instance, are classic insider/outsider tales, with an oscillating perspective that never allows any of the characters' discrepant cosmopolitanisms to take precedence, and this is why she has been so frequently anthologized. Her texts still present problems for critics, because the main representative of the Chinese American perspective can seem flaky and a bit naïve, often serving to undermine available stereotypes but sometimes seeming to reinforce them.[181] The end result may be, as Annette White-Parks puts it, a "counter perspective" that helps "depict the scope of humanity in its diversified range," and, if one reads the stories in this way, one appreciates their literary quality.[182] But if one finds that the texts side too strongly with assimilationist ideas, cater too openly to their original audiences' prejudices, and thereby too thoroughly diminish the full humanity of the protagonist, one is hard-pressed to argue for their literary quality.

Zitkala-Sa (the pen name of Gertrude Simmons Bonnin) claimed she inhabited a "middle ground" between the assimilation policies of the schools and the tribalist views of the reservation.[183] Her texts, which are almost literary, demonstrate the difference between a middle ground and a cosmopolitan overview; her clear position in the debates about assimilation flattens her texts. O. E. Rolvaag includes aspects of Norwegian folklore and literature in *Giants in the Earth* (1927) that were specifically addressed to his Norwegian American readers, as April Shultz has pointed out, but which are balanced by the more American mythic materials. The text embraces aspects of American ideology while refusing to abandon Norwegian fatalism and other parts of Rolvaag's cultural heritage; as Shultz notes, he was writing in the context of the "Americanism" campaigns of the 1920s, and he represents both sides of the argument.[184] Herbert Quick's *Vandemark's Folly* (1922), an unjustly neglected regionalist novel, oscillates among the perspectives of Dutch immigrants and natives, Eastern immigrants to the Midwest and earlier arrivals, and farmers and nonfarmers, all the while broadly distributing folly.

And the same is true of the old canon. Hemingway's *In Our Time* (1925) oscillates between stories set in rural Michigan and vignettes of European war (as well as other urban and rural scenes), with the narratives containing internal oscillations between locals and visitors as well—the breadth and balance of perspectives is precisely what makes this book, in my opinion at least, his masterpiece. Those who find in Hemingway's work a trained incapacity to see the world from nontestosterone-soaked perspectives find his texts, again following the logic of literary cosmopolitanism, not worthy of their reputation. I would argue that *In Our Time* is the Hemingway text that most thoroughly and intentionally deconstructs machismo rather than simply exalting or mourning it (though these options are represented as well). The claims of his men and women in these stories are exquisitely balanced, his view of violence wide-ranging and multifaceted. *In Our Time* is his most significant literary accomplishment, in thorough contrast, for instance, to the beset manhood of *Across the River and into the Trees* (1950). By the time he wrote that novel he had become a parody of his macho press image and had lost all sense of balance.

Some regionalist work in the 1910s, 1920s, and 1930s—particularly novels and stories by Harry Leon Wilson, Irvin S. Cobb, Margaret Deland, Dorothy Canfield Fisher, Booth Tarkington, Mary Hallock Foote, Edna Ferber, Zane Grey, Thomas Dixon, and Zona Gale—flirts with literary quality simply because regionalist fiction had by then become so thoroughly formulaic that it required at least a semblance of literary balance. And I have had to omit many other regionalist works, including late entries by Freeman and Howells, and books by Dreiser, W. E. B. DuBois, Frost, Cahan, Carl Sandburg, John Steinbeck, Walter White, Thomas Wolfe, Viña Delmar, Langston Hughes, Onoto Watanna, Floyd Dell, Wallace Thurman, and others. But the writers I have discussed all too briefly in this section—Cather, Wharton, Johnson, Masters, Frederick, Anderson, Suckow, Lewis, the Twelve Southerners, Glasgow, Kelley, Caldwell, Faulkner, Yezierska, Gold, Toomer, Fauset, and McKay—represent a wide enough, and balanced enough, cross section of American literary production in these decades, I hope, to make my argument clear.

AFTER 1930

The New New Regionalism
and the Future of Literature

"The regional movement never had much substance," Henry Nash Smith told an interviewer in 1980. "Efforts to 'feel the purposeful earth' . . . were preposterous."[1] Reacting against the pastoral, Jeffersonian romanticism of the 1920s and 1930s and the resurgence of back-to-the-land ideas at the end of the 1960s, in which similar "preposterous" ideas would again influence a sizable subculture, Smith was speaking from the perspective of American studies, which, like contemporary cultural studies, is a field that has a certain amount of contempt for the tinkling teacups of literary culture. He was speaking about the way economic depression incited a renewed desire for rootedness, or at least for stories of rootedness, in the 1930s. This literary desire for roots is seen by some leftist critics to be siphoning energies that would be better spent on political action. But others, like Michael Steiner, to whom Smith was talking, read the Federal Writers' Project and the local stories it collected, stories in which farmers and farm laborers "professed a strong attachment" to the land and migrants to the cities held on to memories of the landscapes of their past, as signs that regionalism was "part of a desire for the security of place amid the disorder and stress of the great depression" that permeated all levels of society.[2] The Depression created "a prolonged, insidious fear of rootlessness," Steiner writes, and a "persistent affirmation of place that were the vernacular counterparts to the regional theorizing of the 1930s" (446). But for Smith, this is all beside the point: "Regionalism didn't affect anyone who didn't read," he told Steiner. "It was a fluttering of literary dovecotes and the schemes of a few well-intentioned intellectuals and planners."[3] Literature, for Smith, is not at the crossroads; the literary road, or at least the regionalist literary road, in his view, never quite meets the political.

Included in Smith's attack are literary-regionalist theorists such as Lewis Mumford, but Mumford, at least, was well aware of exactly this kind of criticism. In his 1940 "Roots in the Region," Mumford distinguished between the "two sides" of regionalism, the political, interested in conservation, political responsibility, and community, and the "cultural and sentimental side."[4] He understood that some literary texts were ripe for what would become Smith's critique: "A sentimental regionalism, that dreams dreams without putting a foundation under them, must finally lose its own self-respect" (266). The political program needs the cultural, however, because otherwise, "one might as well intone the *World Almanac* for inspiration" (266), he claims, almost suggesting that literary regionalism exists simply to provide the pep rally fight songs for the "political side."

To cast regionalism in these dichotomous terms, however, though rhetorically useful for a sometime planner, sometime literary critic such as Mumford, is to misunderstand literary regionalism as much as Smith does. The feeling of the purposeful earth can certainly appear preposterous—in fact Hamlin Garland and many other regionalists regularly make fun of their urban characters for just that—but so can its opposite, the urban refusal to understand the attachments people have to the land, which is sometimes also the butt of Garland's jokes. The literary regionalists understood sentimental localism and its problems, knew that cosmopolitan literary texts were not specific calls to action, and knew that this was not the result of a lack of political acuity or attention. The literary regionalists already knew Smith's argument. And Mumford's. And they anticipated the arguments of many other, more recent critiques of "the local" as well. David Simpson's critique of Clifford Geertz, Vince Pecora's of the New Historicism, Patrick Scott's more literary analysis, Michael O'Brien's historiographical arguments, and the burgeoning literature on political and cultural cosmopolitanism cited above have all exposed in great detail, what Pecora calls "the limits of local knowledge."[5] But Mumford and the literary writers from the 1870s through the 1930s, as I hope I have shown, have been well aware of these limits. The literary regionalists were the first proponents of what Clifford would come to call "discrepant cosmopolitanisms"; they understood that all knowledge is necessarily local, all knowledge in the modern world necessarily cosmopolitan.

"Romantic localism," as critics today call it, or "sentimental" localism in Mumford's case, is almost always a rhetorical rod used to beat an author whose work has failed some fundamental literary test. The rejection of sentimental localism was central to the "revolt from the village" novelists in the 1920s and the anti–local color criticism of the 1950s. In each case, the charge is related to what was seen as missing perspectives, a lack of courage in facing all the facts of life, and therefore, a kind of cultural-political cowardice. The test is always not simply of political consciousness or efficacy, in other words, but of fullness and balance. Supposedly hard-hitting, naturalistic, antiromantic representations of local life can easily fail the same test.

Take the case of Robert Schenkkan's *Kentucky Cycle* (1992). After Schenkkan's play won the Pulitzer Prize for Drama in 1992, it was attacked from several quarters for its lack of authenticity. The problem was not that it failed at political truth telling, but that, while its characters' lives were represented with a full consciousness of their real degradation, there was no attention to their dignity or culture. The play offered only "an interpretation of the history of Eastern Kentucky as one of violence, vengeance, and calamity," as one critic put it, not a picture of life as it was actually lived.[6] Schenkkan was, in fact, an outsider who had visited the mining regions of Kentucky for only one weekend before writing his play, and otherwise knew Kentucky only from a stint as an actor at the Actors' Theater of Louisville and some library research. Bobbie Ann Mason, a Kentucky writer with somewhat more authentic credentials (she was born and raised in the state), wrote in the *New Yorker* that the South has long been represented as "a lawless, backward wasteland populated by the Dukes of Hazzard, the Beverly Hillbillies, L'il Abner, the feuding Hatfield and McCoy clans, the feral dimwits in *Deliverance*," and that "the shame these images impose" on Southerners was "compounded with confusion" by the success of Schenkkan's play.[7] For other Kentucky writers, the effect was worse than confusion. John Ed Pearce called the play "the literary equivalent of a drive-by shooting."[8] Finlay Donesky claimed that it was "a classic case of psychosocial projection" or scapegoating.[9] Rodger Cunningham blasted Schenkkan's "pseudocritical attitude" and Herbert Reid his "shallow, 'populist' glorification of the local."[10]

Gurney Norman, a writer and creative writing professor at the University of Kentucky, attacked the play for its exploitative lack of authenticity, saying that it is "only the latest narrative in a century-long stream of narratives that have portrayed the people of this region as mean, quaint, violent, brutish, and generally low-down and sorry."[11] Norman told Mason he felt that Schenkkan was probably well-intentioned but "his boot is in my face and I have to yell." He told the *Washington Post* that the play is "simply political agitprop, which the large audience was just eating up. I think the play serves everyone who feels that they are hip to Schenkkan's little urban sophisticated ultra-liberal agenda. The long-suffering Kentucky people are left out of the equation."[12] What is missing, Norman argues, is balance, a look not just at the lives degraded by poverty and economic exploitation but at the good qualities of Kentuckians, their hospitality, pride, loyalty, and resistance, even though he knows that such talk opens him to charges that he is peddling "pastoral nostalgia."[13] Mason reports on the battle between Schenkkan and Norman, asking each to respond to the other's comments in turn, but finally breaks off, concluding that the divide between them cannot be bridged. When two farmers cannot agree to maintain a common fence, she writes, each builds his or her own, and the land in between is known as "the Devil's lane" (62). This metaphoric land in-between is the region, I have been arguing, the real home turf of literary regionalism.

Another Kentucky author, Chris Offutt, in an interview shortly after Mason's article appeared, said that he distrusted Mason's take, because although she was a Kentuckian, she was a "flatlander" whose life and culture were far removed from the realities of the hill people Schenkkan had tried (and failed) to represent.[14] Offutt respected Gurney Norman for his long attachment to the hills, but Norman, he thought, having spent too much time in academia, was really an outsider himself. Offutt had just published his own critically acclaimed collection of stories, *Kentucky Straight* (1992), and was at the time very much identified with the people in his stories. But these battles over relative authenticity and relative romanticism, over who is really inside and who is outside, who has the right to represent whom, all miss the literary boat. As Schenkkan says in his own defense, the *Kentucky Cycle* is not a play about Kentucky any more than *The Crucible* is a play about New England; it is about the destructive side of the American dream: "What I'm interested in is how much Eastern Kentucky's situation, which can be viewed, and has historically been viewed, as somewhat isolated, is in fact a paradigm for the United States as a whole."[15]

Offutt speaks the same language. He claims that in his own work, he is "trying to write about people in this region in ways that show they are just like everyone else—they have ethical dilemmas, complex feelings, neuroses, just like everyone else."[16] Robert Brustein, no fan of romantic localism or political activism, finds in Schenkkan's work "a laudable desire to universalize" but suggests that Schenkkan fails because of the one-sidedness of his characterizations: his "endless parade of basehearted men eventually becomes a reverse form of sentimentality."[17] What Schenkkan and his various critics, including Offutt and Brustein all share, of course, whether they are concerned about the actual people of the Kentucky hills or not, is a belief that a balancing of local and more universal concerns is central to adequate literary representation.

The same dynamic is at work in battles over ethnic literature, and has been, as I have suggested, since it first appeared on the American literary scene in the late nineteenth century. In 1998, Lois-Ann Yamanaka's *Blu's Hanging* (1997) was awarded the annual literary prize of the Association of Asian American Studies and this caused a furor similar to that which surrounded Carl Van Vechten's *Nigger Heaven* and Claude McKay's *Home to Harlem* in the 1920s, for similar reasons.[18] As Susan Hwang has noted, readers were outraged at what they saw as unduly negative portrayals of Hawaiians of Filipino descent in the novel, written by a Hawaiian of Japanese descent. The condemnations of "sensationalist" Harlem Renaissance texts, in particular the argument that portrayals of rape and other forms of criminality should be avoided because they perpetuate negative stereotypes, are repeated in the debate about Yamanaka's text and prize. Detractors of Yamanaka's work suggested that her antiromantic view of Filipino depravity was a dishonest, exoticizing form of exploitation. The main focus of their ire was Uncle Paolo, a Filipino–Hawaiian character who sells drugs, molests his teenage nieces, and rapes the eight-year-old protagonist, but they note that Yamanaka's earlier work also had negative, stereotypical representations of Filipinos.[19] Ethnic studies professors from the University of Hawaii wrote letters of protest to the Association of Asian American Studies, and the Filipino American Studies Caucus arrived at the award ceremony wearing black armbands, then stood with their backs to the stage in protest. The Filipino caucus had lodged formal complaints against the AAAS board when it nominated Yamanaka in previous years; she had been nominated for *Saturday Night at the Pahala Theater* (1993) and again for *Wild Meat and Bully Burgers* (1996). In 1996 the furor reached such a peak that the award was suspended.[20]

Yamanaka's defenders claimed that the protesters were not reading the texts correctly; they pointed out that the narrator of *Blu's Hanging,* herself a child, was not speaking for the author, but simply representing one set of social attitudes, that the implied author was not agreeing with her view of Filipinos any more than the implied author agreed with the narrator's belief that using someone else's deodorant meant that one would "catch their b.o." In other words, the cosmopolitanism of the text resides in the author-reader interaction, not in the views of the characters. Other defenders attacked what they saw as the protesters' attempt to censor Yamanaka, and by extension all Asian American writers. David Mura complained that the Filipino caucus was acting like all the "others who want to muzzle you, who say you can't write about this or that. . . . The voices of silence each writer confronts are myriad and endless and always potentially silencing."[21] Rodney Morales, a professor at the University of Hawaii, countered: "If anyone wants to talk about censorship, let's talk about the censored voices of Filipinos and Hawaiians (the indigenous people) in Hawai'i's so-called Local Literature scene. Let's talk about who gets published and why." No one argues that there are no Filipino rapists; the argument on both sides concerns the lack of balanced, full representation, both at the textual level and at the level of what Howells called the literary House of Representatives. In 1998, as in 1878, literature's job, and in particular regionalist literature's job, is seen in relation to the rights and obligations of different populations of persons. Similar debates crop up with regularity, as they did in the case of Richard Wright's

Native Son (1940), Maxine Hong Kingston's *Woman Warrior* (1976), Alice Walker's *The Color Purple* (1982), and many other texts.[22] The politics of these debates cannot be transcended by referring to some literary aesthetic that is free from such concerns; literature's reason for being, its readership, its structure, its content, and its force all derive precisely from these interpopulation politics. The bloody crossroads cannot be avoided.

In the 1950s, when there was a concerted effort on the part of some who embraced the New Criticism to avoid the crossroads, local color literature fared quite badly. In 1952, Donald A. Dike, speaking for a growing consensus, wrote in *College English* that "'local color' has nowadays become a term of critical abuse, a way of designating the presence in fiction of irrelevant description or of the merely quaint," in part because the nineteenth-century local colorists failed "to produce a significant literature."[23] Dike's account of the perceived literary paucity of the genre is akin to Smith's left-liberal attack on romantic regionalism as politically ineffective: they are simply two ways of beating what they agreed was the same dying horse. But it is far from accidental that when the politics of these texts is lost on new groups of readers their literary quality seems to diminish. By the 1950s, the fate of farmers was not a key concern for the general culture, and suburbia became the milieu that seemed richest for displaying the culture's fault lines. In the meantime, the center of America's literary history had become the American Renaissance. F. O. Matthiessen, who helped institutionalize that period, had written his first book about Sarah Orne Jewett in 1929; after his *American Renaissance* (1941), critical attention to classic regionalism dwindled to a shallow stream for several decades.[24]

To reject local color for its political concerns, however, was to misunderstand the aesthetic arguments of the New Criticism. As I have suggested, the New Criticism can best be seen as a particular reading of these texts' politics, not a rejection of them. Nonetheless, it was only when the feminist critics in the 1970s began to find in women's regionalist writing a revolt against patriarchy that American literary and cultural historians again took an interest in it. With a return to explicitly historical concerns by many critics in the 1980s, regionalist literature was once again recognized for its literary value and once again became an important focus of critical work.

While regionalism's literary-critical fortunes rose and fell over the decades, its popularity with nonacademic readers remained strong. Through mid-century Faulkner, Warren, Suckow, Edna Ferber, John Steinbeck, and McKinlay Kantor continued writing regionalist texts, and new voices, such as Flannery O'Connor, Eudora Welty, and Carson McCullers in the South, Wallace Stegner and Larry McMurtry in the West, and many others worked the genre. Many texts, from Harriet Arnow's *The Dollmaker* (1954), in which a Kentucky Appalachian family is transplanted to Detroit, and Ken Kesey's *Sometimes a Great*

Notion (1964) about the Pacific Northwest, found popular and critical audiences, as did, to a lesser degree, the nonfiction and poetry of Edward Abbey, Gary Snyder, and Wendell Berry. A large number of more recent writers are also closely associated with the locales that are featured in their fiction and where they (usually) also have a home: Carolyn Chute, Dorothy Allison, Larry Brown, Chris Offutt, Cormac McCarthy, Louise Erdrich, Walter Mosley, Annie Proulx, Mary Swander, Kathleen Norris, Jon Hassler, Richard Russo, Pam Houston, David Guterson, Kent Haruf, Harry Crews, T. R. Pearson, Pat Conroy, John Berendt, Barry Hannah, Mary Stefaniak, Robert Inman, Mary Ward Brown—the list could go on and on. These writers do not fit the profile drawn by Henry Nash Smith any more than the earlier regionalists did. Although some literary essayists, such as Wendell Berry and Gretel Ehrlich, have become important spokespersons for ecologically minded back-to-the-landers, they are far from naïve about what a sentimental localism is. "The regional motive is false," Berry writes, whenever it is akin to nationalism, afloat in its own myths, or "when the region is made the standard of its own experience—when, that is, perspective is narrowed by condescension or pride so that a man is unable to bring to bear on the life of his place as much as he is able to know."[25] The better the book, the more it manages to balance a sense of "the purposeful earth" with a sense of purposeless drudgery. The more literary the book, the more a romantic attachment to locality is juxtaposed to both rootless alienation and something akin to rooted cosmopolitanism, and the more the perspective is widened to as much as one is "able to know."

There is such a thing as romantic regionalism, of course, and it continues to be produced and to find an audience, but it is, I would argue, always subliterary. Tony Early's *Jim the Boy* (2000), for instance, uses many of the local color techniques of the nineteenth century in telling the story, set in the 1930s, of a twelve-year-old boy's coming to consciousness of the beauty of his local world, and from a twelve-year-old's perspective it might seem literary.[26] Some of the issues, such as tensions between the hillbilly kids and the town kids, still have some resonance, as does, in a very basic way, the coming-of-age motif itself. When he visits an area past the next town, "beyond which lay new worlds" (52), Jim begins to have a cosmopolitan awakening: "*People live here,* and he thought, *They don't know who I am.* At that moment the world opened up around Jim like hands that, until that moment, had been cupped around him" (53). The *Bildungsroman* almost necessarily includes a narrative of broadened consciousness, and one assumes that part of the appeal this text has for readers is its invocation of this cosmopolitan trope. The text follows the regionalist model in other ways as well, showing us the incursions of the larger world into the local scene, especially the railroad station being built in the town ("It finally seemed like *somewhere*" [92]) and in the introduction of electricity. The night they first turn on the electricity, "The brightness of the few lights," Jim feels, "only magnified the darkness that still surrounded the town" (148). When Ty Cobb happens one day to be on a train that stops at the new station, his arrival has a profound effect; as soon as the train begins to pull out of the station, "Already Jim could feel how empty the town would be" (168). Jim sees the town from a prospect at the top of the "hillbilly mountain," and "he could not believe how little space Aliceville occupied in the world" (225). These and other scenes—like the evocation of different ages in the form of coal fossils (178), of history in the form of Independence Hall (202), of modernity in the form of the Empire State Building (203), and of migration in the form of a hillbilly wife who is really an educated Philadelphian—all contribute to a typical cosmopolitan perspective.

These moments seem excessively stage-managed in the text, however, and in the end they are negated. In the very last scene, as Jim contemplates the new perspective on his town from the mountain, he is filled with dread: "It's too big," he says, and his uncle immediately reassures him, absolving him of any responsibility to a larger world. "I'm just a boy," says Jim, and his uncle makes that okay: "But you're *our* boy," he says. This is perhaps the key to the book's popular success—the world is bigger than some readers would like it to be, full of dread and difference, and the text suggests that we should not worry, we have our loved ones, our little worlds can always cup their hands around us again. I agree with Henry Nash Smith here—I find such platitudinous reassurance pathetic. The novel uses all the techniques of the cosmopolitan regionalist text, in other words, to absolve its readers emotionally of accepting the very invitations to openness the form affords. Although the novel had a brief vogue, it will not become part of any literary canon unless some critic comes along who can find in it a more complex relation to its themes than I have managed to do.

Chris Offutt's work, conversely, is classic literary regionalism. Every story in his first collection, *Kentucky Straight* (1992), contrasts local and larger perspectives, never settling comfortably. In "Sawdust," the first story in the book, the narrator decides to get his GED, which is being offered at the VISTA center in town. The narrator's confidence in his own knowledge of the woods and his lack of knowledge of the wider world are set against the VISTA worker's urban sophistication and her incomprehension of the people among whom she works. These two basic positions, both with obvious strengths and flaws, are complicated by others: the narrator's father wanted to be a veterinarian but dropped out of school, turned to religion, and committed suicide; his brother works at a factory three hours away and buys satellite dishes, microwaves, and VCRs, but his embrace of modernity does not extend to getting "eat up wit the smart bug" in order to get a GED, which he claims stands for "Get Even Dumber" (10); his mother displays a conventional piety; the townspeople insult the narrator and fight him because of what they see as his uppitiness. These characters represent not just individual choices, but the range of cultural options.

His father was obsessed with maps and collected them, poring over them "till way past dark" (7). When he asks the preacher where the Land of Nod is, the preacher says it was lost in the flood. But the narrator doesn't buy it: in one of Offutt's many formulations of the relation of the local to the larger world, his father insists that "everywhere has to be somewhere" (7). The perspective from "everywhere" gets less attention in these stories than it often did in earlier regionalist texts; the outsider characters are very thinly drawn, but the presence of their world is palpably felt. The assumption is that readers are themselves outsiders, bringing that perspective with them to the text—as Offutt has said, very few of the people he writes about read him. He tells a story of returning home to the hills after publishing his first books, worried that one of his friends, the one most likely to read, might, in fact, have read a story in which he appears as a thinly disguised character, and not in a very good light. He meets him with great trepidation, which only increases when the friend says he has, in fact, read the book. As Offutt sweats, he names the very story. "You know what's funny?" he asks Offutt, who does not know whether to form some kind of reply or just run. "The very same thing happened to me a few years back!" He then goes on to talk about a few minor differences, but remains astounded by the coincidence between the event in his life and that on the page. Literary reading is a particular kind of reading, a kind to which, as this anecdote suggests, Offutt is trained and his hill-dwelling subjects are not; or, we might say, in recognizing his relation to the text, his subject understands better than Offutt himself at that moment that the facts of existence and their literary representation exist in two different orders.

One of the through threads in Offutt's stories is poverty. In one story a boy is ready to fight his teacher because she has suggested he is poor; his father had always told him they were not, and that he should not stand for anyone suggesting they were. The question of value, of whether living in the woods on next to nothing is better or worse than commuting six hours a day to a factory job in order to acquire frivolous electronic goods, is one that is staged in the hills of Kentucky but is obviously central to the general cultural conversation. In much contemporary regionalism, as in earlier decades, the relations among the specific populations represented are less important than the meaning they have as markers in these other debates. Dorothy Allison's *Bastard Out of Carolina* (1992) is informed by an argument about violence against women and the abuse of children that none of the characters quite have the cosmopolitan chops to understand or articulate. Carolyn Chute's *Beans of Egypt, Maine* (1985), like Allison's book, like Yamanaka's, and for that matter like Mary Wilkins Freeman's "Old Woman Magoun" (1909) and a host of regionalist texts in between, stages an argument about sexual violence that is not a local issue but a human one. And thus the regional blindness to these issues represents not so much a regional fact as a national or international one. The politics of these texts thus engage not just the obvious moral precepts against violence, but, in their sympathy for their characters, represent the full complexity of the issues involved. Their literary quality makes them both more and less than simple denunciations. They do not provide manifestos so much as, in Edward Said's words, they "elucidate the contest."[27]

Said, who had a long career as a politically engaged intellectual, claimed recently that the intellectual's role is not to take sides but to make clear the meanings for all participants of their differences, echoing Gerald Graff's decision to do just that vis-à-vis the culture wars.[28] "The intellectual's role," Said wrote, "is first to present alternative narratives and other perspectives on history than those provided by the combatants on behalf of official memory and national identity" (34), and he ended with what I take to be exactly the kind of justification of literature I have outlined here as central to the American literary tradition: "I conclude with the thought that the intellectual's provisional home is the domain of an exigent, resistant, intransigent art into which, alas, one can neither retreat nor search for solutions. But only in that precarious exilic realm can one first truly grasp the difficulty of what cannot be grasped, and then go forth to try anyway" (36). This view of intellectual responsibility is a very particular one, much more likely to be shared by people trained in literary studies in America than intellectuals of other backgrounds, national or disciplinary. This kind of idealism, based in an irresolvable cosmopolitanism, is exactly what Jewett referred to when she told Cather that the highest political motive writers can have is the desire to acquaint people with their neighbors, and that to do so means not being too far inside or too far outside the local scene. Fully engaged, intellectually and aesthetically satisfying literary work eschews political resolution, refuses to stay in or out of agreement with the political commitments of its characters, and this is precisely what leaves the crossroads bloody, precisely why the bloody crossroads are where literature lives.

I am aware that many of my colleagues will find this argument hopelessly benighted and reactionary, reviving the old-school humanism we have all been taught, with the help of the Frankfort School and others, to see as complicit with the worst abuses and inequities of the modern age. They will say I have it backward, that the reason I find this literary ethos in the work of the Southern Agrarians and the New Critics, in the work of elite writers from the nineteenth and twentieth centuries, is because they all share a similar set of class prerogatives, they are all very much like Gramsci's uncommitted cosmopolitan intellectuals, as am I. Some will argue that their own political commitments allow them to read the political unconscious of these texts not because of the literary ethos I describe, but despite it. This is obviously not the place to launch a full-

blown argument in favor of humanism, but it should be clear from my arguments that I am locating the literary ethos squarely in that tradition. Humanism
"has been accused of fostering or tolerating a tyranny of instrumental reason, a
desacralization and exploitation of nature, a colonization by Europeans of the
rest of the world, a patriarchal domination of women, and a class hegemony of
the capitalist bourgeoisie," as Graham Good sums it up, and he and others who
want to revive "liberal humanism" as the informing ethic of academic life do
not attempt to contradict these charges of complicity with historical evils.[29]

Still, as Good argues, "liberal humanist principles" were even more obviously
central to those in the past and the present who have been "working to allevi-
ate or remedy" many of these evils: "The abolition of slavery, the emancipation
of women, and the extension of democratic rights to all classes are examples"
(4). In many ways Good's critique itself reeks of the rearguard rhetoric of those
who fought attempts to broaden syllabi and reading lists and to increase the diversity of faculties and students bodies in the 1970s and 1980s, and who claimed
that all the tools for human liberation and progress already existed in the traditional canon. But unlike those defenders of the status quo, who argued against
the leveling, diluting, or destructive (to use just the most common metaphors)
influences of the further democratization of higher education, Good argues
against what he sees as a resignation to the "carceral vision" of Foucault and others. Good sees a connection between the (self-defined) most progressive groups
in academic life and the creation of the "managerial university" in which "information services" and "targeted client categories" rather than "the disinterested pursuit and preservation of knowledge" are the guiding principles (103).
The arguments that all knowledge is power, that capitalism controls all facets of
life including intellectual life, that economic interest perverts all humanisms,
Good suggests, all support even as they indict commercial civilization, they represent "*de facto* acquiescence in the actually existing system" (103).[30] If academic inquiry is divorced from its humanistic goals of increasing freedom and
equality, he writes, it leaves the university no other function than to service the
needs of corporate culture.

Good's argument here, in which he turns the tables on negative hermeneu-
tics, whatever heuristic value it might have, is not necessary to my own, but his
insistence that liberal humanism provides the basis of progressive politics, even
as it provides a justification of the traditional canon, is similar to my argument
about the nature of literary value in America. What seems to be classic American literature's political indecision is not only central to its aesthetic quality but
central to its political engagement as well. Literary writers in America have not
produced dialectic texts: they have arranged theses and antitheses but not syn-
theses. From Whitman's astoundingly precise formulation—"Do I contradict
myself? Very well, then, I contradict myself. I am large. I contain multitudes"—

to the revolution in syllabi, canons, and scholarship over the last thirty years, the central impulse of American literary culture has been toward multitudinous inclusion, away from the reductive, toward balance and away from resolution. Critics of the various movements within literary criticism over the last half century have been quick to use the term "reductive" as a dismissive adjective, and whether they have been right or wrong in a particular case is less important than the desire they thereby manifest to expand rather than contract.

Canon revision has most often been figured as an expansion of the canon, even though in practice it necessitates replacements and substitutions more than actual expansion—we can get students to read only so many books a term— precisely because the impulse to add representative texts trumps the desire to codify a hierarchy of texts. Literary texts themselves have continued to add Carolina bastards, Jewish authors in adult diapers, gay Republicans, and Islamic fundamentalists to the groups represented, in a communal effort to finish the project Gertrude Stein started in *The Making of Americans,* "a complete description of every kind of human being that ever could or would be living."[31] Stein comically claims that after writing what became the thousand-page text, trying to write a "complete description of everything," she decided that "it would be nice to really have described every kind there is of men and women," but "after all I know I really do know that it can be done and if it can be done why do it" (256). Stein's joke, as I have said, relies on the literal impossibility of the project. But, then again, in a metaphor of Gayatri Chakravorty Spivak's that is itself one image of the boundless literary urge to incorporate, literature's job is to "figure the impossible."[32]

Bruce Robbins, the English professor who has had the longest career defending the idea of cosmopolitanism, suggested in one of his sallies in the culture wars of the late 1980s that attacks against multiculturalism were an attempt to "reprovincialize American culture," and thought there were two strands to the attack. One consisted of distaste for the anthropological (inclusive rather than hierarchical) view of culture, with a return to the canon offered as an antidote to its leveling effect. The other strand relied on a characterization of academics as self-interested ivory tower elitists, tenured radicals out of touch with American society.[33] Robbins convincingly argues that these two halves of the critique do not cohere, that academics cannot at once be too democratic and not democratic enough. But he does not offer an answer to the fundamental question he raises, of how the urge to multicultural representation can be integrated with a "concern for the *value* of the cultural exhibits offered" (357). Some texts continue to seem "better" to us than others, and we end up in the *Animal Farm* position of arguing that all texts are created equal, but that some are more equal than others. The fact is that none of us is ever both committed to an intellectual project of some kind and a true cosmopolitan in some absolute sense. We may feel a desire to be "cosmopolites," in the sense Samuel Johnson defines the term in his *Dictionary* (1755), "*at home* in every place," but we are not, in fact, nor, in a way, would we want to be.[34] The *desire* for a cosmopolitan vista can remain a prime animating force for literature and criticism because we can safely assume that we have never arrived at the ideal prospect that it might afford. To arrive there would make us universalists, after all, and destroy the very democratic desire pushing us in that direction. The cosmopolitan horizon, we might say, is what we look toward, not, thankfully, where we can ever stand or, perhaps, where we would want to stand for long.

It is clear as well that for all our championing of openness to difference, the critical disciplines have never given up the hierarchical bent that has been, through the theoretical necessities of recent years, so noticeably submerged. T. S. Eliot is judged harshly for his anti-Semitism, not simply as a person or personage, but also as an artist. Henry James's *American Scene* is lambasted for its xenophobic, racist pronouncements, for its failure to live up to its title's claims to survey. But if these failures of cosmopolitan vision are the main reason some critics condemn these authors, it is precisely their otherwise quite extraordinary cosmopolitanism that explains their continued reputation over the decades; it is James's ability to keep the competing cultural claims of his Europeans and Americans, his Bostonians and Southerners, his New Women and old, his parents and children, in barely contained, conflictual, argumentative balance that is the essence of his literary accomplishment. His literary cosmopolitanism, more than his vaunted aestheticism or formal speculations, made him a New Critical darling, just as his insufficient cosmopolitanism has, in more recent years, made him a target.

As David Harvey, himself a geographer and theorist of the regional, suggests, "the novel is not subject to the closure in the same way that more analytic forms of thinking are."[35] Harvey makes this claim in relation to Raymond Williams's decision to write regionalist novels, and notes that Williams praised literature that had, in Williams's words, no "imposed resolution—the tension is there to the end, and we are invited to consider it."[36] In *The Country and the City* (1973), Williams, one of the great theorizers of the local novel, gave one of the most forceful articulations of the provincialism of a metropolitan view of the country he called "the rural retrospect," pastoral or traditional descriptions of the beauty of the land that were often "explicitly reactionary."[37] Literary artists, however, are never so reductive. D. H. Lawrence's genius, Williams suggests, was his "restless, often contradictory opposition" to any such easy formulation, and in describing it, he reenacts it: "His is a knot too tight to untie now: the knot of a life under overwhelming contradictions and pressures. But as I have watched it settle into what is now a convention—in literary education especially—I have felt it as an outrage" (271). Williams has often been used as ammunition against this or that writer's reactionary ideology, but at the heart of Williams's own project was a belief that what makes literature artistic is its refusal to settle for either the city or the country. In a similar vein, Sacvan Bercovitch reads Melville's *Pierre* as a satire on pastoral literature that, even if it does not take its cosmopolitan errand seriously enough, ends favoring neither the urban nor the rural.[38] And so on.

Literary cosmopolitanism can sometimes seem to be, and in inadequately literary texts often is, not a dynamic balance of views but a mushy mélange. What does it mean, finally, some have asked, to arrange the many varieties of African American experience in a novel like Ralph Ellison's *Invisible Man* (1953), only to end with an invocation of Enlightenment ideals? What kind of understanding results? Paul Ricoeur addresses this general problem in *History and Truth* (1965) when he warns that

> understanding is a dangerous venture in which all cultural heritages risk being swallowed up in a vague syncretism. Nevertheless, it seems to me that we have given here the elements of a frail and provisional reply: only a living creature, at once faithful to its origins and ready for creativity on the levels of art, literature, philosophy and spirituality, is capable of sustaining the encounter of other cultures—not only of sustaining but of giving meaning to that encounter.[39]

The goal, he suggests, is "a kind of harmony in the absence of all agreement" (283). It is just such an absence of agreement that animates the literary, that elevates a mere story to the level of the literary. *Invisible Man,* "Up the Coulee," *O Pioneers!* and *The Sound and the Fury* retain what Garland called their "literary power" precisely through such lack of agreement.

I have said too little in this work about issues of "literary language," but I hope that my scattered comments (especially my references to Bakhtinian analysis) have been enough to suggest how central my notions of literary cosmopolitanism are to this vexed issue in literary criticism as well. The fact that Theodore Dreiser remains at the center of the American literary canon alongside Henry James confused Lionel Trilling because of the obvious disparity between Dreiser's prosaic clumsiness and James's verbal virtuosity. My argument is that literariness as I have defined it here always trumps other versions of the literary, such as literariness defined as the artful use of language.

The New Critics, in fact, were attempting to codify at the level of language the same forces I have been codifying with reference to plot, theme, and character. Dynamic balance, ambiguity, complexity, multiplicity: these can be achieved at the linguistic level in such a way as to pass New Critical tests only through complex referentiality. To analyze the most complex literary words (in William Empson's sense) in these texts would yield readings very similar to those I have achieved through attention to larger structures and movements.[40] Or, to invoke a slightly different tradition of stylistics, the effects of defamiliarization in these texts are produced by the refusal to reduce thematic issues to one or another familiar ideological position.[41] The cleverest, most rhetorically sophisticated, grammatically elegant sentences, when they are in the service of social and political banality, cannot pass the literary tests set up by the New Critics or the Russian Formalists, any more than they pass my own. As Ransom wrote, poetic language is the union of "logical structure" and "local texture," and requires "rich contingent materiality."[42] Cleanth Brooks, of course, went so far as to suggest that poetry and paradox are virtually identical.[43] My project here has been to outline what I see as the primary logical structures and paradoxes of the American literary text.

To the extent that contemporary literary and cultural criticism locates such fundamental contradiction, such absence of agreement, in the phenomena it studies, it continues to do literary work. We literary academics rightfully lose our larger audience, however, whenever we suggest that we can reduce, for our audience, the cultural debates of their world to any single set of precepts, to any formula, however squarely we might claim that formula to be on the side of justice and social progress. The disgust with which "political correctness" was met in some circles and the alacrity with which it was adopted in others, should rightly give us pause. Our job, finally, is neither to retreat from politics nor, in our literary work, to embrace any politics. We need to honor the blood spilled at the crossroads, to have faith in the power of literary representation, to continue to argue, in response to any ideology, that "the world is more complicated than that." We need to be large, to contain multitudes. To be literary, we need to contradict ourselves. And to be good critics we need to recognize the contradictions of literary texts not as their failure but as essential to their success.

Notes

Discipline and Hubris

1. René Girard, lecture, "Modern Thought and Literature," Stanford University, March 1982. Girard made similar claims in *"To Double Business Bound": Essays on Literature, Mimesis, Anthropology* (Baltimore: Johns Hopkins University Press, 1978), and in *Things Hidden since the Foundation of the World* (Baltimore: Johns Hopkins University Press, 1994).

2. Cary Nelson, Paula A. Treichler, and Lawrence Grossberg, "Cultural Studies: An Introduction," in *Cultural Studies*, ed. Cary Nelson, Paula A. Treichler, and Lawrence Grossberg (New York: Routledge, 1992), 1.

3. Fredric Jameson, *Signatures of the Visible* (New York: Routledge, 1990), 16.

4. Northrop Frye, quoted in Barbara Hernstein Smith, *Contingencies of Value: Alternative Perspectives for Critical Theory* (Cambridge, Mass.: Harvard University Press, 1988), 19. See also Frye, *Anatomy of Criticism: Four Essays* (Princeton: Princeton University Press, 1957), 18; and Philip Smallwood, "Criticism, Valuation, and Useful Purpose," *New Literary History* 28, 4 (1997) 711–22. The only option, according to Terry Eagleton, is "to provide a materialist *explanation* of the bases of literary value," and thus to discuss standards of taste as historical phenomena (Terry Eagleton, *Criticism and Ideology* [New York: Verso, 1998], 162). For Eagleton, literary values are among "the assumptions by which certain social groups exercise and maintain power over others," and so to announce a literary preference is to exercise and maintain the power of the middle class over the lower classes, a burden, in Rudyard Kipling's sense, that most would rather not carry (Terry Eagleton, *Literary Theory: An Introduction* [Minneapolis: University of Minnesota Press, 1983], 16). Instead, we study other people's evaluations: over the last two decades, scholars of literary regionalism have identified a series of what Tony Bennett has called "reading formations" and Stanley Fish "interpretive communities" in an attempt to locate the social, economic, and political commitments of different groups of readers in the late nineteenth century and thereby understand the kinds of aesthetic assumptions and judgments they made (Tony Bennett, "Texts, Readers, Reading Formations," *Literature and History* 9, 2 [autumn 1984]: 214–27; Stanley Fish, *Is There a Text in This Class? The Authority of Interpretive Communities* [Cambridge: Harvard University Press, 1980], 14). Nancy Glazener, analyzing nineteenth-century periodicals such as the *Atlantic Monthly* and the *Arena*, argues that though both magazines found great value in local color literature, they did so for different reasons. They had different politics and therefore different cultural investments in the fictions they printed and reviewed. Glazener does not herself evaluate the texts in literary terms; she is interested in providing contextual

explanations of past evaluations (Nancy Glazener, *Reading for Realism: The History of a Literary Institution* [Durham: Duke University Press, 1997], 190–201). While I too am interested in why American readers have valued certain books more highly than others through the years, in this book, rather than discuss the historical contingencies of literary value in the finely detailed way Glazener does (though I will rely on her study and many like it along the way), I am taking something closer to what Fernand Braudel called the *"longue durée"* approach (Fernand Braudel, "History and the Social Sciences: The *Longue Durée*," in *On History* [Chicago: University of Chicago Press, 1982]), which, as Braudel suggests, implies "putting on seven-league boots and passing over certain short-term realities and episodes" (Braudel, *The Perspective of the World* [New York: Harper & Row, 1984], 20). I describe the elements of a literary ethos that has been at the center of the American literary tradition for the last 150 years, shared by writers and readers across what might seem like enormous cultural divides.

5. For a description of "literary federalism" see William C. Dowling, *Literary Federalism in the Age of Jefferson: Joseph Dennie and* The Port Folio, *1801–1812* (Columbia: University of South Carolina Press, 1999). As part of their resistance to Jeffersonian democracy, writers such as Dennie embraced distinctions of literary representation antithetical to the ethos I am describing.

6. J. H. Morse, "The Native Element in American Fiction [2]," *Century* 4 (July 1883): 365.

7. Alvin Kernan, *The Death of Literature* (New Haven: Yale University Press, 1990); John Ellis, *Literature Lost: Social Agendas and the Corruption of the Humanities* (New Haven: Yale University Press, 1997); Robert Scholes, *The Rise and Fall of English* (New Haven: Yale University Press, 1998); Edward W. Said, "Presidential Forum: Scholarship and Commitment: Introduction," *Profession* (2000): 6–45. For a review of these and other works, see Andrew Delbanco, "The Decline and Fall of Literature," *New York Review of Books,* November 4, 1999.

8. Quoted in Tom McGeveran and Rebecca Traister, "The Droves of Academe," *New York Observer,* January 6, 2003, 8.

Toward a Theory

1. William Carlos Williams, *Imaginations* (New York: New Directions, 1970), 311.

2. Frederick L. Gwynn and Joseph Blotner, eds., *Faulkner in the University* (Charlottesville, Va.: University Press of Virginia, 1959), 197; David Minter, ed., *The Sound and the Fury,* by William Faulkner, Norton Critical Edition (New York: Norton, 1987), 249.

3. Interview, bookreporter.com, April 28, 2000.

4. Http://www.algonquin.com/larrybrown/larry7.html.

5. Larry Brown, Prairie Lights Bookstore, Iowa City, Iowa, October, 1997.

6. Lionel Trilling, "Reality in America," in *The Liberal Imagination* (New York: Viking, 1950), 3; Vernon L. Parrington, *Main Currents of American Thought: An Interpretation of American Literature from the Beginnings,* 3 vols. (New York: Harcourt, Brace, 1927–1930).

7. See Calvin Bedient, *He Do the Police in Different Voices:* The Waste Land *and Its Protagonist* (Chicago: University of Chicago Press, 1986), 73.

8. Carey McWilliams, *The New Regionalism in American Literature* (Seattle: University of Washington Press, 1930), 23.

9. Henry Steele Commager, *Jefferson, Nationalism, and the Enlightenment* (New York: George Braziller, 1975), 178.

10. Hamlin Garland, *Crumbling Idols: Twelve Essays on Art Dealing Chiefly with Literature, Painting, and the Drama,* ed. Jane Johnson (1894; reprint, Cambridge: Harvard University Press, 1960), 140, 44.

11. John Guillory, *Cultural Capital: The Problem of Literary Canon Formation* (Chicago: University of Chicago Press, 1993), 46.

12. Howells to Mitchell, October 20, 1885, in *Howells, Selected Letters 1882–1891,* ed. George Arms et al. (Boston: Twayne Publishers, 1980), 131.

13. William Dean Howells, *Their Wedding Journey* ([1871] Boston: Houghton Mifflin, 1916), 63.

14. Quoted in Nancy K. Harris, "Problems of Representation in Turn-of-the-Century Immigrant

Fiction," in *American Realism and the Canon*, ed. Tom Quirk and Gary Scharnhorst (Newark: University of Delaware Press, 1994), 132—33.

15. Sinclair Lewis, Nobel Prize acceptance speech, in the appendix to James Hutchisson, *The Rise of Sinclair Lewis, 1920—1930* (University Park: Pennsylvania State University Press, 1996), 264.

16. Mark Schorer, *Sinclair Lewis* (Minneapolis: University of Minnesota Press, 1963), 799.

17. M. M. Bakhtin, "Discourse in the Novel," in *The Dialogical Imagination*, ed. Michael Holquist, trans. Caryl Emerson and Michael Holquist (Austin: University of Texas Press, 1981), 259—422.

18. Garland, *Crumbling Idols*, 129.

19. Hamlin Garland, in Paula Blanchard, *Sarah Orne Jewett: Her World and Her Work* (Reading, Mass.: Addison-Wesley, 1994), 231; Elizabeth Stuart Phelps, in Josephine Donovan, *New England Local Color Literature: A Women's Tradition* (New York: Frederick Ungar, 1983), 48.

20. For the latest statement of this position, see Judith Fetterley and Marjorie Pryse, "Introduction," in *American Women Regionalists, 1850—1910: A Norton Anthology*, ed. Judith Fetterley and Marjorie Pryse (New York: Norton, 1992).

21. Richard Brodhead, *Cultures of Letters: Scenes of Reading and Writing in Nineteenth-Century America* (Chicago: University of Chicago Press, 1993); Amy Kaplan, "Nation, Region, Empire," in *Columbia History of the American Novel*, ed. Emory Elliott et al. (New York: Columbia University Press, 1991).

22. Michael Bérubé, *The Employment of English: Theory, Jobs, and the Future of Literary Studies* (New York: New York University Press, 1998), 28.

23. Henry David Thoreau, "Life Without Principle," *Atlantic Monthly* (Oct. 1862), reprinted in *Collected Essays and Poems* (New York: Library of America, 2001), 363. Thoreau's version is closer to mid-nineteenth-century ideals than to the literary ethos that takes shape after the Civil War, more interested in "truth" than in populations of persons. "With respect to a true culture and manhood, we are essentially provincial still, not metropolitan,—mere Jonathans. We are provincial, because we do not find at home our standards; because we do not worship truth, but the reflection of truth; because we are warped and narrowed by an exclusive devotion to trade and commerce and manufactures and agriculture and the like, which are but means, and not the end."

24. Stanley Fish, *Professional Correctness: Literary Studies and Political Change* (New York: Oxford University Press, 1995); the classics of the right-wing attack are Dinesh D'Souza, *Illiberal Education: The Politics of Race and Sex on Campus* (New York: Free Press, 1991), and Roger Kimball, *Tenured Radicals: How Politics Has Corrupted Our Higher Education* (New York: Harper & Row, 1990).

25. Pierre Bourdieu, *Rules of Art: Genesis and Structure of the Literary Field*, trans. Susan Emanuel (Stanford: Stanford University Press, 1996), 297.

26. Barbara Herrnstein Smith, *Contingencies of Value* (Cambridge: Harvard University Press, 1988). Smith's introductory chapter provides a classic literary-cosmopolitan defense of her relativist project; to understand evaluation is to see the relation between our evaluation of texts and the "total economy of our existence" (16), and thus different experiences necessarily result in different evaluations. After all, Smith writes, "experience is a provincialism of its own" (5).

27. Cleanth Brooks, *The Well-Wrought Urn* (New York: Harcourt, Brace & World, 1947), 203, 207; Cleanth Brooks and Robert Penn Warren, *Understanding Poetry* (New York: Henry Holt, 1939), xlv.

28. I am using a notion of literary public here similar to Michael Warner's: a "public that comes into being only in relation to texts and their circulation." Michael Warner, *Publics and Counterpublics* (New York: Zone Books, 2002), 66. Warner, an English professor, relies in his arguments on exactly the kind of literary logic I am outlining here: "A public has a metacritical dimension," he writes, for instance, in that "it gives form to a tension between general and particular that makes it difficult to analyze from either perspective alone" (11).

29. William Dean Howells, *Criticism and Fiction, and Other Essays 1837—1920* (New York: New York University Press, 1959), 68.

30. Henry Giroux, David Shumway, Paul Smith, and James Sosnoski, "The Need for Cultural Studies: Resisting Intellectuals and Oppositional Public Spheres," in *A Cultural Studies Reader: History, Theory, Practice*, ed. Jessica Munns and Gita Rajan (New York: Longman Publishing Group, 1996).

31. Fish, *Professional Correctness*, 41—70, 115—26.

32. Kenneth Frampton, "Towards a Critical Regionalism: Six Points for an Architecture of Resistance," in *The Anti-Aesthetic: Essays on Postmodern Culture*, ed. Hal Foster (New York: New Press, 1998), 16–30; see also Jean-Louis Cohen, "The Search for a Critical Practice," *Casabella* 60 (Jan. 1996): 21–27; Spyros Amourgis, ed., *Critical Regionalism: The Pomona Meetings Proceedings* (Pomona: California Polytechnic State University, 1991); Botond Bognar, "On the Critical Aspects of Regionalism," *A + U* 234 (Mar. 1990): 11–18; Alexander Tzonis and Laine Lefaivre, "Why Critical Regionalism Today?" *A + U* 236 (May 1990): 23–33.

33. See, for instance, Wes Jackson, "Natural Systems Agriculture: The Truly Radical Alternative," in *Recovering the Prairie*, ed. Robert F. Sayre (Madison: University of Wisconsin Press, 1999), 191–99; and Donald Worster, *Nature's Economy: A History of Ecological Ideas*, 2d ed. (New York: Cambridge University Press, 1994).

34. David M. Jordan, *New World Regionalism: Literature in the Americas* (Toronto: University of Toronto Press, 1994), 8; Josephine Donovan, "Breaking the Sentence: Local-Color Literature and Subjugated Knowledges," in *The (Other) American Traditions: Nineteenth-Century Women Writers*, ed. Joyce W. Warren (New Brunswick: Rutgers University Press, 1993), 226–43; Michel Foucault, "Of Other Spaces," *Diacritics* 16 (spring, 1986): 22–27, and idem, "Questions of Geography," in *Power/Knowledge: Selected Interviews and Other Writings, 1972–1977* (New York: Pantheon, 1980), 63–77.

35. See Donovan, *New England Local Color Literature*; Barbara H. Solomon, "Introduction," in *Short Fiction of Sarah Orne Jewett and Mary Wilkins Freeman*, ed. Barbara H. Solomon (New York: New American Library, 1979), 1–42; Marjorie Pryse, "Women 'at Sea': Feminist Realism in Sarah Orne Jewett's 'The Foreigner,'" *American Literary Realism* 15, 2 (autumn 1982): 244–52; Kate McCullough, *Regions of Identity: The Construction of America in Women's Fiction, 1885–1914* (Stanford: Stanford University Press, 1999).

36. Jordan, *New World Regionalism*; and David Jordan, *Regionalism Reconsidered: New Approaches to the Field* (New York: Garland, 1994); Fetterley and Pryse, "Introduction." See also Bruce Levy's excellent article on Edward Eggleston, "The Country of Corner Lots: *The Mystery of Metropolisville*, the Single Tax, and the Logic of Provincial Realism," *American Literary Realism* 30 (winter 1998): 77–94.

37. Twelve Southerners [John Crowe Ransom, Allen Tate, Robert Penn Warren, Donald Davidson et al.], *I'll Take My Stand* (New York: Harper, 1930; reprint, Baton Rouge: Louisiana State University Press, 1977).

38. Stephanie Foote, *Regional Fictions: Culture and Identity in Nineteenth-Century American Literature* (Madison: University of Wisconsin Press, 2001), 3.

39. See Louis Renza, *"A White Heron" and the Question of Minor Literature* (Madison: University of Wisconsin Press, 1984); Emily Toth, ed., *Regionalism and the Female Imagination: A Collection of Essays* (New York: Human Sciences Press, 1985); Ann Douglas Wood, "The Literature of Impoverishment: Women Local Colorists in America," *Women's Studies* 1 (1972): 3–45; Sandra Zagarell, "Narrative of Community: The Identification of a Genre," *Signs: A Journal of Women in Culture and Society* 13, 3 (1988): 498–527; Richard M. Weaver, "Realism and the Local Color Interlude," *Georgia Review* 22 (1968): 301–5; Floyd C. Watkins, *In Time and Place: Some Origins of American Fiction* (Athens: University of Georgia Press, 1977); Louis Wann, *The Rise of Realism: American Literature from 1860 to 1888* (New York: Macmillan, 1933), 1–17; Michael Davitt Bell, *The Problem of American Realism: Studies in the Cultural History of a Literary Idea* (Chicago: University of Chicago Press, 1993); B. A. Botkin, "Regionalism: Cult or Culture?" *The English Journal* 25 (March 1936): 181–85; Donald Dike, "Notes on Local Color and Its Relationship to Realism," *College English* 14, 2 (1952): 81–88; David Marion Holman, *A Certain Slant of Light: Regionalism and the Form of Southern and Midwestern Fiction* (Baton Rouge: Louisiana State University Press, 1995); Christopher Lasch, *The True and Only Heaven: Progress and Its Critics* (New York: Norton, 1991); Eric J. Sundquist, "Realism and Regionalism," in *Columbia Literary History of the United States*, ed. Emory Elliott et al. (New York: Columbia University Press, 1988), 501–24; Frederick Turner, *Spirit of Place: The Making of an American Literary Landscape* (San Francisco: Sierra Club Books, 1989); Donna M. Campbell, *Resisting Regionalism: Gender and Naturalism in American Fiction* (Athens: Ohio University Press, 1997).

40. The single most important text in this development is Raymond Williams, *The Country and the City* (New York: Oxford University Press, 1973). Many of the texts cited in the previous note are also fundamentally concerned with this issue, as are Raymond Williams, "Region and Class in the Novel," in

The Uses of Fiction: Essays on the Modern Novel in Honour of Arnold Kettle, ed. Douglas Jefferson and Graham Martin Milton (Keynes, England: Open University Press, 1982), 59–68; Philip Fisher, *Still The New World: American Literature in a Culture of Creative Destruction* (Cambridge: Harvard University Press, 1999); June Howard, ed., *New Essays on "The Country of the Pointed Firs"* (Cambridge: Cambridge University Press, 1994); Philip Joseph, "Landed and Literary: Hamlin Garland, Sarah Orne Jewett, and the Production of Regional Literatures," *Studies in American Fiction* 26, 2 (autumn 1998): 147–70; Nancy Glazener, *Reading for Realism;* Kate McCullough, *Regions of Identity.*

41. Brodhead, *Cultures of Letters*, 144, 145.

42. Amy Kaplan, "Nation, Region, Empire," in Elliott et al., ed., *Columbia History of the American Novel*, 252.

43. Fetterley and Pryse, "Introduction"; see also Donovan, *New England Local Color Literature.*

44. Glazener, *Reading for Realism.*

45. June Howard, "Unraveling Regions, Unsettling Periods: Sarah Orne Jewett and American Literary History," *American Literature* 68, 2 (June 1996): 365–84. Howard suggests that a literary history "both capacious and critical" (365) can only be achieved through attention to our own sociohistorical positions as critics; I am going to argue that the texts already contain both perspectives.

46. Joni Kinsey, *Plain Pictures: Images of the American Prairie* (Washington, D.C.: Smithsonian Institution Press, 1996).

47. Bakhtin, "Discourse in the Novel," 263 and passim. Cheryl Herr talks about oscillation in the regional novel in a somewhat different way, taking her cue from Gilles Deleuze; see Cheryl Herr, *Critical Regionalism and Cultural Studies: From Ireland to the American Midwest* (Gainesville: University Press of Florida, 1996).

48. Pryse has come closer to this argument in other writings: in "'Distilling Essences': Regionalism and 'Women's Culture'" (*American Literary Realism* 25, 2 [1993]: 11).
she writes that "in general the regionalist writers incorporated inclusivity as a cultural value."

49. Irvin S. Cobb, "Local Color," in *Local Color* (New York: George Doran, 1916), 20.

50. Mary Catherwood, "Pontiac's Lookout" (1894) in *American Local Color Writing, 1880–1920*, ed. Elizabeth Ammons (New York: Penguin, 1998), 179.

51. Mary Austin, "Regionalism in American Fiction," *English Journal* 25 (Feb. 1932): 97–107. Austin contrasted the bird's-eye view to a subliterary "automobile-eye view": "Time is the essence of the undertaking, time to live into the land and absorb it; still more time to cure the reading public of its preference for something less than the proverbial bird's-eye view of the American scene, what you might call the automobile-eye view, something slithering and blurred, nothing so sharply discriminated that it arrests the speed-numbed mind to understand, characters like garish gas stations picked out with electric lights" (107).

52. The standard work on professionalization is still Burton J. Bledstein, *The Culture of Professionalism: The Middle Class and the Development of Higher Education in America* (New York: Norton, 1976); for the relation to literature and the magazine market see Richard J. Ohmann, *Selling Culture: Magazines, Markets, and Class at the Turn of the Century* (New York: Verso, 1996); and Christopher P. Wilson, *The Labor of Words: Literary Professionalism in the Progressive Era* (Athens: University of Georgia Press, 1985).

53. Pierre Bourdieu, *Rules of Art: Genesis and Structure of the Literary Field,* trans. Susan Emanuel (Stanford: Stanford University Press, 1996). In the 1880s in France, the "literary and artistic field is constituted as such in and by opposition to a 'bourgeois' world which had never before asserted so bluntly its values and pretension to control the instruments of legitimation, both in the domain of art and in the domain of literature" (58). Bourdieu's prescriptive postscript is itself in the literary vein, with its calls for an "Internationale of intellectuals" that, "by increasing their autonomy . . . can increase the effectiveness of a political action whose ends and means have their origin in the specific logic of the fields of cultural production" (340).

54. C. M. Thompson, "New Figures in Literature and Art: Hamlin Garland," *Atlantic Monthly* 76 (Dec. 1895): 840–44; reprinted in *The Critical Reception of Hamlin Garland 1891–1978*, ed. Richard Boudreau, Charles L. P. Silet, and Robert E. Welch (Troy, N.Y.: Whitson, 1985), 28.

55 Review of Charles Egbert Craddock, *Where the Battle Was Fought, Nation* 39, 1006 (1884): 314.

56. Review of Charles Egbert Craddock, *Raid of the Guerilla, New York Times,* June 9, 1912, 358.

57. William Malone Baskervill, "Charles Egbert Craddock," in *Southern Writers: Biographical and Critical Studies* (1897; reprint, New York: Gordian Press, 1970), 357–404.

58. Henry C. Vedder, "George Washington Cable," in *American Writers of To-day* (New York: Silver, Burdett, 1894), 261–74.

59. Review of Bret Harte, *In the Carquinez Woods, Nation* 37, 951 (1883): 255–56.

60. Review of Kate Chopin, *Bayou Folk, Atlantic Monthly* 73 (April, 1894): 559.

61. Willa Cather, review of Kate Chopin, *The Awakening,* in *The World and the Parish,* vol. 2: *Willa Cather's Articles and Reviews, 1893–1902,* ed. William M. Curtin (Lincoln: University of Nebraska Press, 1970), 694–99.

62. Alice Brown, review of Sarah Orne Jewett, *The Country of the Pointed Firs, Book Buyer* 15 (Oct. 1897): 248–50.

63. Horace E. Scudder, "Miss Jewett," *Atlantic Monthly* 73 (Jan. 1894): 133.

64. Horace S. Fiske, *Provincial Types in American Fiction* (New York: Chautauqua Press, 1903).

65. William Dean Howells, review of Hamlin Garland, *Main-Travelled Roads, Harper's New Monthly Magazine* 83, 496 (September, 1891): 638–42.

66. Howells, *Criticism and Fiction,* 20–21.

67. Grace Isabel Colbron, "Across the Colour Line," *Bookman* 8 (Dec. 1898): 339.

68. "Garland in Ghostland," *Arena* 34 (Aug. 1904): 206–16.

69. Harry Aubrey Toulmin, "Charles Egbert Craddock," in *Social Historians* (Boston: Gorham Press, 1911), 59–97.

70. *Overland Monthly,* 2d ser., 8, 46 (Oct. 1886): 440.

71. Vedder, *American Writers of To-day,* 268; William Malone Baskervill, *Southern Writers,* vol. 1 (Nashville: Publishing House of M.E. Church, 1897), 318; Randolph Bourne, "From an Older Time," *Dial* 65 (Nov. 2, 1918): 363; all reprinted in *Twentieth-Century Literary Criticism,* vol. 4 (Detroit: Gale Research, 1981), 24–25.

72. Norman Foerster, *Toward Standards: A Study of the Present Critical Movement in American Letters* (New York: Farrar & Rinehart, 1930), ix.

73. Horace E. Scudder, "New Figures in Literature and Art," *Atlantic Monthly* 75 (May 1895): 658.

74. T. S. Perry, review of Wilhelm Jensen, *Fluth und Ebbe, Atlantic Monthly* 40 (Nov. 1877): 636.

75. Horace E. Scudder, review of Francis Marion Crawford, *Saracinesca, Atlantic Monthly* 60 (Sept. 1887): 414.

76. Walt Whitman, *Democratic Vistas* in *Complete Poetry and Collected Prose* (New York: Library of America, 1982) 943.

77. Howells, *Literature and Life* (New York: Harper, 1952), 46.

78. John De Forest, "The Great American Novel," *Nation* (Jan. 9, 1868).

79. Julian Hawthorne, "The American Element in Fiction," *North American Review* 139 (Aug. 1884), 178.

80. Edward Eggleston, "Formative Influences," *Forum* 10 (Nov. 1890): 284–85.

81. James Lane Allen, "Local Color," *Critic* 8 (Jan 9, 1886): 13–14.

82. *Overland Monthly,* 2d ser., 1, 1 (Jan. 1883): 97; *Overland Monthly,* 2d ser., 2, 9 (Sept. 1883): 331; *Overland Monthly,* 2d ser. 8, 46 (Oct. 1886): 440.

83. James Taft Hatfield, "Scholarship and the Commonwealth," *PMLA* 17 (1902): 391, 398.

84. Henry C. Vedder, *American Writers of To-day,* 26, 164, 22.

85. Bliss Perry, *A Study of Prose Fiction* (1902; rev. ed. (Boston: Houghton Mifflin, 1920), 5.

86. George Woodberry, "The Language of All the World," *Torch* (1905), reprinted in *Contemporary American Criticism,* ed. James Bowman (New York: Henry Holt, 1926) 315. As Kenneth Cmiel has shown, debates about the value of literature in these years was also explicitly a debate against overspecialization. See Kenneth Cmiel, *Democratic Eloquence: The Fight over Popular Speech in Nineteenth-Century America* (New York: Morrow, 1990), 148–75.

87. William McFee, "The Cheer-Leader in Literature," *Harper's Magazine* (March 1926), reprinted in *Contemporary American Criticism,* 255.

88. H. L. Mencken, "Criticism of Criticism of Criticism," in *Prejudices: First Series* (New York: Knopf, 1919), 12.

89. J. E. Spingarn, *The New Criticism* (New York: Columbia University Press, 1911).

90. Davidson, "A Mirror for Artists," in Twelve Southerners, *I'll Take My Stand*, 28–60; see also Donald Davidson, *Regionalism and Nationalism in the United States: The Attack on Leviathan* (1938; reprint, New Brunswick, N.J.: Transaction Publishers, 1991); and idem, "Regionalism and Nationalism," in *"Still Rebels, Still Yankees" and Other Essays* (Baton Rouge: Louisiana State University Press, 1957).

91. Allen Tate, "The New Provincialism," in *Essays of Four Decades* (Chicago: Swallow, 1968), 545.

92. John Crowe Ransom, "The Aesthetic of Regionalism" (1934), in *Selected Essays of John Crowe Ransom*, ed. Thomas Daniel Young and John Hindle (Baton Rouge: Louisiana State University Press, 1984), 46.

93. John T. Frederick, "Introduction," in *Out of the Midwest*, ed. John T. Frederick (New York: McGraw-Hill, 1944), xv.

94. John Crowe Ransom, *The World's Body* (New York: Charles Scribner's Sons, 1938), x.

95. Ezra Pound, "Provincialism the Enemy," *New Age* 12 (July 26, 1917), reprinted in *Selected Prose: 1909–1965*, ed. William Cookson (London: Faber, 1973), 159; see Hans-Werner Ludwig, "Province and Metropolis, Centre and Periphery: Some Critical Terms Re-examined," in *Poetry in the British Isles: Non-Metropolitan Perspectives*, ed. Hans-Werner Ludwig and Lothar Fietz (Cardiff: University of Wales Press, 1995), 47–69.

96. Elliott et al., ed., *Columbia Literary History*, xii.

97. Robert E. Spiller, Willard Thorp, Thomas H. Johnson, and Henry Seidel Canby, eds., *Literary History of the United States* (New York: Macmillan, 1948), vi.

98. William P. Trent, John Erskine, Stuart P. Sherman, and Carl Van Doren, eds., *The Cambridge History of American Literature* (New York: Macmillan, 1933), xi.

99. *Heath Anthology of American Literature*, ed. Paul Lauter (Boston: Houghton Mifflin, 1998), 3rd. ed., xxxvi.

100. I compiled these phrases before giving a talk at the University of South Carolina, all culled from critical work of that university's faculty: Robert Newman has recently suggested a public relations campaign based on these arguments and elsewhere has claimed that Herman Melville and Brockden Brown write in ways that disturb the basic social categories of good and evil, savagery and civilization, Indian and white; his colleague at the time, Pamela Barnett, finds "the impossibility of resolution" to be "the impetus" in Larsen's *Quicksand*, and that Toni Morrison's *Beloved* "explodes the dichotomies" between male and female, rapist and victim. Cynthia Davis suggests that Jewett explodes the dichotomies of hetero- and homosexuality and hetero- and homosociality. Amittai Aviram's preference for Kant over Hegel is based on the way Kant helps us see illuminating paradox in our fictions, while Meili Steele's preference for Hegel over Kant is based on the way it provides a new, "recuperative" theoretical "framework that recasts the crippling opposition" between sociological and dialogical vocabularies "into a productive incommensurability." Robert Newman, "Reviving the State of the Profession" *ADE Bulletin* 122 (spring 1999): 35–38; and idem, "Indians and Indian-Hating in *Edgar Huntly* and *The Confidence Man*," *MELUS* 15, 3 (fall 1988): 65–74; Pamela E. Barnett, "Figurations of Rape and the Supernatural in *Beloved*," *PMLA* 112, 3 (May 1997): 418–27; and idem, "'My Picture of You Is, after All, the True Helga Crane': Portraiture and Identity in Nella Larsen's *Quicksand*," *Signs* 20, 3 (spring 1995): 575–600; Cynthia J. Davis, "Making the Strange(r) Familiar: Sarah Orne Jewett's 'The Foreigner,'" in *Breaking Boundaries: New Perspectives on Women's Regional Writing*, ed. Sherrie A. Inness and Diana Royer (Iowa City: University of Iowa Press, 1997), 88–108; Amittai Aviram, "Asking the Question: Kant and Postmodernism?" paper delivered at the Northeast American Society for Eighteenth-Century Studies, Durham, New Hampshire, Dec. 12, 1999; Meili Steele, "How Philosophy of Language Informs Ethics and Politics: Richard Rorty and Contemporary Theory," *Boundary 2* 20, 2 (summer 1993): 140–72.

101. All from *Profession* (2002): Mary Louise Pratt, "The Traffic in Meaning: Translation, Contagion, Infiltration," 25, 35; Sherry Simon, "Crossing Town: Montreal in Translation," 23; Doris Sommer, "Bilingual Aesthetics: An Invitation," 12; Dianna Taylor, "Translating Performance," 49; James F. Slevin, "Keeping the University Occupied and Out of Trouble," 70.

102. Nancy K. Harris, "Problems of Representation in Turn-of-the-Century Immigrant Fiction," in *American Realism and the Canon,* ed. Tom Quirk and Gary Scharnhorst (Newark: University of Delaware Press, 1994), 138, 137.

103. Lisa Lowe, *Immigrant Acts: Asian American Cultural Politics* (Durham: Duke University Press, 1996), 173.

104. Susan Gillman, "Regionalism and Nationalism in Sarah Orne Jewett's *Country of the Pointed Firs,*" in Howard, ed., *New Essays on "Country of the Pointed Firs,"* 115.

105. Amanda Anderson, "Cosmopolitanism, Universalism, and the Divided Legacies of Modernity," in *Cosmopolitics: Thinking and Feeling beyond the Nation,* ed. Pheng Cheah and Bruce Robbins (Minneapolis: University of Minnesota Press, 1998), 286.

106. Julia Kristeva, *Nations without Nationalism,* trans. Leon S. Roudiez (New York: Columbia University Press, 1993), 5.

107. David Harvey, "Cosmopolitanism and the Banality of Geographic Evils," *Public Culture* 12, 2 (summer, 2000): 529; Paul Rabinow, "Representations Are Social Facts: Modernity and Post Modernity in Anthropology" in *Writing Culture: The Poetics and Politics of Ethnology,* ed. James Gifford and George E. Marcus (Berkeley: University of California Press, 1986), 258.

108. Immanuel Kant, "Toward Perpetual Peace: A Philosophical Sketch," in *Kant's Political Writings,* ed. Hans Reiss, trans. H. B. Nisbet (New York: Cambridge University Press, 1970), 105.

109. Martha Nussbaum, *For Love of Country: Debating the Limits of Patriotism,* ed. Joshua Cohen (Boston: Beacon Press, 1996), 8. Hereafter cited in the text.

110. Sissela Bok's and Kwame Anthony Appiah's responses are in Cohen, ed., *For Love of Country,* 40, 21–29.

111. Robert Pinsky, Gertrude Himmelfarb, and Benjamin Barber are cited in Cohen, ed., For *Love of Country,* 88, 87–88, 77, 75, 30.

112. Keith Michael Baker and Peter Hans Reill, eds., *What's Left of Enlightenment? A Postmodern Question* (Stanford: Stanford University Press, 2001), 1.

113. David A. Hollinger, "The Enlightenment and Cultural Conflict," in Baker and Reill, eds., *What's Left of Enlightenment?* 8. See also Tzvetan Todorov, *The Imperfect Garden: The Legacy of Humanism* (Princeton: Princeton University Press, 2002), and the discussion below of Graham Good, *Humanism Betrayed: Theory, Ideology, and Culture in the Contemporary University* (Montreal: McGill-Queen's University Press, 2001).

114. Judith Butler, "Universality in Culture," in Cohen, ed., *For Love of Country,* 45–52; see also Axel Honneth, "Is Universalism a Moral Trap? The Presuppositions and Limits of a Politics of Human Rights," in *Perpetual Peace: Essays on Kant's Cosmopolitan Ideal,* ed. James Bohman and Matthias Lutz-Bachmann (Cambridge: MIT Press, 1997), 155–78; and Dena Goodman, "Difference: An Enlightenment Concept," in *What's Left of Enlightenment?* eds. Baker and Reill, 129–47.

115. Gayatri Spivak, "Can the Subaltern Speak?" in *Marxism and the Interpretation of Culture,* ed. Cary Nelson and Lawrence Grossberg (Urbana: University of Illinois Press, 1988); Homi K. Bhabha, *The Location of Culture* (New York: Routledge, 1994); Dipesh Chakrabarty, "Universalism and Belonging in the Logic of Capitalism," *Public Culture* 12, 3 (fall 2000): 653–78; Scott L. Malcomson, "The Varieties of Cosmopolitan Experience," in *Cosmopolitics,* ed. Cheah and Robbins, 234.

116. Arnold Krupat, *Ethnocriticism: Ethnography, History, Literature* (Berkeley: University of California Press, 1992), 3.

117. Ross Posnock, *Color and Culture: Black Writers and the Making of the Modern Intellectual* (Cambridge: Harvard University Press, 1998), 9, 11.

118. K. Anthony Appiah, "Cosmopolitan Reading," in *Cosmopolitan Geographies: New Locations in Literature and Culture,* Essays from the English Institute, ed. Vinay Dharwadker (New York: Routledge, 2001), 202.

119. Cohen, ed., *For Love of Country,* 56.

120. Ibid., 122.

121. Pheng Cheah, "Introduction, Part II: The Cosmopolitical—Today," in *Cosmopolitics,* ed. Cheah and Robbins, *Cosmopolitics,* 31.

122. Karl Marx and Friedrich Engels, *The Communist Manifesto,* in *The Marx-Engels Reader,* 2d ed., ed. Robert C. Tucker (New York: Norton, 1978), 476.

123. Antonio Gramsci, *Selections from the Prison Notebooks,* ed. and trans. Quintin Hoare and Geoffrey Nowell Smith (New York: International Publishers, 1971), 17–18, 274.

124. Frantz Fanon, *The Wretched of the Earth,* trans. Constance Farrington (New York: Grove Press, 1963), 149–50.

125. Howard Fast, "Cosmopolitanism," *Daily Worker,* April 26, 1956.

126. Timothy Brennan, *At Home in the World: Cosmopolitanism Now* (Cambridge: Harvard University Press, 1997); Sheldon Pollock, "Cosmopolitan and Vernacular in History," *Public Culture* 12, 3 (fall 2000): 591–626. Brennan's book is an interesting case of academic disciplining. His earliest work on cosmopolitanism was clearly in favor of the concept (cf. "Cosmopolitans and Celebrities," *Race and Class* 31, 1 (1989): 1–19), but by the time the book was published he had adopted a more critical line, to the point where one reviewer suggested that the book is not a critique of cosmopolitanism but a critique of "pseudo-cosmopolitanism" (Ross Posnock, "The Dream of Deracination: The Uses of Cosmopolitanism," *American Literary History* 12 [winter 2000]: 802–8). In his acknowledgments, Brennan writes, in what I imagine is a somewhat wistful tone, "The early chapters of this book were written five years ago and have been revised under the withering comments of people whose perspicacity and care astounded me." In the conclusion he completes his about-face: "The pages above have been about how an elusive and malleable construct like cosmopolitanism has served to limit a necessary confrontation with alternative values implicit in the reception of the 'third world.' While making it more difficult to talk about the concept convincingly, the term's very malleability and elusiveness were central to the success of its role as an arbiter of bad faith" (310). And then, flopping once more, he hopes for a future "cosmopolitanism worthy of the name . . . a global cultural outlook that respects autonomy and contestatory values" (309).

127. Robert Reich, *The Work of Nations: Preparing Ourselves for Twenty-First–Century Capitalism* (New York: Knopf, 1991), 309–10. Una Chaudhuri also offers the image of "cell-phone toting frequent-flyer cosmopolitans who seem to be the prophets of a *Postethnic*-postmodern world, one of those about whom contemporary identity is being theorized as a matter of 'aerials, not roots.'" Una Chaudhuri, "Theater and Cosmopolitanism: New Stories, Old Stages," in Dharwadker, ed., *Cosmopolitan Geographies,* 182.

128. Christopher Lasch, *The Revolt of the Elites and the Betrayal of Democracy* (New York: Norton, 1995), 46–47.

129. Friedrich Nietzsche, *The Will to Power,* trans. Walter Kaufmann (New York: Random House, 1967), 47.

130. Bruce Ackerman, "Rooted Cosmopolitanism," *Ethics* 104 (1994): 516–35; Mitchell Cohen, "Rooted Cosmopolitanism: Thoughts on the Left, Nationalism, and Multiculturalism," *Dissent* (fall 1992): 478–83.

131. Homi Bhabha, "Unsatisfied: Notes on Vernacular Cosmopolitanism," in *Text and Nation: Cross-Disciplinary Essays on Cultural and National Identities,* ed. Laura García-Moreno and Peter C. Pfeiffer (Columbia, SC: Camden House, 1996), 198; Bruce Robbins, "Introduction, Part I: Actually Existing Cosmopolitanisms," in *Cosmopolitics,* ed. Cheah and Robbins, 1–19; James Clifford, *Routes: Travel and Translation in the Late Twentieth Century* (Cambridge: Harvard University Press, 1997); David A. Hollinger, *Postethnic America: Beyond Multiculturalism* (New York: Basic Books, 1995). The argument for "already existing cosmopolitanism" had been made by Hannah Arendt in her *Lectures on Kant's Political Philosophy,* ed. Ronald Beiner (1982; Chicago: University of Chicago Press, 1989): "In the last analysis, one is a member of the world community by the sheer fact of being human; this is one's 'cosmopolitan existence'" (75).

132. Harvey, "Cosmopolitanism and the Banality of Geographic Evils," 530. See Sheldon Pollock, "The Cosmopolitan Vernacular," *Journal of Asian Studies* 57, 1 (Feb. 1998): 6–37; Rob Wilson, "A New Cosmopolitanism Is in the Air: Some Dialectical Twists and Turns," in *Cosmopolitics,* ed. Cheah and Robbins, 351–61; Robert R. Edwards, "The Metropol and the Mayster-Toun," in *Cosmopolitan Geographies,* ed. Dharwadker, 33–62; Bruce Robbins, "The Weird Heights: On Cosmopolitanism, Feeling, and Power," *differences* 7, 1 (1995): 167.

133. Jacques Derrida,"On Cosmopolitanism," in *On Cosmopolitanism and Forgiveness*, trans. Mark Dooley and Michael Hughes (NewYork: Routledge, 2001), 4.

134. Posnock,"The Dream of Deracination," 802–8.

135. Idem, *Color and Culture*, 21.

136. Celia Thaxter, *Among the Isles of the Shoals* (1873; reprint, Portsmouth, N.H.: Peter E. Randall, 1994), 29. Hereafter cited in the text.

137. Harvey,"Cosmopolitanism and the Banality of Geographic Evils."

1850-1900

1. Harry R.Warfel and G. Harrison Orians, *American Local-Color Stories* (NewYork: American Book Company, 1941), xxiv.

2. Claude Simpson edited an anthology in 1960 with a very similar list: Jewett, Alice Brown, Stowe, Freeman, Cooke, Deming, Catherwood,Woolson, Garland, Page, Chesnutt, Murfree, Harris, Cable, Bonner, Chopin, Harte, and Alfred Henry Lewis. Claude M. Simpson, ed., *The Local Colorists: American Short Stories, 1857–1900* (NewYork: Harper, 1960).

3. Elizabeth Ammons, "Introduction," in Ammons, ed., *American Local Color Writing, 1880–1920*, viii. See Mary Louise Pratt, *Imperial Eyes: Travel Writing and Transculturation* (NewYork: Routledge. 1992); by autoethnography, Pratt means texts in which "colonized subjects undertake to represent themselves in ways that *engage with* the colonizer's own terms" (7). Pratt's work began my own thinking on these issues.

4. Spiller et al., eds., *Literary History of the United States*, 2:1017.

5. The major exception to this statement is Nancy Glazener's *Reading for Realism*. Also pertinent is Quentin E. Martin's "Hamlin Garland's 'The Return of the Private' and 'Under the Lion's Paw' and the Monopoly of Money in Post-CivilWar America," *American Literary Realism* 29 (fall 1996), in which Martin discusses Garland's "woefully unappreciated and misunderstood work," dismissed by the New Critical "'apolitical' criticism of the past and the 'political' criticism of the present," which relegates him to the status of "white male writer" (63, 74). "As a result," Martin suggests, in typical literary-cosmopolitan fashion, "literary studies and America's very sense of its own past continue to be impoverished" by his exclusion.

6. Hamlin Garland, *Main-Travelled Roads* (1891; reprint, NewYork: New American Library, 1962), 54.

7. Brodhead, *Cultures of Letters*, 139–41.

8. Bill Brown, "The Popular, the Populist, and the Populace—Locating Hamlin Garland in the Politics of Culture," *Arizona Quarterly* 50 (autumn 1994): 101.

9. Foote, *Regional Fictions*, 42. Foote's argument is the most interesting recent reading of Garland's methods. She argues that "a representational literary economy and a national market economy combine to produce an ambivalent idea of the local" (43); I am suggesting that the productive combination is more complex, and that the result is something more than ambivalence, but in many other ways our two readings are compatible.

10. Glazener, *Reading for Realism*, 193. See also John L. Sutton, "The Regional Form as a Commodified Site in Hamlin Garland's *Main-Travelled Roads*," *MidAmerica* 23 (1996): 56–63, for Garland's work in the context of the politics of the *Arena*.

11. Hamlin Garland, *Son of the Middle Border* (NewYork: P.F. Collier & Son, 1917), 94.

12. It is also interesting, given Brodhead's argument about tourism, that Rob has left Wisconsin for the far Western plains because "Waupac is a kind of summer resort, and the people that use' t' come in summer looks down on us cusses in the fields an' shops" (102). It is this class resentment that provokes the speech that Seagraves finds inspiring.

13. William Dean Howells,"Editor's Study," *Harper's* (Sept. 1891), reprinted in *Editor's Study*, ed. James W. Simpson (Troy:Whitston Publishing, 1983), 333.

14. *NewYork Tribune*, June 28, 1891, 14. Many other critics praised his breadth and balance. E. F. Harkins,

in *Famous Authors (Men)* (Boston: LC Page & Co, 1901), writes that even the list of his public lectures in the 1890s "show us the breadth of mind which he had reached just as he entered citizenhood" (42).

15. Arthur Inkersley, "The Gospel according to Hamlin Garland," *Education* 15 (June 1895): 21.

16. C. M. Thompson, "New Figures in Literature and Art: Hamlin Garland," *Atlantic* 76 (Dec. 1895): 840–44, 842.

17. H. L. Mencken, "Six Members of the Institute," in *Prejudices, First Series* (New York: Knopf, 1919), 63.

18. Harriet Beecher Stowe, "Uncle Lot" (1834), in Fetterley and Pryse, eds., *American Women Regionalists: 1850–1910*, 4.

19. Bret Harte, "M'liss: An Idyl of Red Mountain," in *The Outcasts of Poker Flat* (1870; reprint, New York: New American Library, 1961), 81.

20. Carrie Tirado Bramen, *The Uses of Variety: Modern Americanism and the Quest for National Distinctiveness* (Cambridge: Harvard University Press, 2000), 130; Maria Amparo Ruiz de Burton, *The Squatter and the Don* (Houston: Arte Publico, 1992. Ruiz de Burton's novel is back in print for cultural-historical reasons; its cosmopolitanism, and thus its literary appeal, is very limited. Bramen's discussion of regionalism and cosmopolitanism is very valuable, especially in linking Jamesian pragmatism to cosmopolitan ideals; her approach and goals are different than mine here, however.

21. Mary Noailles Murfree [Charles Egbert Craddock], "The Star in the Valley" (1878), in Fetterley and Pryse, eds., *American Women Regionalists, 1850–1910*, 257.

22. Sarah Orne Jewett, "Introduction," *Deephaven* (Boston: Houghton Mifflin, 1893)

23. Sarah Orne Jewett, "Miss Peck's Promotion," in *The King of Folly Island and Other People* (Boston: Houghton Mifflin, 1888), reprinted in *Short Fiction of Sarah Orne Jewett and Mary Wilkins Freeman*, ed. Barbara H. Solomon (New York: New American Library, 1979), 233.

24. Sarah Orne Jewett, *Country of the Pointed Firs*, in Solomon, ed., *Short Fiction*, 47.

25. Sandra A. Zagarell, "Crosscurrents: Registers of Nordicism, Community, and Culture in Jewett's *Country of the Pointed Firs*," *Yale Journal of Criticism* 10, 2 (1997): 355–70.

26. June Howard, "Unravelling Regions, Unsettling Periods: Sarah Orne Jewett and American Literary History," *American Literature* 68, 2 (June 1996): 378.

27. Howard, ed., *New Essays*.

28. Sandra A. Zagarell, "*Country's* Portrayal of Community and the Exclusion of Difference," in ibid., 55, 40.

29. Michael Davitt Bell, "Gender and American Realism in *Country of the Pointed Firs*," in ibid., 76–77.

30. Elizabeth Ammons, "Material Culture, Empire, and Jewett's *Country of the Pointed Firs*," in ibid., 81–99; Susan Gillman, "Regionalism and Nationalism," 109.

31. Howard, "Introduction," in Howard, ed., *New Essays*, 30.

32. Charles Chesnutt, "The Goophered Grapevine," originally published in *Atlantic Monthly* in 1887; and *The Conjure Woman* (1899), reprinted in *Charles W. Chesnutt: Stories, Novels, & Essays* (New York: Library of America, 2002), 6.

33. This point had been made about Chesnutt by earlier critics, such as William L. Andrews, *The Literary Career of Charles W. Chesnutt* (Baton Rouge: Louisiana State University Press, 1980).

34. Kenneth M. Price, "Charles Chesnutt, the *Atlantic Monthly*, and the Intersection of African American Fiction and Elite Culture," in *Periodical Literature in Nineteenth-Century America*, ed. Kenneth M. Price and Susan Belasco Smith (Charlottesville: University Press of Virginia, 1995), 257–74.

35. Eric J. Sundquist, *To Wake the Nations: Race in the Making of American Literature* (Cambridge, Mass.: Harvard University Press, 1993), 273.

36. Mary Wilkins Freeman, "A Mistaken Charity," in *A Humble Romance and Other Stories* (New York: Harper and Brothers, 1887), reprinted in Solomon, ed., *Short Fiction*, 308.

37. E. C. Steadman, "Constance Fenimore Woolson," *Critic* (Jan. 3, 1894): 73–74.

38. J. H Morse, "The Native Element in American Fiction [2]," *Century* 4 (July 1883): 369.

39. "Worship of Local Color," *Nation* 84 (Jan 24, 1907): 76.

40. *Overland Monthly,* 2d ser., 4, 22 (Oct. 1884): 447.

41. Excerpted in "Chronicle and Comment," *Bookman* 10 (Jan. 1900): 429.

42. Nancy Huston Banks, "The New York Ghetto," *Bookman* 4 (Oct. 1996): 157.

43. C., "'Lowly' Poets," *Poet Lore* 9, 2 (1897): 298.

44. J. H. Morse, "Recent American Fiction," *Atlantic Monthly* 55 (Jan. 1885): 125.

45. Meredith Nicholson, "Edward Eggleston," *Atlantic Monthly* 90 (Dec. 1902): 804–9.

46. Morse, "The Native Element in American Fiction," 288–98.

47. Charles W. Coleman Jr., "The Recent Movement in Southern Literature," *Harper's* 74 (May 1887): 837–38. Hereafter cited in the text.

48. William Dean Howells, "Paul Laurence Dunbar," *Harper's Weekly* (June 27, 1896), 280.

1900-1930

1. "Local Color and After," *Nation* 109 (Sept. 27, 1919): 426–27.

2. Carl Van Doren, "Contemporary American Novelists: X. The Revolt from the Village: 1920," *Nation* 113 (Oct. 12, 1921): 407–12. To take just one example: within three months *Survey* published the Alain Locke collection of essays that became *The New Negro* (New York: Albert & Charles Boni, 1925) and an issue on "Regional Community," edited by Lewis Mumford (*Survey* 14, 3 [May 1, 1925]).

3. Robert L. Dorman, in *Revolt of the Provinces: The Regionalist Movement in America, 1920–1945* (Chapel Hill: University of North Carolina Press, 1993), xii.

4. Robert H. Wiebe, *The Search for Order, 1877–1920* (New York: Hill and Wang, 1967), xiii, xiv.

5. B. A. Botkin, "Regionalism: Cult or Culture?" *English Journal* 25 (March 1936): 182.

6. Mary Austin, "Regionalism in American Fiction," *English Journal* 25 (Feb. 1932): 97.

7. Howard W. Odum and Harry Estill Moore, *American Regionalism: A Cultural-Historical Approach to National Integration* (New York: Henry Holt, 1938), 3.

8. Patrick Mazza, "Uncovering the Hidden History of Regionalism: The American Regionalist Insurgency of the 1920s–40s," *Cascadia Planet* (Jan. 15, 1997), http://www.tnews.com.

9. Quoted in Botkin, "Regionalism, Cult or Culture?" 182. See also Dorman, *Revolt of the Provinces:* "Regionalism must be considered not only as a critique of modernization, and not only as a noteworthy contribution to the historic dialogue over pluralism, but also as marking a significant stage in the still unfolding history of conservationism, preservationism, urban planning, and environmentalism" (xiii).

10. Lewis Mumford, "The City," in *Civilization in the United States,* ed. Harold Stearns (New York: Harcourt, Brace, 1922), 17.

11. John Dewey, "Americanism and Localism," in *Characters and Events: Popular Essays in Social and Political Philosophy,* vol. 2 (New York: Holt, 1929), 538, 541.

12. Ernest H. Gruening, ed., *These United States* (New York: Boni & Liveright, 1923, 1925), reprinted as Daniel Borus, ed., *These United States: Portraits of America from the 1920s* (Ithaca: Cornell University Press, 1992); for the relationship to *Civilization in the United States,* see Borus's introduction, 19–21.

13. Editors of the *Nation,* "Divided We Stand," in Borus, ed., *These United States,* 27.

14. This series is collected in Tom Lutz and Susanna Ashton, eds., *These "Colored" United States: African American Essays from the 1920s* (New Brunswick: Rutgers University Press, 1996).

15. See Posnock, *Color and Culture,* for his slightly different version of the cosmopolitanism of the Harlem Renaissance.

16. Willa Cather, *O Pioneers!* (New York: Penguin, 1989), 3. Parts of this section were originally published as Tom Lutz, "Cosmopolitanism Vistas: Willa Cather, Hamlin Garland, and the Literary Value of Regionalism," in *Recovering the Prairie.*

17. Cf. Frank's newspaper reading, 111–12, and Mrs. Lee's reading, 140–41.

18. Review of *O Pioneers!* [anon] *Nation* 97 (Sept. 4, 1913), 210–11.

19. Ronald Weber, *The Midwestern Ascendancy in American Writing* (Bloomington: Indiana University Press, 1992), 229.

20. Review of *McTeague*, *Courier*, April 8, 1899, reprinted in *Willa Cather: Stories, Poems, and Other Writings* ed. Sharon O'Brien (New York: Library of America, 1992), 925.

21. Willa Cather, "An Heir Apparent," *Courier*, April 7, 1900, reprinted in ibid., 931.

22. Willa Cather, "Henry James," *Courier*, Nov. 16, 1895, reprinted in ibid., 905.

23. Willa Cather, "Miss Jewett," reprinted in ibid., 854, 855.

24. Willa Cather, "Walt Whitman," *Nebraska State Journal*, Jan. 19, 1896, reprinted in ibid., 902–3.

25. Willa Cather, preface to *Alexander's Bridge* (1922), reprinted in *Alexander's Bridge*, ed. Marilee Lindeman (New York: Oxford University Press, 1997), 95.

26. Willa Cather, "My First Novels (There Were Two)," *Colophon*, June 1931, reprinted in *Willa Cather: Stories, Poems, and Other Writings*, 965.

27. Quoted in L. Brent Bohlke, ed., *Willa Cather in Person: Interviews, Speeches, and Letters* (Lincoln: University of Nebraska Press, 1986), 44.

28. Willa Cather, *My Ántonia*, in *Willa Cather: Early Novels and Stories*, ed. Sharon O'Brien (New York: Library of America, 1987), 712.

29. See Glen A. Love, "Jim Burden: A Rare Modern," in *Approaches to Teaching Cather's* My Ántonia, ed. Susan J. Rosowski (New York: MLA, 1989), 146–49.

30. "How wonderful if we could throw all the furniture out of the window; and along with it, all the meaningless reiterations concerning physical sensations, all the tiresome old patterns, and leave the room as bare as a stage of a Greek theater, or as that house into which the glory of Pentecost descended; leave the scene bare for the play of emotions, great and little." Willa Cather, "The Novel Démeublé" (1922), reprinted in Willa Cather, *Not Under Forty* (New York: Knopf, 1936), 51.

31. Sharon O'Brien, *Willa Cather: The Emerging Voice* (New York: Oxford University Press, 1987); James Woodress, *Willa Cather: A Literary Life* (Lincoln: University of Nebraska Press, 1987).

32. Anne E. Goldman, *Continental Divides: Revisioning American Literature* (New York: Palgrave Macmillan, 2000), 137.

33. Elizabeth Ammons, "Cather and the New Canon: 'The Old Beauty' and the Issue of Empire," *Cather Studies* 3 (1996): 258, 265. See also, for instance, Walter Benn Michaels's more complex reading in *Our America: Nativism, Modernism, and Pluralism* (Durham: Duke University Press, 1995); Loretta Wasserman, "Cather's Semitism," in *Cather Studies*, vol. 2, ed. Susan J. Rosowski (Lincoln: University of Nebraska Press, 1993); and Toni Morrison, *Playing in the Dark: Whiteness and the American Literary Imagination* (New York: Vintage, 1992).

34. Joan Acocella published "Cather and the Academy" in the *New Yorker* in 1995 and expanded it for *Willa Cather and the Politics of Criticism* (New York: Vintage: 2000).

35. Acocella, *Willa Cather*, 29.

36. Jewett, *Letters*, 248.

37. Edith Wharton, *Ethan Frome* (New York: New American Library, 2000), 3. Hereafter cited in the text.

38. Judith Fryer, *Felicitous Space: The Imaginative Structure of Edith Wharton and Willa Cather* Chapel Hill: University of North Carolina Press, 1986), 106–7.

39. R. W. B. Lewis, *Edith Wharton: A Biography* (New York: Harper & Row, 1975), 397.

40. Edith Wharton, *Summer*, in *Edith Wharton: Novellas and Other Writings*, ed. Cynthia Griffin Wolff (New York: Library of America, 1990).

41. Alfred Kazin, *A Writer's America: Landscape in Literature* (New York: Knopf, 1988).

42. Eric J. Sundquist, "Realism and Regionalism," in Elliott, ed., *Columbia Literary History of the United States*, 523.

43. Thadious M. Davis, "Race and Region," in Elliott et al., ed., *The Columbia History of the American Novel*, 407–36.

44. Weber, *The Midwestern Ascendancy in American Writing*, 170.

45. Anthony Channell Hilfer, *The Revolt from the Village, 1915–1930* (Chapel Hill: University of North Carolina Press, 1969).

46. James Weldon Johnson, *The Autobiography of an Ex-Colored Man* (New York: Sherman, Good, 1912; reprint, New York: Vintage, 1989), xl.

47. Posnock, *Color and Culture*, 76.

48. See also Siobhan Somerville, *Queering the Color Line: Race and the Invention of Homosexuality in American Culture* (Durham: Duke University Press, 2000).

49. Eve Kosofsky Sedgwick, *Epistemology of the Closet* (Berkeley: University of California Press, 1990).

50. See Max Putzel, *The Man in the Mirror: William Marion Reedy and His Magazine* (Columbia: University of Missouri Press, 1998).

51. William Marion Reedy, "The Writer of Spoon River," *Reedy's Mirror* (Nov. 20, 1914): 1; quoted in John E. Hallwas, "Introduction," *Spoon River Anthology: An Annotated Edition* ed. John E. Hallwas (Urbana: University of Illinois Press, 1992), 3.

52. Hallwas, "Introduction," 4ff.

53. "The Origin of Spoon River," *St. Louis Post-Dispatch,* March 29, 1918, 21; quoted in Hallwas, "Introduction," 15.

54. Amy Lowell, *Tendencies in Modern American Poetry* (1921; reprint, New York: Haskell House, 1970), 139; William Stanley Braithwaite, "Spoon River Anthology," *Forum* 55 (Jan. 1916): 118–20. More recently both these passages have been used to argue for the Bakhtinian dialogism of the text, which is to say something much like what Braithwaite describes. See Patrick D. Murphy, "The Dialogical Voices of Edgar Lee Masters' *Spoon River Anthology,*" *Studies in the Humanities* 15 (June 1988): 13–32.

55. Edgar Lee Masters, "The Genesis of Spoon River," *American Mercury* 28 (Jan. 1933): 53.

56. See Ian F. A. Bell for a reading of *Spoon River* in relation to Ezra Pound's poetic theories and Pound's writings about Masters. "In the Real Tradition: Edgar Lee Masters and Hugh Selwyn Mauberly," *Criticism* 23, 2 (spring 1981): 141–54.

57. "Not only does the mock-heroic style jar against the predominantly serious tone of the epitaph-poems, it undercuts one of the great strengths of *Spoon River Anthology*—the description of everyday people as fit subjects for poetic analysis." John E. Hallwas, "Introduction," 10. This jarring and undercutting can also be read as a balancing act.

58. Quoted in John E. Hallwas, "Introduction," 10.

59. Edgard Lee Masters, quoted in K. Narayana Chandran, "*Revolt from the Grave: Spoon River Anthology* by Edgar Lee Masters," *Midwest Quarterly* 29 (summer 1988): 438–47. For the relation of the *Anthology* to the life, see Hallwas and the numerous articles by Charles E. Burgess in *Papers on Literature and Language, Western Illinois Regional Studies,* and elsewhere.

60. The *Midland* was published monthly except for double issues, and in one case a quadruple issue; the first issue was published in January 1915 and the last in March–April–May–June 1933. The magazine was printed in Iowa City even when the editorial offices moved with Frederick. Circulation ranged from two hundred to five hundred until the move to Chicago, when the subscription list swelled to twelve hundred and as many as two thousand copies were printed. The price was $1.50 per year, which was raised to $2.00 in 1920 and to $3.00 in 1924. Portions of this section were originally published as "The Cosmopolitan *Midland,*" in *Little Magazines and Modernism,* ed. Adam McKible and Suzanne Churchill (Columbus: Ohio State University Press, 2004).

61. *Midland* 1, 1 (Jan. 1915): 1.

62. Edward J. O'Brien, ed., *The Best Short Stories of 1915 and the Yearbook of the American Short Story* (Boston: Small, Maynard, 1916), 9.

63. H. L. Mencken, in Frederick papers, University of Iowa Special Collections; *Smart Set* (July 1923): 141.

64. Frederick J. Hoffman, Charles Allen, and Carolyn F. Ulrich, *The Little Magazine: A History and a Bibliography* (Princeton: Princeton University Press, 1946), 133; they dismiss the entire local color movement as preregionalist: "One seeks reality, the other a conscious distortion of reality" (136).

65. John Tebbel, *The American Magazine: A Compact History* (New York: Hawthorne Books, 1969), 9.

66. Edward J. O'Brien, ed., *The Best Short Stories of 1930 and the Yearbook of the American Short Story* (New York: Dodd, Mead, 1930), 9.

67. Milton M. Reigelman, *The Midland: A Venture in Literary Regionalism* (Iowa City: University of Iowa Press, 1976), 4.

68. Hoffman et al., *The Little Magazine*, 140; Royce's talk was published as a pamphlet by the university and in Royce's *Race Questions, Provincialism, and Other American Problems* (New York: Macmillan, 1908.

69. Letter from Ruth Suckow to John T. Frederick, Sept. 29, 1925, Frederick papers.

70. Frank Luther Mott, who would later achieve academic fame as a chronicler of American journalism, was an early contributor to the magazine and moved from his job as editor of the Grand Junction, Iowa, newspaper to the Iowa faculty at Frederick's urging, becoming coeditor of the *Midland* in 1925; Reigelman, *The Midland*, 22. The magazine had a debt of $263 the first year, and ran $100–200 short each year through the 1920s; in the 1930s, although circulation increased, red ink climbed to about $1000 a year; Frank Luther Mott, *A History of American Magazines, V: Sketches of 21 Magazines 1905–1930* (Cambridge: Harvard University Press, 1968), 142.

71. Marquis Childs, in Reigelman, *The Midland*, 26.

72. "Regionalism—notes," Frederick papers.

73. Philip Joseph, "Landed and Literary: Hamlin Garland, Sarah Orne Jewett, and the Production of Regional Literatures," *Studies in American Fiction* 26 (autumn 1998): 147–70.

74. Quoted in Hoffman et al., *The Little Magazine*, 130.

75. Lewis Mumford, *Technics and Civilization* (New York: Harcourt, Brace, 1934), 292.

76. I am playing on Gerald Graff's phrase; see his *Literature against Itself: Literary Ideas in Modern Society* (Chicago: University of Chicago Press, 1979).

77. Sherwood Anderson, "Ohio: I'll Say We've Done Well," in Borus, ed., *These United States,* 292.

78. The Editors, "Divided We Stand," in ibid., 28.

79. Willa Cather, "Nebraska: The End of the First Cycle," in ibid., 226.

80. Dorothy Canfield Fisher, "Vermont: Our Rich Little Poor State," in ibid., 373.

81. Sherwood Anderson, Winesburg, Ohio: Text and Criticism, ed. John H. Ferres (New York: Viking, 1967)

82. Irving Howe, *Sherwood Anderson: A Biographical and Critical Study* (1951; reprint, Stanford: Stanford University Press, 1966), 107.

83. M. A. [Maxwell Anderson], "A Country Town," *New Republic,* June 25, 1919, reprinted in *Winesburg, Ohio: Text and Criticism,* 254.

84. Rebecca West, *New Statesman,* July 22, 1922, reprinted in ibid., 262.

85. H. L. Mencken, *Smart Set* (Aug. 1919), reprinted in ibid., 257.

86. On the characters' complicity with their oppression, see Weber, *The Midwestern Ascendancy in American Writing,* 91–117.

87. See Mark Schorer, *Sinclair Lewis: An American Life* (New York: McGraw-Hill, 1961), 500–501.

88. Austin, "Regionalism in American Fiction," 99.

89. Sinclair Lewis, *Babbitt* (New York: Harcourt, Brace, 1922), 182.

90. Sinclair Lewis, *Arrowsmith* (1925; reprint, New York: Harcourt, Brace, 1952), 283.

91. R. W. B. Lewis and Nancy Lewis, eds., *The Letters of Edith Wharton* (New York: Charles Scribner's Sons, 1988), 455.

92. Schorer, *Sinclair Lewis,* 268.

93. Related by George Jean Nathan, quoted in ibid., 284.

94. H. L. Mencken, letter to Frederick, Frederick papers, Box 16.

95. Quoted in Weber, *The Midwestern Ascendancy in American Writing,* 181.

96. H. L. Mencken, "The Library," *American Mercury* 9 (Nov 1926), 383.

97. Ruth Suckow, "The Uprooted," in *Iowa Interiors* (New York: Knopf, 1926), 109.

98. Ruth Suckow, *The John Wood Case* (New York: Viking, 1959), 45, 31.

99. Ruth Suckow, *The Odyssey of a Nice Girl* (New York: Knopf, 1925), 57.

100. John T. Frederick, "Ruth Suckow and the Middle Western Literary Movement," *English Journal* 20 (Jan. 1931): 8.

101. Ruth Suckow, "A Rural Community," in *Iowa Interiors,* 57.

102. H. L. Mencken, "The Sahara of the Bozart" (1917), in *Prejudices: Second Series* (New York: Knopf, 1920), 136, 140.

103. Twelve Southerners, *I'll Take My Stand,* xliii.

104. Frank Lawrence Owsley, "The Irrepressible Conflict," in ibid., 62, 91.

105. Donald Davidson, "Regionalism and Nationalism," in *"Still Rebels, Still Yankees" and Other Essays* (Baton Rouge: Louisiana State University Press, 1957), 270–71.

106. Davidson, "A Mirror for Artists," in Twelve Southerners, *I'll Take My Stand,* 57.

107. Allen Tate, "Remarks on the Southern Religion," in ibid., 155.

108. In Allen Tate, *On the Limits of Poetry* (1948; reprint, Freeport, N.Y.: Books for Libraries Press, 1970).

109. Allen Tate, "The New Provincialism" (1945), in *Essays of Four Decades* (Chicago: University of Chicago Press, 1968), 535–46.

110. John Crowe Ransom, "Reconstructed but Unregenerate," in Twelve Southerners, *I'll Take My Stand,* 15.

111. John Crowe Ransom, "The Aesthetic of Regionalism," in *Selected Essays of John Crowe Ransom* (1934; reprint, Baton Rouge: Louisiana State University Press, 1984), 46.

112. Here Ransom is also echoing Margaret Mead's arguments about the relation of complex cultures to choice in *Coming of Age in Samoa* (1928).

113. John Crowe Ransom, "Preface," in *The World's Body,* x–xi.

114. Idem, "The Mimetic Principle," in ibid., 198n.

115. Idem, "Forms and Citizens," in ibid., 46.

116. René Wellek and Austin Warren, *Theory of Literature,* 3d ed. (New York: Harcourt Brace Jovanovich, 1962), 30.

117. I. A. Richards, *Principles of Literary Criticism* (London: Routledge and Kegan Paul, 1924), 250.

118. Brooks, *The Well-Wrought Urn,* 226–38; Murray Krieger, *The Institution of Theory* (Baltimore: Johns Hopkins University Press, 1994), 93.

119. John Crowe Ransom, "Art and Mr. Santayana," in *The World's Body,* 326. I have omitted the two words "of nature" at the ellipses; Ransom means by nature the entirety of the material and animal world, which he opposes in his writings to abstraction, so the sentence without the two words captures his meaning.

120. Douglas Anderson, "Alienation and Abundance: American Farm Fiction, 1900–1930," Ph.D. diss., University of Iowa, 2002. Edna Ferber's *So Big* (1924) also portrays a farm-owning woman; other agricultural novels with female protagonists in these years include Jack London's *Valley of the Moon* (1913), Edith Summers Kelley's *Weeds* (1923) O. E. Rolvaag's *Giants in the Earth* (1927), Phil Stong's *State Fair* (1932), and Ferber's *American Beauty* (1931).

121. Ellen Glasgow, *The Woman Within* (New York: Harcourt, Brace, 1954), 129.

122. The text provides a running commentary on sexual repression from the moment Dorinda's mother "fell victim to one of those natural instincts which Puritan theology has damned but never wholly exterminated" (9), through a description of how Dorinda is disgusted and frightened by her father's attempt to take her on his knee (40–41), to the clear and repeated connections among repressed sexuality, the mother's religious fantasies, and Dorinda's own obsessive industry. Ellen Glasgow, *Barren Ground* (1925; reprint, New York: Harcourt Brace, 1985).

123. Edith Summers Kelley, *Weeds* (1923; reprint, Carbondale: Southern Illinois University Press, 1972), 152.

124. Matthew J. Bruccoli, "Afterword," in Kelley, *Weeds,* 343.

125. Erskine Caldwell, *God's Little Acre* (New York: Grosset & Dunlap, 1933), 278.

126. See the Erskine Caldwell website (http://id.mind.net/~fletch/) and the site for the Caldwell birthplace museum: http://newnan.com/ec/.

127. William Faulkner, *The Sound and the Fury* (1929; reprint, New York: Random House, 1956), 401.

128. Quoted in Joseph Blotner, *Faulkner: A Biography* (New York: Random House, 1974). Nothing could be more wrong, in my mind, than concluding, as Myra Jehlen did in 1976, that the text represents Faulkner's "failure to visualize the past in other than conventionalized terms which we have already seen contain no answers to his questions." The lack of answers is, instead, as Jehlen suggests about his am-

bivalence, an important element of his success. Jehlen is right, at any rate, to see Faulkner's achievement as in line with the American literary tradition: "Faulkner's seems to me . . . one of the most troubled and unresolved visions in America's troubled and unresolved literature" Myra Jehlen, *Class and Character in Faulkner's South* (New York: Columbia University Press, 1976), 46, 20n.

129. Quoted in Malcolm Cowley, *The Faulkner-Cowley File: Letters and Memories, 1944–1962* (New York: Viking, 1978), 15.

130. William Faulkner, "An Introduction to *The Sound and the Fury*," *Mississippi Quarterly* 26 (summer 1973): 410–15 (410).

131. Quoted in *Lion in the Garden: Interviews With William Faulkner, 1926–1962*, ed. James B. Meriwether and Michael Mitigate (New York: Random House, 1988), 140.

132. Robert Penn Warren, "William Faulkner," *New Republic* 12 (Aug. 1946), reprinted in *Literature in America*, ed. Philip Rahv (New York: Meridian Books, 1957), 416.

133. Irving Howe, *William Faulkner* (New York: Random House, 1951), 25.

134. Frederick L. Gwynn and Joseph Blotner, eds. *Faulkner in the University: Class Conferences at the University of Virginia, 1957–1958* (Charlottesville: University Press of Virginia, 1959), 269.

135. Mourning Dove (Hum-Ishu-Ma), *Cogewea: The Half-Blood* (1927; reprint, Lincoln: University of Nebraska Press, 1981), 71.

136. Student evaluations of my courses have consistently singled out *Cogewea* as the text I should drop in future versions of the course.

137. Alfred Kazin, "Introduction," in Michael Gold, *Jews Without Money* (1930; reprint, New York: Carroll and Graf, 1996), 5.

138. Elizabeth Ammons, *Conflicting Stories: American Women Writers at the Turn into the Twentieth Century* (New York: Oxford University Press, 1992), 166.

139. Anzia Yezierska, *The Bread Givers* (1925; reprint, New York: Persea Books, 1975), 10.

140. Michaels, *Our America*, 72.

141. Michael Rogin, "Blackface, White Noise: The Jewish Jazz Singer Finds His Voice," *Critical Inquiry* 18 (spring 1992): 426.

142. Lucinda H. MacKethan, "*Cane*: A Pastoral Problem," *Mississippi Quarterly* 35 (fall 1975): 423–34; reprinted in *Cane: A Norton Critical Edition*, ed. Darwin Turner (New York: Norton, 1988), 230.

143. Letter to the *Liberator*, quoted in Darwin T. Turner, "Introduction [to the 1974 Edition of *Cane*]," in Turner, ed., *Cane: A Norton Critical Edition*, 129.

144. Letter to Waldo Frank, quoted in Turner, "Introduction," 129

145. Jean Toomer, "Outline of Autobiography," 58–59, quoted in Brian Joseph Benson and Mabel Mayle Dillard, *Jean Toomer* (Boston: Twayne, 1980), 97–98.

146. Waldo Frank, "Introduction," reprinted in Turner, ed., *Cane: A Norton Critical Edition*, 138.

147. Alfred Kreymborg, *Our Singing Strength* (New York: Macauley, 1929), 575.

148. John Armstrong, "The Real Negro," *New York Tribune*, Oct. 14, 1923, 26, reprinted in *The Merrill Studies in Cane*, ed. Frank Durham (Columbus: Charles E. Merrill, 1971), 27–28.

149. W. E. B. Du Bois and Alain Locke, "The Younger Literary Movement," *Crisis* 27 (Feb. 1924): 162.

150. Quoted in Turner, "Introduction," 121.

151. Jean Toomer, "On Being an American," in *The Wayward and the Seeking: A Collection of Writings by Jean Toomer*, ed. Darwin T. Turner; letter to the *Liberator*, quoted in Turner, "Introduction," 128.

152. Jean Toomer, *Cane*, in Turner, ed., *Cane: A Norton Critical Edition*, 108–9.

153. Thadious Davis, "Foreword to the 1989 Edition" in Jessie Redmon Fauset, *There Is Confusion* (1924; reprint, Boston: Northeastern University Press, 1989), xiii.

154. Zona Gale, "Introduction," in Jessie Redmon Fauset, *The Chinaberry Tree* (1931; reprint, New York: AMS Press, 1969), viii.

155. Fauset, *The Chinaberry Tree*, ix.

156. Fauset, *There Is Confusion*, 226.

157. Quoted in Deborah E. McDowell, "Introduction," in Jessie Redmon Fauset, *Plum Bun: A Novel without a Moral* (1928; reprint, Boston: Beacon Press, 1990), xi.

158. McDowell, "Introduction," xi.

159. For a reading of Fauset's *Plum Bun* based on this theory of literary cosmopolitanism, see Erica Still, "The Literary Cosmopolitanism of Jessie Redmon Fauset," manuscript.

160. W. E. B. Du Bois, *The Souls of Black Folk,* in *Writings,* ed. Nathan I. Huggins (New York: Library of America, 1996).

161. Quoted in Tyrone Tillery, *Claude McKay: A Black Poet's Struggle for Identity* (Amherst: University of Massachusetts Press, 1992). 87.

162. Quoted in ibid., 87; Marcus Garvey, "*Home to Harlem,* Claude McKay's Damaging Book Should Earn Wholesale Condemnation of Negroes," *Negro World* (Sept. 29, 1928), 1.

163. Claude McKay, *Banjo: A Story without a Plot* (1929; reprint, New York: Harcourt, Brace, 1957), 324. Portions of this section were originally published as Tom Lutz, "Claude McKay: Music, Sexualities, and Literary Cosmopolitanism," in *Black Orpheus: Music in African American Fiction from the Harlem Renaissance to Toni Morrison,* ed. Saadi Simawe (New York: Garland, 2000).

164. Wayne M. Cooper, "Foreword," in Claude McKay, *Home to Harlem* (1928; reprint, Boston: Northeastern University Press, 1987), xiii.

165. Joyce Hope Scott, "Black Folk Ritual in *Home to Harlem* and *Black Thunder,*" in *Claude McKay: Centennial Studies,* ed. A. L. McLeod (New Delhi: Sterling, 1992), 123–34.

166. McKay, *The Negroes in America* (1923; reprint, Port Washington, NY: Kennikat Press, 1979), 43.

167. McKay, review of *Shuffle Along,* in *The Passion of Claude McKay,* ed. Wayne F. Cooper (New York: Schocken, 1973), 63.

168. Sherley Anne Williams, *Give Birth to Brightness: A Thematic Study in Neo-Black Literature* (New York: Dial Press, 1972), 137.

169. Kathy J. Ogren, "Controversial Sounds: Jazz Performance as Theme and Language in the Harlem Renaissance," in *The Harlem Renaissance: Revaluations,* ed. Amritjit Singh, William S. Shiver, and Stanley Brodwin (New York: Garland, 1989), 170, 179.

170. Posnock, *Color and Culture,* 242–43.

171. For a discussion of the relation of race, civilization, and physical energy, see Tom Lutz, "Curing the Blues: W. E. B. Du Bois, Fashionable Diseases, and Degraded Music in 1903," *Black Music Research Journal* 11 (1991): 137–56; and idem, *American Nervousness, 1903: An Anecdotal History* (Ithaca: Cornell University Press, 1991), 3–13, 244–75.

172. Melvin Dixon, *Ride Out the Wilderness: Geography and Identity in Afro-American Literature* (Urbana: University of Illinois Press, 1987), 46ff.

173. McKay, *Home to Harlem,* 228.

174. McKay, *Banjo,* 192.

175. Wayne F. Cooper, *Claude McKay: Rebel Sojourner in the Harlem Renaissance: A Biography* (Baton Rouge: Louisiana State University Press, 1987), 153.

176. D. H. Lawrence, *Women in Love* (1920; reprint, New York: Viking Press, 1950), 330–31.

177. Sherwood Anderson, *Poor White* (1920; reprint, New York: Viking, 1969), 106.

178. Claude McKay, *A Long Way from Home* (1970; reprint, London: Pluto, 1985), 247.

179. James Clifford, *Routes: Travel and Translation in the late Twentieth Century* (Cambridge: Harvard University Press, 1997), 36.

180. Addison Gayle Jr., *Claude McKay: The Black Poet at War* (Detroit: Broadside Press, 1972), 17.

181. See Sean McCann, "Connecting Links: The Anti-Progressivism of Sui Sin Far," *Yale Journal of Criticism* 12 (spring 1999): 73–88; for other readings of Sui Sin Far, see Carol Roh-Spaulding, "Wavering Images: Mixed-Race Identity in the Stories of Edith Eaton/Sui Sin Far," in *Ethnicity and the American Short Story,* ed. Julia Brown (New York: Garland, 1997), 155–76; Ammons, *Conflicting Stories;* Martha Patterson, "Survival of the Best Fitted: The Trope of the New Woman in Margaret Murray Washington, Pauline Hopkins, Sui Sin Far, and Mary Johnston," Ph.D. diss., University of Iowa, 1996.

182. Annette White-Parks, "A Reversal of American Concepts of 'Other-ness' in the Fiction of Sui Sin Far," *MELUS* 20, 1 (spring 1995): 17.

183. Zitkala-Sa, "Impressions of an Indian Childhood," *Atlantic Monthly* 85 (1900), 37–47.

184. See April Schultz, "'To Lose the Unspeakable'": Folklore and Landscape in O. E. Rolvaag's *Giants in the Earth*," in *Mapping American Culture*, ed. Wayne Franklin and Michael Steiner (Iowa City: University of Iowa Press), 89–111.

After 1930

1. Quoted in Michael Steiner, "Regionalism in the Great Depression," *Geographical Review* 73 (1983): 441.

2. Ibid., 443.

3. Quoted in ibid., 437.

4. Lewis Mumford, "Roots in the Region," in *Faith for Living* (New York: Harcourt Brace, 1940), 266.

5. David Simpson, "Being There?: Literary Criticism, Localism, and Local Knowledge," *Critical Quarterly* 35, 3 (1993): 3–17; Vincent P. Pecora, "The Limits of Local Knowledge," in *The New Historicism*, ed. H. Aram Veeser (New York: Routledge, 1989), 243–76; Patrick Scott, "Tennyson, Lincolnshire, and Provinciality: The Topographical Narrative of *In Memorium*," *Victorian Poetry* 34, 1 (1996): 39–51; Michael O'Brien, "On Transcending the Mollusc: Cosmopolitanism and Historical Discourse," *Gettysburg Review* 1, 3 (1988): 457–68.

6. Bobbie Ann Mason, "Recycling Kentucky," *New Yorker* 69 (Nov. 1, 1993): 50.

7. Ibid., 50–51.

8. John Ed Pearce, "A Prize-Winning Slander," *Louisville Courier-Journal*, Oct. 5, 1993, quoted in Finlay Donesky, "America Needs Hillbillies," in *Confronting Appalachian Stereotypes: Back Talk from an American Region*, ed. Dwight B. Billings, Gurney Norman, and Katherine Ledford (Lexington: University of Kentucky Press, 1999), 285.

9. Donesky, "America Needs Hillbillies," 297.

10. Rodger Cunningham, "The View from the Castle: Reflections on the *Kentucky Cycle* Phenomenon," in Billings, ed., *Confronting Appalachian Stereotypes*, 308; Herbert Reid, "Regional Consciousness and Political Imagination: The Appalachian Connection in an Anxious Nation," in Billings, ed., *Confronting Appalachian Stereotypes*, 319.

11. Gurney Norman, "The *Kentucky Cycle* Still Perplexes," *Lexington Herald-Leader*, June 6, 1993, D6.

12. Ibid., 68, 62.

13. Quoted in Mason, "Recycling Kentucky," 61. Interestingly, Norman's major credit to date is the novel *Divine Right's Trip*, serialized in *The Whole Earth Catalog*, which was the prime site of "think locally, act globally" culture in the late 1960s and which combined back-to-the-land ideology with an explicit cosmopolitanism.

14. Chris Offutt, interview with the author, Nov. 1993.

15. Quoted in Mason, "Recycling Kentucky," 56.

16. Chris Offutt, interview with the author, Nov. 1993.

17. Robert Brustein, "Hillbilly Blues" (1993), in *Dumbocracy in America: Studies in the Theater of Guilt, 1987–1994* (Chicago: Ivan R. Dee, 1994), 198.

18. I am indebted in what follows to Susan Hwang's discussion of the Yamanaka controversy in "Defining Asian American Fiction: Ethnic Literary Studies, The Book Industry, and the Production of Value," Ph.D. diss., University of Iowa, 2003, 143–56.

19. For instance, in her collection of poetry, Lois-Ann Yamanaka, *Saturday Night at the Pahala Theater* (Honolulu: Bamboo Ridge Press, 1994).

20. See Hwang, "Defining Asian American Fiction," 147.

21. Quoted in Hwang, "Defining Asian American Fiction," 153.

22. Richard Wright, *Native Son* (New York: Harper, 1940); Maxine Hong Kingston, *The Woman Warrior: Memoirs of a Girlhood among Ghosts* (New York: Knopf, 1976); Alice Walker, *The Color Purple* (New York: Harcourt, Brace, Jovanovich, 1982).

23. Donald A. Dike, "Local Color and Its Relation to Realism," *College English* 14, 2 (1952): 81.

24. F. O. Matthiessen, *Sarah Orne Jewett* (Boston: Houghton Mifflin, 1929); and idem, *American Renaissance: Art and Expression in the Age of Emerson and Whitman* (New York: Oxford University Press, 1941).

25. Wendell Berry, "The Regional Motive," *Southern Review* 6 (1970): 974.

26. Tony Early, *Jim the Boy* (Boston: Little, Brown, 2000).

27. Edward Said, "The Public Role of Writers and Intellectuals," *Nation* (Sept. 17/24, 2001): 31.

28. Gerald Graff, *Beyond the Culture Wars: How Teaching the Conflicts Can Revitalize American Education* (New York: Norton, 1992). I am of course aware of Said's early life abroad, but the argument that follows, which claims that his view of intellectual responsibility is of a particularly American literary form, is based not on his background as a Middle Easterner, but on his education from secondary school on in American institutions and his subsequent career in an American English department.

29. Graham Good, *Humanism Betrayed*, 2001), 3.

30. See also Judith Butler, Ernesto Laclau, and Slavoj Zizek, *Contingency, Hegemony, Universality: Contemporary Dialogues on the Left* (New York: Verso, 2000), for debates on this topic.

31. Gertrude Stein, "The Gradual Making of the Making of Americans" (1935), in *Selected Writings of Gertrude Stein*, ed. Carl Van Vechten (New York: Vintage, 1990), 253.

32. Gayatri Chakravorty Spivak, *A Critique of Postcolonial Reason: Toward a History of the Vanishing Present* (Cambridge: Harvard University Press, 1999), 112.

33. Bruce Robbins, "Othering the Academy: Professionalism and Multiculturalism," *Social Research* 58 (1989): 359.

34. See John Bryant, "'Nowhere a Stranger': Melville and Cosmopolitanism," *Nineteenth-Century Fiction* 39 (1984): 289.

35. David Harvey, *Justice, Nature, and the Geography of Difference* (Malden, Mass.: Blackwell Publishers, 1996), 28.

36. Raymond Williams, *The Long Revolution* (New York: Columbia University Press, 1961), 157.

37. Williams, *The Country and the City*, 271.

38. Sacvan Bercovitch, "How to Read Melville's *Pierre*" in *Herman Melville: A Collection of Critical Essays*, ed. Myra Jehlen (Englewood Cliffs, N.J.: Prentice Hall, 1994), 116–25.

39. Paul Ricoeur, *History and Truth*, trans. Charles A. Kelbly (Evanston: Northwestern University Press, 1965), 283.

40. William Empson, *The Structure of Complex Words* (Ann Arbor: University of Michigan Press, 1967).

41. See Victor Shklovsky, "Art as Technique," in *Russian Formalist Criticism: Four Essays*, ed. L. T. Lemon and M. J. Riis (Lincoln: University of Nebraska Press, 1965), 3–24.

42. John Crowe Ransom, in *The Intent of the Critic*, ed. Donald A. Stauffer (Princeton: Princeton University Press, 1941), 92.

43. Brooks, *The Well-Wrought Urn*, 203.

Index